Gandhi and Tagore

This book brings together the political thought of Gandhi and Tagore to examine the relationship between politics, truth and conscience. It explores truth and conscience as viable public virtues, with regard to two exemplars of ethical politics, addressing in turn the concerns of an evolving modern Indian political community.

The comprehensive and textually argued discussion frames the subject of the validity of ethical politics in inhospitable contexts, such as the fanatically despotic state and energised nationalism. The book studies in nuanced detail Tagore's opposition to political violence in colonial Bengal, the scope of non-violence and *satyagraha* as recommended by Gandhi to Jews in Nazi Germany, his response to the complexity of protest against the Jallianwala Bagh massacre and the differently constituted nationalism of Gandhi and Tagore. It presents their famous debate in a new light, embedded within the dynamics of cultural identification, political praxis and the capacity of a community to imbibe the principles of ethical politics.

Comprehensive and perceptive in analysis, this book is a valuable addition for scholars and researchers of political science, with specialisation in Indian political thought, philosophy and history.

Gangeya Mukherji is Reader in English at Mahamati Prannath Mahavidyalaya, Mau-Chitrakoot, Uttar Pradesh, India.

Gandhi and Tagore

Politics, truth and conscience

GANGEYA MUKHERJI

NEW DELHI LONDON NEW YORK

First published 2016
by Routledge
2 Park Square, Milton Park, Abingdon, Oxon OX14 4RN

and by Routledge
711 Third Avenue, New York, NY 10017

Routledge is an imprint of the Taylor & Francis Group, an informa business

© 2016 Indian Institute of Advanced Study (IIAS), Shimla

The right of Gangeya Mukherji to be identified as author of this work has been asserted by him in accordance with sections 77 and 78 of the Copyright, Designs and Patents Act 1988.

All rights reserved. No part of this book may be reprinted or reproduced or utilised in any form or by any electronic, mechanical, or other means, now known or hereafter invented, including photocopying and recording, or in any information storage or retrieval system, without permission in writing from the publishers.

Trademark notice: Product or corporate names may be trademarks or registered trademarks and are used only for identification and explanation without intent to infringe.

British Library Cataloguing-in-Publication Data
A catalogue record for this book is available from the British Library

Library of Congress Cataloging-in-Publication Data
A catalog record has been requested for this book.

ISBN: 978-1-138-94617-0 (hbk)
ISBN: 978-1-315-67097-3 (ebk)

Typeset in Adobe Garamond Pro
by Apex CoVantage, LLC

Dedicated to

Manas Mukul Das
Rama Charan Tripathi
Sibesh Chandra Bhattacharya

Contents

Foreword by Peter Ronald deSouza	viii
Preface	xiii
Acknowledgements	xxiv
1. Cuspidal imaginings of political community in modern India: Bankimchandra and Vivekananda	1
2. Politics: truth and non-violence	40
3. Nationalism: ethics and responsibility	114
4. In argument: considerance of the political	173
Bibliography	219
Index	229

Foreword

It is not often that one gets the privilege and the pleasure of writing a foreword for a book in the history of ideas. The privilege comes from being given an early glimpse of the four conversations that Gangeya Mukherji has staged of the intellectual life of early twentieth-century India. These are first that between Indian thinkers and social reformers primarily of Bengal and the thought traditions of ancient India; second, internally between this group of thinkers themselves on what they regard as the sources of the problems that confront India and on the different ways that each suggests for the country to move forward; third, between these thinkers and their contemporaries in the West, especially those in Europe, where the formulation of the question itself is to be argued over (What does it require to be modern? What should modernity look like in India?); and fourth, between thinkers across the globe of the contemporary that Gangeya holds can shed light during his elaboration of an idea that was first articulated in an earlier historical period. For example, he believes Bernard Williams must intrude in a conversation between Tagore and Gandhi on truth and politics because he has something valuable to offer. And from the argument as it develops intrude he must.

These are the four conversations that take place concurrently in the book as Gangeya has thinkers from the past speak to the future and also, in reverse, thinkers from the present speak to the past. His discussion of the ideas of Bankim, Vivekananda, Tagore and Gandhi and some others that emerge in the book is fascinating not just because it illumines the concerns of the period but also because it invites us to distinguish between concerns that have only period relevance from those that are more perennial. As an able interlocutor, Gangeya introduces their ideas on ethics and politics and also interrogates them from several vantage points. In the process, he entices the reader to enter a world of our recent past where some of India's 'public intellectuals' – to use a modern descriptor which I feel is not out of place for that period – articulated a dream of India's post-colonial future. When in my opening statement I had said it was a privilege to write this foreword, it was for the privilege of this early glance was what I was referring to.

Foreword　❉　ix

The pleasure, however, comes from a different direction. Gangeya's work that I have had the opportunity to read, over the last six years, has in these years freed itself from what I would like to call an exegetical diffidence and has evolved into one that I can best describe as exegetical expansiveness. His idiom and conceptual vocabulary has come into its own. This, I believe, is indicative of the maturation of his ideas. He does not now seek to include every comment that he finds interesting – a problem that many of us struggle with and few can overcome – but allows his judgement to decide what to exclude and what to include in his analysis. As a consequence, the text does not become overloaded. This is a tough call, and only those who have developed their own social philosophy can display such confidence especially when the interlocution is with deep thinkers such as Gandhi and Tagore. As a result, the text shows a maturity of understanding that one begins to admire and I daresay sometimes even envy. (I wish I had thought of that connection!) In this book, one can see Gangeya's deep and continuous engagement with the antinomies of the human condition. While his scholarship, even in the past, was never in doubt, given the expanse of his reading, this work places him in a select scholarly circle that only those who first strictly follow classical protocols of first mastering the text to be discussed, then locating it in its social and intellectual context, then identifying possible persons it can speak to, and finally elaborating extensively on its concerns, are admitted. In this book, Gangeya has earned his place in that select circle. This is what gives me so much pleasure.

Having offered my understanding of the large canvass of the book, let me now engage with some of the ideas expressed in it. Since I have no intention of presenting a synopsis of the chapters – one has to savour each section for oneself – let me instead respond to three ideas from the book. The first is his borrowing Hannah Arendt's phrase 'dark times' to refer to a period when the moral fabric of a society is under stress, and perhaps worse, under threat. Gangeya believes that the time of Tagore and Gandhi was such a dark time when they were called upon to defend the moral fabric of Indian society. His adoption of this term to describe the period is attractive because it not only connects with the changes taking place in Europe, during the same period, but it also brings into the centre of our discussion the ethical element in politics. He holds that a time when it is believed that there is a basic contradiction between 'politics' and 'truth' is a period that portends ill for the polity. He seems to suggest, ever so subtly, that in our own times the belief in the public

x ❖ Foreword

discourse is of the existence of such a contradiction. Does he wish to warn us that we are entering a period of dark times? Rather than view this as a warning, I would like to see it as an invitation to study the ideas of the intellectual stalwarts of an earlier age who too struggled with questions similar to the ones that we are struggling with but who responded to them in creative ways. They were always mindful of the need to align their commitment to the ethical with their desire for social and political transformation. In their vision of the future, ethics and politics were aligned. Engaging with the ideas of this period would help us enormously in finding ways to think through the problems of India today. This is the value of the book.

This brings me to the second big idea that has preoccupied each of these four conversations and that constitutes a running theme in the book. It is the place of 'conscience' in public life. Gangeya regards conscience as being cultivated by knowledge and ethical practice. This is a dense and layered statement and in opening it up, we would find a plethora of questions on the nature of subjectivity. For example, when does one know that it is conscience that speaks in ethical ways and when is it the attempt by the subconscious to attempt a cover up, a process of rationalisation of action that we are only too familiar with rather than the critical judgement that Gangeya is hopeful for? In our times, this role of conscience needs to be debated more than it has been by contemporary political theorists. I say this not only because I see the value of conscience for what it is, as the moral arbiter of action, but also because the dynamics of agents, and of social agency, in our thinking about institutions, needs to be subjected to a more consistent interrogation. By drawing attention to 'conscience', he has drawn attention to the complex problem of the nature of such agency. For Gangeya, if I read him correctly, pragmatism seems to have replaced ethical politics. I see this observation again as an invitation to open up another complex problem in our study of ethical politics. Perhaps a clue is available in Gandhi's views on 'ashram observances' where he argues, in the little booklet, that ashram rules must be strictly followed and must become a habit and when that happens, 'then and only then is one ready for public life'. In true Buddhist dialectics, we must spend a lot of effort thinking about the meaning of 'then'. Gandhi seems to be saying that only when one has developed the habit of following rules (moral or legal?), when they become second nature and not burdens, then and only then will the conscience emerge as a guide? This is an area of enquiry that is gestured to in the book.

Foreword　❉　**xi**

The third large idea in these conversations is their thoughts regarding the making of 'political community'. This is the core of the book because Gangeya, as a historian of ideas, tries to give us the different answers propounded by Bankim, Vivekananda, Tagore and Gandhi on how to build and sustain a political community and on what should be its nature. This concern is at the centre of political debates in India today. There are rumours in 2015 that the current dispensation is seeking to restructure the secular and plural political community that was built by the members of the constituent assembly and move us towards a more muscular majoritarian polity. Be that as it may, this book, *Gandhi and Tagore: Politics, Truth and Conscience*, is a valuable contribution to the debate.

I want to end this foreword with a lament and a hope. The lament is of our intellectual practices of inadequate interrogation by our academy of the social and political thought of India, of the implicit assumption by modern scholars in the humanities and the social sciences that the thinkers of modern India have little illumination to offer our times and that if we wish to understand our present it is better to look across the oceans. This borrowing of ideas is in itself not a problem as long as, following the injunction of K. C. Bhattacharya, we subject them to critical scrutiny. But we do not. We borrow uncritically and as a result, our minds 'get enslaved'. D. L. Sheth in his essays has shown the costs we have had to pay for this uncritical borrowing of the idea of 'development' from the West. With deep pathos, Tagore describes this condition, in his essay on the Eastern University:

> The training we get in our schools has the constant implication in it that it is not for us to produce but to borrow. And we are casting about to borrow our educational plans from European institutions. The trampled plants of Indian corn are dreaming of recouping their harvest from the neighbouring wheat fields. To change the figure, we forget that, for proficiency of walking, it is better to train the muscles of our own legs than to strut upon wooden ones of foreign make.[1]

Gangeya's book is a step in the other direction. Because it is a text in the history of ideas of early twentieth-century India and one developed through four conversations, it stands without the burden of 'strutting around upon wooden legs of foreign make'. My hope is that the scholarly approach adopted by this book, of mastery of text and of staging a conversation between a thinker and a range of others, will be the direction taken by more studies in the intellectual history of India. This way of returning, recovering and reconstructing a world of ideas from our past (both recent and distant) is, I believe, the best defence against an obscurantism that seeks to appropriate our past to control the present. We desperately need such defences in India today.

Peter Ronald deSouza
27 July 2015

Peter Ronald deSouza is Professor at the Centre for the Study of Developing Societies and holds the Dr. S. Radhakrishnan Chair of the Rajya Sabha till April 2017.

Note

1. Rabindranath Tagore, 'An Eastern University' in ed. Sisir Kumar Das, *The English Writings of Rabindranath Tagore* (Delhi: Sahitya Akademi, 2001), 3: 562.

Preface

The present volume has emerged from a fellowship at the Indian Institute of Advanced Study. The progression of this project on the political thought of Gandhi and Tagore increasingly conveyed to me the necessity and propriety of a modification in the earlier plan, and the focus in this book has become thereby sharper on the relationship of politics with truth and conscience in the political writings of Gandhi and Tagore. The choice of the thematic itself might appear as anomalous, oxymoronic even, inasmuch as imagining the possibility of disabusing politics from power seems, not any the less particularly in our age, more impossibly difficult. The political community, manifestly, is little disposed to value integrity of position along with logicality of argument and fairness of method, and with political shades now gradually acquiring a pervasive opacity, it is almost as if the conditions that drew Hannah Arendt's comment are once again forming on the periphery of our collective political vision: 'History knows many periods of dark times in which the public realm has been obscured and the world become so dubious that people have ceased to ask any more of politics than that it show due consideration for their vital interests and personal liberty.'[1] On the plane of politics, however, it will not only bode ill for its very concept, but also wholly limit the possibility of politics, if the equation between politics and truth comes to be unqualifiedly accepted as having been historically contradictory. Nevertheless, it might quite clearly be discernible on the plane of philosophy that the division between politics and truth is not equal.[2] As to this, a resilient conscience in the political actors might provide leverage to politics to approximate itself to the virtue of truth. It may be appropriate to mention at this point that the virtue of conscience, in the conceptual world of both Gandhi and Tagore, is united more with a general human inclination to ethical purpose than overtly informed/formed by a particular tradition of knowledge or ethics. Through a Western epistemic analogy, this virtue can be perhaps described as something akin to *syndersis*, as understood in terms of an instinctive and immediate comprehension of first moral principles. Subsequent interpretations, in the West, of this faculty of positive discrimination imbued it with authority which connected with ethical

xiv ❖ Preface

decisions. Hannah Arendt has indicated the inherence and development of this faculty in Western conceptions. 'Conscience, as we understand it in moral or legal matters, is always present within us, just like consciousness. And this conscience is also supposed to tell us what to do and what to repent; before it became the *lumen naturale* or Kant's practical reason, it was the voice of God.'[3] Both Gandhi and Tagore regarded conscience as primarily being an impulse that could be so naturally potent as to become even an imposition on the mind of the individual and an imperative on his actions. Hence, their confidence as to the demonstrable rectitude of the untutored human mind, and in its latent and durable ethicality even when faced with close situations, is strikingly illustrated in one of Tagore's short stories, *Ramkanaier Nirbuddhita* (*The Folly of Ramkanai*).[4] Conscience in their understanding would, however, not be limited by this definition to an instinctual response only and was considered to be further cultivatable by knowledge and ethical practice. The six ancient schools of Hindu philosophy have broadly agreed that the conscience (*antahkarana*) is an amalgamation of mind (*man*), intellect (*buddhi*), consciousness (*chitta*) and ego (*ahamkara*). Motivated mainly by the soul (*atman*), it is determined in its reach and power by the play of the three archetypal human qualities (*gunas*) of goodness (*sattva*), passion (*rajas*) and ignorance (*tamas*). Inherent thus in all humans, conscience is formed in proportion to the quality of goodness in an individual and sustained in large degrees through knowledge and reflection. Emmanuel Levinas perceives conscience as a transcendent quality beyond the certitude of the self and a facilitator of truth through its recognition of the finitude and frailty of the cognitively located individual. 'Conscience welcomes the Other. It is a revelation of a resistance to my powers that does not counter them as a greater force, but calls in question the naïve right of my powers, my glorious spontaneity as a living being. Morality begins when freedom, instead of being justified by itself, feels itself to be arbitrary and violent. The search for the intelligible and the manifestation of the *critical* essence of knowing, the movement of a being back to what precedes its condition, begin together.'[5] This aptitude for cultivation provides for translation of conscience from an operational discrimination in practical situations to a faculty for reasoning and choice on the plane of concept and principle. These twin aspects of conscience may be thought for them to effectively cover, in the sphere of politics, the gamut from philosophical understanding to individual action.

Preface ❖ xv

It is at the same time both reasonably evident and acknowledged that Gandhi as well as Tagore had a certain distrust of the practice of politics as it obtained in the political class in India. Gandhi's famous early dismissal of English parliamentary democracy, the indiscriminate emulation of which he along with Tagore was highly critical of and its political officers is well known: 'they [Prime Ministers] have neither real honesty nor a living conscience'. Tagore's political writings are usually not as well accessed as his literary oeuvre, but he was a serious political thinker and also a critic of the prevailing political practices, as in this comment on Indian politics: 'those whom we call *bhadra* (genteel) have decided that politics is the division of India's throne'. But to present these two opinions as finally indicating their binary opposition to the methodology of politics will be inaccurate and preclude the nuance and detail of their consideration of politics. Associating them with entirely unrealistic aspirations and judgements and therewith describing them through the metaphor of wistfulness will constitute them as political exotica. Unfortunately, such an impression is not wholly uncommon in our academic discourse on polity. The lives of both Gandhi and Tagore intersected the decades that witnessed massive political crimes against humanity and which were included in the definition of dark times as given by Hannah Arendt. Any notion of the elision, in their political thought of crucial ethical issues and moral choices, required in the political world of those years, will categorise them at best as ineffectual and unconcerned moral dreamers. In the case of Tagore particularly, the obscuring of his insistent and informed interrogatory offered to the political community might inadvertently depict him as a *flaneur* on the political landscape of his times. Even their contemporary evaluators on occasions either misunderstood or misrepresented their positions. In a recent study, Sean Scalmer has described the deliberate construction of an abridged Gandhism – as against Gandhi's splendour and vastness of range conveyed in his *Collected Works* – through censorship or reportage and in carefully written official reports, including imputations of violence, for consumption in the West during Gandhi's own lifetime.[6] Tagore was perceived by a sympathetic biographer as a prisoner of his sensibilities.

Although the organisation of their political thought, the definiteness of its position and the directness of its articulation distinguishes serious intent from platitude, some scholars have tended to attribute quaintness to the metaphysical associations which are otherwise intrinsic to their

xvi ❖ Preface

positions. Gandhi had said on record, while explaining the reasons for writing an autobiographical narrative, that his internationally known experiments in the sphere of politics were of far less value to himself than his spiritual experiments which had to a great extent enabled his political experiments: 'But I should certainly like to narrate my experiments in the spiritual field which are known only to myself, and from which I have derived such power as I possess for working in the political field.'[7] The metaphysics inherent to their politics reinforced their ethical positions, and they thus simultaneously abstained from and transformed the purely political. Leszek Kolakowski has, in another context, indicated at the complication of wholly dismissing metaphysics from politics, particularly when evaluating issues relating to political ethics.[8] Affairs have nevertheless come to such a pass that, notwithstanding the astonishing subtlety and hardness of their political thought, Gandhi and Tagore have, in some sections of scholarship, gradually transformed to become more of a conscience than pathfinders in the world of politics.

The present study seeks to explore the first principles of ethical politics as conceived by Gandhi and Tagore and thereby contextually explores truth and conscionableness as viable public virtues. For these two thinkers, the citizen and member of political community were not different in ethical quality from the apolitical individual. The affiliations of state and nation do not necessarily compromise the ethical positions of the individual, and the political thought of our two protagonists foregrounds the tradition of truth telling, which provides the plane of the reconciliation of politics with truth and conscience. The reincarnation of tradition was, however, not unproblematic for them, and the imagining of the values of responsibility and participation on their part involved the attempt to redraw the conversational parameters of the ancient sophisticated cultures of India to enable a conversation between the different intellectual traditions of East and West. This was perhaps sequential and also necessary to make this redefining of identity sustainable on the philosophical as well as the practical plane. Gandhi and Tagore prominently highlighted that which had begun to gather increasing attention since the last few decades of the nineteenth century, the unethicality of expediency being allowed to deny equal political energy to the abolition of gender and caste hierarchies, as was otherwise being directed to the aim of decolonising India politically. India is currently engaged with working out issues of representation and participation across diverse secular and religious classes/communities. Sustained efforts are underway among communities to think through innovative positions regarding identity and belonging. In the thinking of concepts/ideas of future communities, the foundational thinking as of nineteenth- and twentieth-century India regarding the modern Indian community may be thought to acquire some relevance as new situations keep currently unfolding. It is difficult to relegate the debates centred on the defence of traditional political ethics in the early nineteenth century as mere worship of an imaginary past. The major protagonists of the debates were engaging with the Euro-centric claims of the superior morality of Western social and political systems and in attempting to reject the unqualified applicability of such claims were also opening the discourse to a future examination of both traditional and modern social and political institutions. Certain later Indian thinkers, in addition to those who completely rejected traditional institutions as exploitative and immoral, focussed on both the deleterious and the creative aspects of traditional Indian political thought in their explorations of alternative conceptual resources. C. A. Bayly has drawn attention to the significance of this early defence of tradition, highlighting the roles of P. Raghavia, an official in the British administration, and Ram Raz, an Indian judge in Bangalore, during the second and third decades of the nineteenth century. It is relevant to refer to Bayly in detail with regard to the implications of the debate and its reception in contemporary scholarship in the field of India studies.

> One reason the patriotic political debates of the early nineteenth century have been overlooked by historians is that politics has been rather narrowly defined. It is this that makes it possible for writers such as Partha Chatterjee and Peter van de Veer (sic) to privilege religion in a narrow sense in their accounts of early anti-colonial resistance. But cultural debates were equally important. The rejection of British claims to hegemony in arts and sciences was a highly political act, since the British 'empire of opinion' was explicitly legitimized in these terms. In this sense the numerous attempts by Indian authorities of the early nineteenth century to protect Indian learning both physically and intellectually from the ravages of the colonizers deserve attention.[9]

A discussion on Bankimchandra Chatterjee and Vivekananda opens this study. Their thinking comprises an early outsider intervention in the discussion on the concept of national politics, involving mainly a sense of ethics and responsibility. One can perceive, as reflected in these thinker-activists, the trajectory of modern Indian thought from an early

xviii ❋ Preface

effort to define Indian identity, which involved a preoccupation with the glorification of past epistemology and tradition, to a more pressing concern with the operability of certain ethical principles in the present Indian political community. Awareness of discriminatory arrangements in social and knowledge structures and responsibility towards their eradication emerge as crucial ethical qualities in their imagination of the political community in modern India. Notably, both of them were among those who extended their historical sense from the generally prevalent tendency to craft histories in either Hindu or Islamic themes while responding to British pictures of past/present Indian community. There was no ambivalency in their imagination of the religious community in modern India. Vivekananda's ceaseless attempts to instil the quality of religious tolerance and harmony in the discourse of community, for instance, can be appreciated when the potential of religious bitterness in the context of culture conflict under colonialism is recognised. A case in point is the anti-Christian riots in Tinnevelly in 1857, which were not of a character as can be immediately described under the broad rubric of communalism, but could be, still dangerously for the future, defined as being relatable with a single specific issue that was possibly explicable as one of cultural resistance, a resentment against what has been described with inevitable irony as the burial of 'polluted outcasts in the sacred land and the procession of their biers along royal streets'.[10]

The next two chapters discuss the politics of Gandhi and Tagore as conceived and practised on the plane of truth and conscience and by logical extension that of non-violence. The discussion attempts to demonstrate the validity of their politics in two theoretically inhospitable situations, in the context of nationalism generally, and more specifically the position of Tagore concerning the attraction of political violence as retributive justice in the charged atmosphere of colonial discrimination and racial humiliation in India in the early twentieth century, and second, that of Gandhi on *satyagraha* against the terrible persecution of Jews in Nazi Germany where all possibilities of non-violence were believed to be verging on the impossible, if not downright extinction. The discussion has tried to include the conceivable aspects of the two situations and foregrounds how they visualised politics and the political conscience, if one can deploy such a terminology, in a perspective of eternity that renders unworkable any justification for its yoking it with violence or destructive nationalism. I have not here considered the idea of constructive nationalism to be a mere terminological inexactitude and have argued that the

Preface ❖ xix

nationalistic ethos of the Indian freedom movement is largely a differently constructed nationalism, at the same time remaining identifiable under the broad rubric of nationalism. Gandhi and Tagore can be seen to endorse this variety of nationalism.[11] In positing this idea, one will have to negotiate certain serious theoretical problems which have been identified in the past and as for instance have been appositely raised by Ashis Nandy. Nandy has argued that Gandhi and Tagore had essentially imagined a post-nationalist India after decolonisation and that it was only the contemporary limitations of vocabulary obtainable to them that cause what is to him a misreading of their otherwise pronouncedly anti-nationalistic writings. 'It is true that some of their writings allow a casual reader to classify them as nationalists – official India has already done so and got away with it – they both were at best imperfect or bad nationalists. To call them nationalists is to vend a local, vernacular version of territoriality, a patently ersatz nationalism.'[12] The present study acknowledges the difficulties perhaps only too logically associated and borne out as well in a few cases in twentieth-century India, with the imagination of a variety of constructive nationalism, but endeavours to extend itself beyond this constraint, insofar as it appreciates the spirit of inclusivity that so prominently inhabits the nationalistic vision in colonial India. From Bankimchandra onwards, with the growth of the ideal of modern India, the leading protagonists in this narrative tended to transcribe nationalism in a sense that was opposed to the dominant European variety, which they acknowledged as being primarily a destructive force in the character of communities. The presidential address of C. R. Das in 1922 at the Gaya Session of the Congress is illustrative in this regard. He described the ideal nationalism as the expression of a nation's identity, not in opposition but in assistance, to the similar 'self- expression and self-realisation' of other nations, clarifying that this concept of nationalism was especially different from the variant of nationalism prevailing in Europe: 'Nationalism in Europe is an aggressive nationalism, a selfish nationalism, a commercial nationalism, of gain and loss.'[13] National interests, he said, were erroneously perceived as being intractably contrary among nations, and it was therefore not realised that to inflict hurt on another nation was to hurt humanity and ultimately therefore to hurt one's own nation. 'That is European nationalism; that is not the nationalism of which I am speaking to you today. I contend that each nationality constitutes a particular stream of the great unity, but no nation can fulfil itself unless and until it becomes itself and at the same time

xx ☉ Preface

realises its identity with Humanity. The whole problem of nationalism is therefore to find that stream and to face that destiny.'[14] He described the growth of Indian nationality in terms of an amalgamation of forces, only apparently hostile, over the centuries. This process moulded a common culture from binaries that included the Aryan and the non-Aryan, the Brahmanic and the Buddhist, the Hindu and the Islamic; and finally, English culture which initially shocked the feeling of Indianness, but then concluded the unification of the Indian spirit. Underwriting political non-cooperation with the philosophy of *swaraj* and *sadhana*, Das argued that non-cooperation could be explained on the plane of ethics and spirituality as a withdrawal from elements injurious at once to the good of a particular nation, and therefore humanity as well, and as isolating from forces that were extraneous to one's nature, 'an isolation and withdrawal which is necessary in order to bring out from our hidden depths the soul of the nation in all her glory'.[15] For the present, without entering into the problematic of extraneity and heterogeneity, it is perhaps possible to speculate on the aspiration for a responsible national state that was in evidence in the nationalistic discourse, with Gandhi and Tagore as its exemplars, of the period under study.

An overview of their mutual argument over political praxis, most notably reflected in non-cooperation, concludes the study. The manifest and cultivable capacity of the majority of people to imbibe the principles of ethical politics appears to be a major concern in the debate between them, embedded significantly within the dynamics of cultural identification on the part of communities. Gandhi, arguably one of the finest practitioners of mass politics, appears with his political movements to pose at times a serious puzzle to Tagore, who was frankly sceptical as to Gandhi's understanding of the human material he was dealing with in his politics. However, it should not by this interrogation alone be presumed that the preparation of the political participants was any less crucial for Gandhi as it was for Tagore. As will be seen in the discussion, Tagore was disinclined to any dilution, in the name of either mass suitability or mass concern, of content and style in the sphere of literature and the arts. He believed that accessibility to the finest literature encouraged the cultivation of sophisticated tastes and appreciation in the wider reading public, and conversely, literary sensibilities were impeded and devalued by accustomed exposure to superficial literature. There could not be separate categories of literature for the aristocracy and the proletariat. His view of mass politics was both similar and different from his position on 'people's' literature, insofar as he disagreed with any kind of ethical devaluation of political campaigns on the grounds of expediency even while remaining sceptical of the restraint of communities during inflammable political situations. He, therefore, disfavoured mass campaigns such as *swadeshi* and the non-cooperation movement. Gandhi, agreeing undeviatingly with the principles of ethics and preparation, effectively relied on his intuitive grasp of public feeling, a grasp which can be considered to have been generally authenticated by events. Isaiah Berlin once described the political behaviour of highly successful statesmen as analogous to artists who understood their medium.[16] Gandhi was, of course, much more than a statesman in the usual sense of the term. However, political artistry can, with reasonable sustainability, be included in a description of his qualities, and it might be possible to draw some explanation of his political imaginativeness by his reasoning of his political decisions.

John Rawls had very cogently described his approach to understanding political philosophy and its relevant texts. This excerpt can indicate a helpful cartography of scholarship: 'We learn moral and political philosophy, and indeed any other part of philosophy by studying the exemplars – those noted figures who have made cherished attempts – and we try to learn from them, and if we are lucky, to find a way to go beyond them. My task was to explain Hobbes, Locke and Rousseau, or Hume, Leibniz and Kant as clearly and forcefully as I could, always attending carefully to what they actually said.'[17] In this study, I have tried to bind all along the two main protagonists of our story to their own texts and to the details of their positions during some of the most difficult tests that confronted their political thought in their lifetimes.

Notes

1. Hannah Arendt, *Men in Dark Times* (San Diego: Harcourt Brace and Company, 1968), 11.
2. I am reminded in this context of Lucien Febvre's initial comment to Fernand Braudel on his choice of topic for research: 'Philip II and the Mediterranean, a good subject. But why not the Mediterranean and Philip II? A much larger subject. For between these two protagonists, Philip and the middle sea, the division is not equal.' Oswyn Murray, 'Introduction', in Fernand Braudel, *Memory and the Mediterranean*, trans. Sian Reynolds (New York: Vintage Books, 2001), x.

xxii ❧ Preface

3. Hannah Arendt, *The Life of the Mind* (San Diego: Harcourt Inc., 1978), 190.

4. Rabindranath Tagore, *Rabindra Rachanabali* (125th anniversary edition), 15 vols. (Kolkata: Visva-Bharati, 1986–1992 [1393–1398 Bengali Era]), 8: 504–507. The tragic story narrates humorously the innate but unconscious ethicism of a simple villager Ramkani who, even though unwilling at one level, feels compelled in his heart to truthfully write the will of his semi-conscious and dying elder brother Gurucharan who bequeaths his entire property to his wife, frustrating the hopes of Ramkanai and his family regarding his son's inheritance of the property. Ramkanai, the only witness to the will, carefully hands it over to his widowed sister-in-law, admonishing her to preserve it safely. His honesty is resented by his wife and son. The habitually ill-treated Ramkanai is afterwards compelled to go to Benaras. Meanwhile, his son and wife conspire to forge a will and challenge in court the claims of Gurucharan's widow, and Ramkanai is summoned back home to testify in support of his son. Astounded and stupefied by their action, he abstains for the next two days from all food and drink, till the time he is required to present himself in court. Exceedingly weak, and facing the circumlocutory interrogation of the opposing counsel, Ramkanai cuts him short and addressing the judge, testifies that the will in favour of Gurucharan's widow is genuine and written in Ramkanai's own hand and also that the one produced by his son is a forgery. His son his sent to prison. Ramkanai returns home to lapse into a severe illness and dies shortly afterwards, lamenting for his son and himself unlamented by his family and relatives.

5. Emmanuel Levinas, *Totality and Infinity: An Essay on Exteriority*, trans. Alphonso Lingis (Pittsburgh, Pennsylvania: Duquesne University Press, 1969), 84.

6. Sean Scalmer, *Gandhi in the West: The Mahatma and the Rise of Radical Protest* (New Delhi: Cambridge University Press, 2011).

7. M. K. Gandhi, *An Autobiography or The Story of My Experiments with Truth* (Ahmedabad: Navjivan Publishing House, 1988), vi.

8. Kolakowski is apparently engaging with the problematic of an overriding ideology in politics: 'If we reject the principle that the end justifies the means, we can only appeal to higher, politically irrelevant moral criteria: and this, Trotsky says, amounts to believing in God.' Leszek Kolakowski, 'Leibniz and Job: The Metaphysics of Evil and the Experience of Evil', in Leszek Kolakowski, *Is God Happy? Selected Essays* (London: Penguin Books, 2012), 170.

9. C. A. Bayly, *Origins of Nationality in South Asia: Patriotism and Ethical Government in the Making of Modern India*, in *The C. A. Bayly Omnibus* (Delhi: Oxford University Press, 2009), 70–71.

10. Bayly, *Origins of Nationality in South Asia*, 76–77.

Preface ❖ **xxiii**

11. I am, in this context, consciously avoiding discrimination between patriotism and nationalism. Admitting of the subtle variations occasionally indicated in the usage of these two terms, it is still possible to argue that, for the purposes of the present discussion, they are here not meaningfully opposed to each other. On another note, and with this caveat, my perception of the nationalism of Gandhi and Tagore approximates to the position taken by Hilary Putnam in the symposium on patriotism and cosmopolitanism initiated by Martha Nussbaum, where Putman argues for what can be defined as a located openness: 'In sum, we do not have to choose between patriotism and universal reason; critical intelligence and loyalty to what is best in our traditions, including our national and ethnic traditions, are interdependent.' Hilary Putnam, 'Must We Choose?', in Martha C. Nussbaum, *Love of Country*, ed. Joshua Cohen (Boston: Beacon Press, 1996), 97.

12. Ashis Nandy, *Regimes of Narcissism, Regimes of Despair* (Delhi: Oxford University Press, 2013), 16.

13. *Congress Presidential Addresses*, ed. A. M. Zaidi, 5 vols. (New Delhi: Indian Institute of Applied Political Research, 1986–1989), 2: 55–56.

14. *Congress Presidential Addresses*, 2: 56.

15. *Congress Presidential Addresses*, 2: 58.

16. Berlin describes many of their political courses, which can be seemingly unexplainable on the plain of theory, as proceeding from a combination of factors, including a leaping but accurate empirical understanding of players and situations. 'Judgement, skill, sense of timing, grasp of the relation of means to results depend upon empirical factors, such as experience, observation, above all on that "sense of reality" which largely consists in semi-conscious integration of a large number of apparently trivial or unnoticeable elements in the situation that between them from some kind of pattern which of itself "suggests" – "invites" – the appropriate action. Such action is, no doubt, a form of improvisation, but flowers only upon the soil of rich experience and exceptional responsiveness to what is relevant in the situation – a gift without which neither artists nor scientists are able to achieve original results.' Isaiah Berlin, 'Realism in Politics', in Isaiah Berlin, *The Power of Ideas*, ed. Henry Hardy (Princeton, NJ: Princeton University Press, 2002), 139–140.

17. Samuel Freeman, *Rawls* (Delhi: Routledge, 2007), 7.

Acknowledgements

Manas Mukul Das has initiated and encouraged my engagement with this area of study that continues to occupy my life so fruitfully. Rama Charan Tripathi intervened at a crucial moment to enable me to pursue research and has since then unhesitatingly provided sustenance in difficult situations. Sibesh Chandra Bhattacharya's exactness in both widening my intellectual horizon and restraining my enthusiastic conclusiveness has only been matched with his invaluable guidance over conceptual terrain. The dedication of this book refers to a cherished relationship with these three remarkable individuals and my deep sense of gratitude for their unstinting *vatsalya* for me.

Peter Ronald deSouza made possible the writing of this book and invited me to look more closely and then beyond my initial project. He presented me with difficult questions and helped me to negotiate through them. The sections on Gandhi's position on Jew resistance in Nazi Germany and Jallianwala Bagh were written in dialogue with him. It is not easy to adequately convey the generosity and affection of his friendship. He has been both a mentor and intellectual interlocutor and largely influenced my intellectual cartography. I remain indebted to him.

I remember with undiminished pleasure the enlightening and delightful conversations with Surabhi Sheth and D. L. Sheth, while savouring warm hospitality in their homes in Shimla and Delhi. They have helped the understanding of the wider thematic of the book. I am grateful to them. The book has been some time in gestation. Its argument has been presented in papers before seminars in Shimla, Delhi, Visva Bharati, Cochin, Varkala and Allahabad. For comments and illuminating discussion, I am particularly grateful to U. R. Ananthamurthy, Sudhir Chandra, Basudeb Chatterjee, Uma Das Gupta, Rajmohun Gandhi, Gopal Guru, Sudipta Kaviraj, Ashis Nandy, Kanchana Natarajan, Bhalchandra Nemade, Sari Nusseibeh, Sanjay Palshikar, Manas Ray, Tapan Raychaudhuri, Sundar Sarukkai, Amiya P. Sen, Chetan Singh, Tridip Suhrud and Vir Bharat Talwar. Harish Trivedi has been ever generous with kind affection. Arindam Chakrabarti and Vrinda Dalmiya are difficult and valued interlocutors and remain concerned and supportive of my personal and intellectual well-being. I am grateful to them.

My special thanks to Upamanyu Basu, Murali Manohar Dwivedi, Arvind Gupta, Pankaj Mishra, Surya Narain, Vijender Singh Rana, Debarshi Sen, Ashok Sharma, Girija Shankar, Rajendra Singh, S. B. Singh, Shashank Thakur and Diwakar Tripathi for their kindness and ample support over the last many years and to Shashank Sinha and Shoma Choudhury at Routledge for their support and undiminished courtesy while I delayed repeatedly over the many timelines during the writing of this book. I remain grateful to Susheela Vyas and Ram Narain Vyas for their simple and abiding affection and to little Kartikeya for sharing his childhood with me.

My parents were concerned with the progress of the book, occasionally even to the extent of camouflaging their indisposition in ensuring supportive environment for my project. My gratitude towards them for everything in life remains now blended with my preoccupation with their happiness and prayers for their life and safety. I am thankful to Deepshikha and Madhumita for lending their active support for realising these prayers. Working on this project has, as always, been made possible with support from Nandini and her taking all responsibility during my long absences from home.

I ✹

Cuspidal imaginings of political community in modern India

Bankimchandra and Vivekananda

The early imaginings of the political community in modern India are perhaps better understood within the relationship of politics with the values of truth and conscience. The political imagination evolved as a part of conceptional nationalism that envisaged the centrality of reform and the reimagining of tradition and social arrangements. It is widely acknowledged that the most meaningful intellectual engagement in nineteenth-century India related to the reform of the social, religious and political community.

We now live in an age of hardened positions regarding ideas and concepts. Many of our ideas of protest and social/systemic change are indeed as they should be a matter of faith for us. But this has an unfortunate complication of creating barriers in a conversation of ideas even while guarding against any dilution in the ideological commitment, so much so that the baggage of historical/ideological contradistinctions threatens to choke all rapprochements. Monolithic doctrines generate opposition and protest. And with the growing harshness of assertion, this may naturally follow that intractable ideological dispute may find its manifestation in violence. Needless to say this is happening. The question of the relevance of the value of reconciliation in social change may not be altogether irrelevant. Reconciliation might ultimately serve as impost for situating of truth and conscience at the centre of politics, meeting a crucial condition for non-violent change in human affairs. It is true that for many in the academy, the Indian nationalist idea has been divested of nearly all regard, but analyses of its workings may not entirely fail to reveal the glimmerings of truth and conscionableness. Sudhir Chandra has seen a somewhat similar value in the phenomenon of Indian nationalism:

2 ❋ Cuspidal imaginings of political community

'Seeing through the magic of an idea or ideology is important to knowing. But recognising the efficacy and glory of the magic while it lasted, is no less important.'[1] I do not thereupon intend, however, to allude to any ephemerality or unreality regarding the concern for justice and restitution that I find solidly reflected in a major trajectory of Indian nationalism and the pragmatism of its politics.

Nationalism qua reform

Charles Griswold represents true reconciliation as being dependent on truthful memory: 'Without honest assessment of the past, no memory worth having; without honest memory, no present worth living; without apology for injuries done, no future worth hoping for.'[2] For our present purpose, reconciliation may be viewed as an attitudinal concept with regard to the social world, or to 'one's own social world'. Looking at Hegel's social philosophy as a project of reconciliation, Michael Hardimon has examined the question of social attitude. 'Ones attitude towards one's social world may be implicit, expressed by the way in which one relates to the central institutions and practices of the society. "Relating to an institution" is a matter of conducting oneself in a certain way with a certain frame of mind with regard to that institution.'[3] But the issue of adopting a particular attitude is again imbued with different layers of consciousness and could even sound amorphous, especially in cases where the attitude may be one of unqualified acceptance of social arrangements and institutions. However, the idea of relating to the political order is in Hardimon's view comparatively easy to depict within a political order, like that of Nazi Germany which forces answers to basic questions of compliancy, complacency and resistance to an evidently evil regime: 'How can I avoid complicity in its evil?'[4] Reconciliation has also been taken to mean 'resignation', 'submission' or 'consolation'. I have chosen to use reconciliation not in these terms but have rather seen it as both a process and a situation. As a process, reconciliation seeks to overcome conflict, division and alienation, whereas the restoration of harmony and equity is the state of reconciliation. It would be preferable for the discussion to view it also as a form of protest and as a positive concept that Hardimon finds best expressed in the German term *versohnung* (conciliation), which conveys transformative possibility in that it does not presuppose a return to earlier circumstances in reconciling but rather reconciling in transformation. Hardimon speculates on the foundational attitudes of this transformation:

> This, in turn, allows us to articulate further our understanding of the conditions the social world must meet if it is to be a home. It seems natural to suggest that if the social world is to be a home, there must be no class of people who are excluded from participating in its central arrangements. We might try to convey this point by suggesting that, in assessing our relation to the social world, the guiding question should not be, Can *I* be reconciled to the social world? but rather, Can *we* be reconciled to the social world?[5]

In the early years of the Congress, the apex organisation of Indian nationalism, there was a general acknowledgement of the moral necessity of merging social reform with nationalism. But it should not be imagined that the imperativeness of such merging were unanimously accepted in the policy planning sessions of the highest level. This indifference, manifested as objection on grounds of expediency and practicability, persisted till the first decade of the twentieth century in spite of the general and expressed feeling among many of the intellectuals and leaders of the disprivileged groups that the largely casteist nationalist movement had no commonality with the crucial issues affecting their society. Jotirao Phule was writing in 1873 in *Gulamgiri* (*Slavery*) of the great benefit of English rule in ending caste oppression in India, and of his gradual disillusionment, as against his boyhood enthusiasm, with nationalist exhortations directed at the unity of all classes to free India from colonial subjection. Phule terms English rule as a great social leveller and harbinger of opportunities for the *shudras* and counsels them to avail of the avenues of advancement till English rule lasted. He is rather caustic about mainstream nationalist politics as it obtained till his time: 'Thank God that He helped the brave English to subdue the rebellion of the *bhat* Nana [Saheb]. Otherwise those enlightened brahmans who worship the phallus would surely have sentenced many mahars for life for tucking their dhotis at one side or for having uttered Sanskrit shlokas in their kirtanas.'[6] In the Congress session in 1886 at Calcutta, Dadabhai Naoroji, notwithstanding his stated awareness to its necessity, flatly denied the propriety of the desire of delegates to admit questions of social reform on the Congress platform, as they had met as a political organisation to plead for political representation, and not to confer on social reform, and criticism for ignoring social issues would be analogous to '[blaming] the House of Commons for not discussing the abstruser problems

4 ❖ Cuspidal imaginings of political community

on mathematics or metaphysics'.[7] Badruddin Tyabji, as president in the Congress session at Madras in 1887, reiterated Naoroji's position on the grave objection of the delegacy to Congress not discussing the issues related to social reform.[8] The most detailed expositional refusal to the persistent demand to prominently incorporate social reform issues in the Congress proceedings came from W. C. Bonnerjee in his presidential address in the Allahabad session in 1892. Bonnerjee informed the delegacy that this issue had been 'discussed threadbare' in the inaugural Bombay session with prominent social reformers including Mahadev Govind Ranade, and it was decided not to 'meddle' with the question, leaving delegates, however, free to confer informally on the topic in the Congress hall after the formal session. This position was adopted mainly because of the controversial nature of the issue and the potential fractiousness that could accrue from formal involvement of Congress sessions with the topic of social change. Bonnerjee pointedly mentioned the variety of concerns linked to this theme, based on individual as well as community attitudes, ranging from women education, child marriage to widow remarriage. Significantly, he refuted the argument that all political reform had to be preceded by social reform. This position is of course deservedly open to analysis on the plane of political philosophy; however, Bonnerjee here referred to the sustainability of the linkage in the context of purely legal measures that the Congress had been consistently proposing, such as the separation of judicial and executive powers up to a level and amendments in laws relating to land and forests. He asked suggestively: 'I ask again, what have these to do with social reforms? Are we not fit for them because our widows remain unmarried and our girls are given in marriage earlier than in other countries? because our wives and daughters do not drive about with us visiting our friends? because we do not send our daughters to Oxford or Cambridge?'[9] Bonnerjee did not in this context raise the issue of the humiliation and exploitation of the perpetually oppressed castes in India. But, as amply indicated by the persistent presence of the issue of social reform even at the highest levels of the political leadership, such questions were being earnestly discussed in the political community. In a few years, the strongest criticism by a political leader of caste oppression was presented by Gopal Krishna Gokhale in 1903 at the Dharwar Social Conference. Gokhale was scathingly critical of the social arrangements that were responsible for such discrimination from the standpoint of justice, humanity and 'national self-interest'. He lamented that the attitude of the educated youth towards the depressed classes as particularly painful and that it was 'monstrous' that certain castes were permanently debarred by social sanction from all opportunity to liberate themselves from their degradation. 'This is deeply revolting to our sense of justice. I believe one has to put oneself mentally into their place to realise how grievous this injustice is.'[10] He mentioned the almost ready endorsement for Gandhi's movement in South Africa and restated what he said had been his privilege to hear during a meeting in Bombay – a speech by Ranade wherein Ranade had drawn comparisons with the treatment of the depressed classes in India with the degradation of Indians in South Africa. Gokhale rejected the analogy of caste as in India and class as in the West, as caste in India was rigid and no movement was possible within its scope: 'A great writer has said that castes are eminently useful for the preservation of society, but that they are utterly unsuited for purposes of progress.'[11] National interest, too, required that opportunities be made available for realising the potential of every inhabitant of the country, and it was to the detriment of the higher aspirations of the nation to keep the 'low castes' at their present level of ignorance and incapacity. Gokhale now touched on the issue of a larger section of Indians remaining unenthused about what were the greater goals of national revival: 'Can you not realize that so far as the work of national elevation is concerned, the energy, which these classes might be expected to represent, is simply unavailable to us? I understand that that great thinker and observer – Swami Vivekananda–held this view very strongly.'[12] He appealed to the university-educated young men to join the movement for elevation of the disprivileged and hoped that at least some of them would dedicate their lives to the noble endeavour of educating and promoting the well-being of the 'unhappy low castes'.

I propose to examine Bankimchandra and Vivekananda, who stand as it were outside the formal political community, as being among the early contributors to the idea of ethical politics, which at its best sought to promote ideas of equal participation of the diverse religious communities, castes and classes in Indian society, not through a hegemonical vision of assimilation within a hierarchical social structure but through a subtler and attitudinal reconciliation. It is possible to see the trajectory of their thought as assisting to conduce the harmonious coexistence of the diverse social groups in India, who have still not come to terms with transactions of claim and consideration which had commenced under a colonial regime during the early decades of the nineteenth century, as also an increasing recognition in the writings of most of these thinkers

6 ❖ Cuspidal imaginings of political community

that the said transactions were motored by the awareness on the part of many social groups that particular facets of the dominant culture of the land actively abetted and upheld their degradation and exploitation. They evidence an acute sensitivity to a central problem with reincarnating traditions with contested histories, a problem which is captured in Jean Amery's comment in a different historical context: 'It will not do to claim national tradition for oneself where it was honorable and deny it where, as dishonor incarnate, it cast a probably imaginary and certainly defenseless opponent from the community of man.'[13] It is in this sense mainly that Bankim and Vivekananda can be construed as precursors of the reconciliation of an injured dignity and threatened privilege. They reflect a natural respect for Indian traditions and evince a sense of pride in their intellectual heritage. However, even when it is in large measure so that the inclusivist philosophies of Indian origin inhabit and inspire their thought, it is not India alone which stimulates their intellect and fashions their thought but also the ideas from the West that inform their sensibility. It is as if that like some other Indian thinkers they seem to have had embarked on a metaphorical journey, to discover their identity, across space and time. This journey seems to have generated their responses to their historical situation. The tussle with tradition underlies the writings of almost all the thinkers of this period, and it is manifested in various shades. Their situation is strikingly similar to what was later described by Nikos Kazantzakis in his autobiographical novel *Report to Greco*.[14]

Nineteenth-century India has been said to be 'a seed time rich in possibilities', when the first tentative steps were being taken to 'induce change against tremendous odds' and towards 'imagining a nation which would be based on the willing union of diverse cultures'.[15] Bankimchandra and Vivekananda examined their social institutions emerging from history, not only to offer ideas of reform which would facilitate social reconciliation but also to speculate on their own position in the schema of history. In the case of Vivekananda, this included an attempt to effect a plan of action for implementing his ideas. Their response to their respective contemporary situations also perhaps had a deeper psychological dimension and, particularly in the case of Vivekananda, to a reconciling of their own existence with the world they found themselves placed in. Their views are variously germinative, speculative, socially engaged and polemical. When seen as living on two different planes, the two men appear at times also very dissimilar.

Bankimchandra: the social conscience

In a discussion of Bankimchandra's vision of the modern political community in India, it becomes of crucial importance to negotiate through the more or less general impression in the academy that Bankimchandra was a Hindu revivalist who manifested reactionary prejudice against social change and hostility towards Muslims. Even a sympathetic scholar of Bankim, such as Sisir Kumar Das, while exonerating him from the charge of being a Muslim baiter, has perceived him as being imprisoned within fastidious prejudices in his regard for established social customs.[16] Bankimchandra is primarily known as one of the greatest novelists in Bangla. But in the history of ideas, he is no less important as an acute thinker in the realm of society and politics who offered subtle analysis of the complex response of the Indian mind to the cross currents of politics and culture in nineteenth-century India. A bibliographic reading of Indian nationalism almost unfailingly turns to him as a significant resource indicative of the attitudinal shades of the Indian mind towards the clefted modernity of colonial India.[17] The aspirations and anxieties that became central to the Indian political community in its dual experience of colonial rule, and what Tagore later described as the velocity of Western ideas, substantially engaged Bankim's attention, and this is directly as well as tangentially evident in both his novels and essays. It is undeniable that he was, on one plane, overly concerned at the withering away of many of the salutary traditional attitudes and the inevitable tectonical shifting in the social terrain of the country generally and Bengal particularly during this potentially mutative period. And it has been agreed that his focus was on a possible plane of reconciliation of social divisions: 'Bankim Chandra aimed at easing tensions in the community and looked for harmony.'[18] His concerns, therefore, clearly translated into an interrogation of the ethical failure of Indian social systems in the twin frames of history and contemporariness. Empathy and responsibility had been already considered as defining social qualities in the early nineteenth century by thinkers such as Rammohun Roy and Ishwarchandra Vidyasagar, but these two qualities became absolutely central in Bankim's concept of human relationships that evolved from the family to the entire world. Since the country was the preceding unit in this matrix of relationship, and more practicable with defined borders and cultural linkages, the principle of responsibility was more cogently operable in the capacity of a citizen within the country.

8 ❖ Cuspidal imaginings of political community

Rachel van Baumer has defined in this context Bankim's concept of the political community of the nation:

> The object of political action was defined, and indeed, the completely foreign concept of political action was brought within the fold of traditional Hindu dogma. At a latter period, Aurobindo was to write in emotional terms of Bankimchandra's having given the mantra and converting the whole nation in a day; but the fact cannot be denied that with Bankim's doctrine of dharma, an acceptable philosophical, religious, and psychological basis had been laid for the twentieth-century nationalist movement.[19]

Among the predictable options open before the typical nationalist of a colonised country are either the uninhibited embracement of the new ideas of vitality and prowess or the equally unambiguous intellectual retirement into the glorious traditions of the national past. Bankim opted for neither of them. He was uncomfortable with the dubious features of the traditions of his own country and sceptical of the promise of modernity extended by the colonising West. He is, in this regard, in his element in his public controversy with Reverend Hastie on his crude commentary of Hindu ritual. Although the controversy popularly arouses interest for the sharpness of Bankim's language, the argument is more remarkable equally for its organisation and clarity, as well as for the general fairness and restraint of its tone. After admonishing Hastie in delightful satire for his substitution of fact by claim, Bankim engaged with the issue in graceful prose. Hastie, he said, had diverted the argument with his excessive advocacy not only of the competence of European scholarship in Sanskrit but also of the superior comprehension of Sanskrit in Europe and America than in India: 'No one questions their scholarship. I can assure him that men like Max Muller and Goldstucker, Colebrook and Muir, Weber and Roth do not stand in need of a champion like Mr Hastie.'[20] Bankim said further that it would be extremely ungrateful on his part not to acknowledge the selfless devotion of these scholars to Sanskrit and their immense contribution to spreading it in the West. But it was simply ridiculous to comment on the general superiority of their erudition and that too based on a very limited awareness of Indian scholarship in Sanskrit in the Indian languages.

> The existence and the scholarship of those who choose to write in their own vernacular, in preference to Mr Hastie's, remain to him and to those who think with him as things unknown. I am also willing to confess that the native

scholars have written much less than Europeans, and that the intellectual culture of the mass of the readers whom they seek to instruct being inferior to that of the highly educated class whom European writers address, the scientific value of their writings is necessarily proportionately inferior. But the inference does not follow that native scholars are less at home in the language and literature of their own country than European Sanskritists.[21]

Notwithstanding his demonstrated admiration for the knowledge systems of modern Europe, he offered a robust epistemic challenge to its parochiality in the reading of alternative paradigms and challenged the conscience of his own countrymen regarding the inequality and injustice habitually suffered by the disprivileged sections of their own nation. Bankim was witnessing the very early days of nationalist politics and he was fairly distrustful of its formality and sterile loquacity. He considered the political class as wholly unconnected with the reality of Indian villages. This distrust of his was completely in common with his two illustrious compatriots, Tagore and Gandhi. He regarded a thoughtful political community as an essential component of the responsible state. Bimanbehari Majumdar has viewed Bankim's national awareness as focussed in a search for ethical politics: 'According to Bankim, a good people is the foundation of a good government. He seeks, therefore, to inculcate political capacity, political habits, and political morality in the Bengali people. He did not believe in any short cut to political power.'[22]

Throughout his literary career, Bankim wrote exposé after exposé on the inequalities of gender and caste and a savage critique on the exploitation of the peasantry. He, along with certain of his peers in the chronological vicinity, represents the initial steps towards social reconciliation, through an acknowledgement of inequality, which had been produced and reinforced through attitudes and norms created by the dominant sections of society and the creation of norms of social responsibility on the part of the privileged. Especially in the context of community divisions, even his construction of the character of Krishna in *Krishna Charitra* overturns many of the notions which constitute the contemporary idea of cultural *Hindutva*. The formulation of his social critique is at many points oblique, and Hayden White's description of Alexis de Tocqueville's style as in his study on the *ancien regime* and the French revolution might be applicable to a certain extent to Bankimchandra's thought and expression: 'The point of view was manifestly Liberal, but the tone was Conservative. The mood, though ostensibly objective and impartial,

10   ✦   Cuspidal imaginings of political community

was modulated from a Tragic acceptance of the inevitable to an Ironic admonition of the devotees of the old order to look to their best interests and to act accordingly.'[23] Bankim understood traditional Indian practices as a congeries of the inspirational and the banal. He viewed the present partly as derelict of the original splendour of ancient Indian civilisation, but it should nowhere be obscured that Bankim conceives the historical traversing of the path of civilisation as having been mediated through the attitudes of acceptance and relinquishment. This coheres with one of the patterns of nationalist envisioning of the trajectory of its nation's past, as described by Seton-Watson: 'The great community held together by a splendid civilisation extending over a vast territory, which suffers eclipse (from social or cultural decay, internal discord, foreign invasion or several of these together), and then seeks to reappear in a new guise as a modern nation.'[24]

In Vedic literature, the *mantras* (verses), which refer to the term *Rashtra* in the modern context translated as nation, centre around the twin themes of material consolidation for a unit of population and its invulnerability to the attacks of external enemies. In Sanskrit, the etymological root of the term *Rashtra* is *raj*, which associates essentially with the quality of being resplendent. Thus, the mantras regarding the *rashtra* possibly refer variously to a group or tribe and wish it to be vested with material endowments and resplendency. The term *rashtra* is defined in the Sanskrit lexicon variously as kingdom, realm, district, region, the people, nation and subjects. The mantras in Vedic literature would probably refer to *rashtra* in the sense of a people or a tribe.[25] It perhaps needs to be clarified that in Sanskrit literature the term mantra is applied to that category of *shloka* (the general Sanskrit term for verse), the incantation of which was believed to be bestowed with divine power. All the *shlokas* in the Vedic corpus are referred to as mantras. I have retained the established nomenclature in this regard.[26] In the *Rigveda*, the mantras referring to the nation generally constitute an appeal from the public to a king and essentially wish for material well-being and prowess for the king as leader and protector of the nation. This mantra, addressed to a king to be, is representative of such references in the *Rigveda*: '[O King] we have received you as the lord of the nation. You become a lord among us. Stay constant and determined in the nation. May all the subjects like you. May the nation never be separated from you.'[27] The verses referring to nation in the *Yajurveda* and the *Atharvaveda* have a similar concern with prosperity and well-being. They invoke the gods to bestow the nation

Cuspidal imaginings of political community ❖ 11

with denizens that are variously, according to their prescribed social order, dutiful, productive, brave and, in the case of women, those that are beautiful and fortunate; and well-endowed horses and kine; bountiful rains and plentiful crops and herbs.[28] There are of course large swathes of social groupage missing from the definition of the denizen. Those named are without exception, Brahmins and Kshatriyas, and the other *varnas* (castes) are not mentioned. Significantly, there is a single instance of the nation being alluded to in the feminine form in the *Rigveda*.[29] There is a prominent and somewhat exceptional instance of the identification of a nation with an individual personality in the later and epic age of Sanskrit literature – perhaps unsurprisingly so, given the fact of the tendency to venerate great heroes in epics across civilisations. King Dashratha terms Rama as the defining value of the Kosala nation, admonishing his queen Kaikeyi: 'The place [Ayodhya] where Rama was not king would cease to be a nation, the forest where Rama resided would become a nation.'[30]

According to Raychaudhuri's evaluation of Bankimchandra's role and contribution as a writer, Bankim comes across as perhaps one of the earliest examples of the public intellectual in modern India. Referring in this context to Bankim's introduction to *Bangadarshan*, the journal found by him, Raychaudhuri has summed up Bankim's concept of the obligations of scholar-citizen: 'As a writer and an educated Bengali, he perceived one duty as incumbent on the people of social class – instructing his countrymen about the nation's past achievements, current problems, and one's duties to the nation. Even his later philosophical writings were unmistakably dedicated to the same task.'[31] With his knowledge of the ancient texts, Bankim could probably have situated himself in the tradition of the wakeful *purohitas* (priests/intellectuals) – in a possible connotation of the term to include within its rubric the intellectual counsellor to the king and society at large and in this context in the sense of a modern interpreter of values – who prayed in the *Yajurveda* for capacitating themselves for unceasing intellectual vigilance regarding the ethical and cultural ethos of the nation, as in this incantation during a sacrificial rite performed for the realisation of the highest values of a Brahmin: 'Prajapati who is the progenitor of food, generated since genesis, *Soma* most resplendent in all herbs and liquids. May those herbs be succulent and nourishing as honey for us; nourished on them, may we the purohitas be ever vigilant in our nation.'[32]

Bankim's critique of inequality and his nuanced analysis of the validity of socio-legal constructions have the tendency to appear in the most

12 ❖ Cuspidal imaginings of political community

unexpected of places, with no ambiguity as to the point the author wishes to make. Considering the structure of the critique, which surrounds Bankim on the count of excessive orthodoxy and even reactionism, it might be pertinent to illustrate very briefly his major premises of social critique in a representative text, keeping superfluous interpretation to a minimum and letting the text speak for itself. In an essay entitled *Bharatbarsher Swadhinata o Paradhinota* ('India's Autonomy and subjection'), Bankim begins rather innocuously, with what can be a value-neutral statement: 'Formerly, India was autonomous. Now, for hundreds of years, she has been in subjection. Modern Indians consider this to be a great sorrow. We wish to make a comparison between that ancient autonomy and this modern subjection, and examine it in order to discern the sorrow and the happiness of it.' Bankim enquires into the real implication of autonomy and subjection through a comparison to 'discover whether or not there is more happiness in modern India than there was in ancient India'. In a tone almost calculated to be provocative, he acknowledges that many will, because of his question, become 'enraged' with him, as he who doubts that 'autonomy is happiness' is by the very fact 'a heretic, a vile man, etc'. But Bankim is unrepentant: 'We agree. But it is difficult to satisfactorily prove that autonomy is better than subjection.' It is not so because India was earlier under a 'tyrannical rule' under Muslims, because of the exploitative system present under 'Hindu rule'. The kingdom which is free from oppression by foreigners is regarded as autonomous; conversely, even countries under home rule can be said to be in subjection, as 'England under the Normans, or India under Aurangzeb'. Conversely, it could be correctly said that 'North India, subjugated by Kutubuddin, was foreign-ruled and in subjection, and that India ruled by Akbar was home-ruled and autonomous'.[33] Although agreeing to the fact that 'ancient India was home ruled and autonomous; modern India is foreign ruled and in subjection', Bankim does not concede that foreign rule is necessarily pernicious because of its foreign character and that indigenous rule is necessarily benign. Even in ancient India, rulers were occasionally 'cruel', 'greedy for wealth' and 'voluptuous', who lived in 'women's apartments' and 'Ancient India used to suffer much from all this. In modern India, it is unlikely that whatever faults the distant king or queen may have will bear fruit in India'. Bankim does not have kind words for Prithviraj, a *Hindutva* icon: 'Prithviraj, for his own pleasure, abducted Jayachandra's daughter, and because of it, battle flared up between them, and they both suffered harm and loss of vigour. As a consequence, both fell into

Cuspidal imaginings of political community ❖ 13

the hands of the Muslims. There is no likelihood, in modern India, of any misfortune arising from the demands of the distant ruler's pleasure.'[34] Bankim acknowledges that under British rule 'the local people are bowed down before them' and that 'the pleasure of the English is responsible for any reduction of happiness of Indians', but this statement of his only serves to foreground the issue of caste oppression in India. There may not have been racial supremacy, 'but there was a similar oppression of caste'.[35] The subsequent critique is strikingly similar in tone to that of Phule and bears quotation in some detail:

> It is not likely that there is something sweet in being oppressed by one's own race, and something bitter only when oppressed by a different race. But we do not wish to make this reply. If anyone is fond of being oppressed by his own race we have no objection. Our only aim is to say that in the place of the racial oppression in modern India, there was caste oppression in ancient India. From the point of view of the majority of the people the two are equivalent.[36]

This essay problematises the colonial system as well, but mainly it is an invitation to Indians to first look closely at the indigenous system of hierarchy and discrimination that had been uninterruptedly in operation over centuries. He wrote that the denial of opportunity to the educated Indian elite under England was similar to caste oppression in ancient India, only that the elite then were not the victims of oppression. It was remarkably prescient, anticipating the demands for self-rule which were to follow and perhaps was indicating that the delinking of political autonomy from social reform would not only not improve the lives of the disprivileged sections of Indian society but would also be dishonest and vitiate the entire political process in the future. The foregrounding of the structural inadequacies of Indian society does not relegate the question of colonialism; it refreshingly prioritises the discourse of social reform, in the concluding section of his essay.

> Many will retort angrily, are autonomy and subjection the same, then? Why do so many people in the world sacrifice their lives for autonomy? To those we speak thus, we humbly submit that we are not engaged in seeking the evolution to this question. We are a nation in subjection – we will be in subjection for a long time – we do not need the answer to that question. Our inquiry was only this: were the people of ancient India, by reason of its autonomy happier than the people of modern India, or not?

14 ☀ Cuspidal imaginings of political community

> We have arrived at this conclusion, that in modern India the Brahmins and Kshatriyas are depressed; and the Sudras, that is, the common people, are somewhat better off.[37]

In fact, even the ill effects of colonialism are more intensely experienced by the disprivileged. The peasants, whose cruel suffering is described in cruel starkness by Bankim, have been named by him significantly as Hasim Sheikh and Rama Kaibarta and Paran Mandal in his essay on agricultural deprivation, *Bangadesher Krishak* ('Bengal's Peasants'). It ironically contrasts the development under British rule with the cruel deprivation of the peasants of Bengal and graphically describes the terrible conditions of their lives. The Bengali *babu* and the colonial official might have profited and do enjoy the fruits of science and urbanisation, but they had failed completely to ameliorate the lives of the people of the country: 'Whose prosperity is the country's prosperity? I see your prosperity and mine, but are you and I the country?'[38] *Muchiram Gurer Jibancharit* (*The Life of Muchiram Gur*) is a fable on the basic ineffectuality of the colonial government ensnared by the ineptitude of its officials, who are well meaning but ill informed and gullible, and a type of spineless, crass and amoral native sycophant who can travel upwards in officialdom and society by feeding literally on the fears of his own countrymen and figuratively on the initiatory diffidence of his rulers.

Inexplicably, Bankim occasionally tended to glorify kingship in ancient India, particularly when analysing Zamindari, which he viewed as a particular attribute of the so-called Muslim period. It is rather bizarre that he sometimes made graphic descriptions of caste oppression, which were by his own admission implicit in the previously prevalent norms of jurisprudence, in coexistence with references to 'benevolent kings', but it is also incongruous to his overall critique and can only be understood in the peculiar dynamics of colonial politics.[39] It is unfortunate, because Bankim otherwise has a flair for nuanced objective analysis on questions like legality of customs, which was a very important issue in nineteenth-century India. I am consciously opting for the interpretation that his occasional laudatory references to 'benevolent Hindu Kings' was cosmetic rather than constitutive of his psyche because had it been otherwise, the expose that he presented of Indian society could hardly have had been possible. We shall return to this aspect later, but I would like to mention here that in almost all of his writings, *Dharmashastras* are not only not approved of, they are hardly ever mentioned, and on the few occasions they do find mention, it is in a pejorative sense. Similarly, in *Samya* (Equality), it is the inequality among castes and more prominently between men and women, which is subjected to clinical analysis by Bankim:

> There is unnatural inequality between Brahmin and Sudra. The killing of a Brahmin is a grave sin, the killing of a Sudra is a lesser sin; this is not according to natural law. Why is it forbidden to kill a Brahmin and not to kill a Sudra? Why is only the Sudra the giver, and only the Brahmin the receiver? Why, instead of this, has there not come into being a law that he who has the capacity to give should be the giver, and he who has need should be the receiver?[40] (my translation)

Significantly, child marriage and women's education are enmeshed in Bankim's analysis; according to him, because of notions of 'chastity' and 'conduct', there was a horror in the minds of the educated Bengali of sending girls to schools, and even many of those who were not averse to the idea found it difficult to send their daughter's to colleges, howsoever much they may desire higher education for their sons: 'Where are their colleges for girls?' The obvious solution lay for Bankim in either having 'separate schools for women' or in educating girls in the college for men. The mere mention of this option would inflame the residents of Bengal. They have no doubt whatever that girls being educated in men's colleges will conduct themselves like prostitutes. Most of the boys will similarly indulge in vices. Even if these objections are not raised if the first option is followed, even then women education is foredoomed in a flurry of questions regarding the succour of children. 'Bengali girls turn mothers and house wives at the age of fourteen. Whatever schooling can be had by the thirteenth year is all that is open to them. Or, even that is not possible – because in what way in even her thirteenth year can the bride or a daughter of a good family, step out of home with book in hand to study?' (my translation).[41] It is unfortunate that the chapter on women was among the three chapters of *Samya* that Bankim later chose to excise from the subsequent publication of his writings. Contrary to general impression, although he withdrew *Samya* entirely from publication, two of its chapters were later incorporated in *Bangadesher Krishak*. Even though the complete text of *Samya* is readily available, it has regrettably not been commensurately analysed in Bankim scholarship. Bankim himself retracted his original view of the position of women in his later writing on the topic in *Dharmatatva*. That he was apprehensive of the social divisiveness of some of his views is apparent, but it might

16 ❖ Cuspidal imaginings of political community

be relevant to also include in the focus his increasing introspectiveness on the theme of individual praxis as social instrument, and according to one scholarly analysis: 'It would be a mistake not to take into account Bankim Chandra's understanding of the ethics of equality in the light of a new kind of religious humanism towards which he was feeling his way after 1876–1880.'[42]

In the last phase of his life, Bankim concentrated on formulating, through the writing of religio-political treatises, a modern Hindu code of conduct, which he thought would outline the ethical life of a political community besides conveying the ideals of a Hindu way of life. But even in this phase, when novels such as *Anandamath* were written, he never supported any kind of orthodoxy. Differentiating between European patriotism and the ideal love of one's country, Bankim presented in the *Dharmatatva* his concept of harmony between universal love and love of country. The citizen would be a citizen of the world, insofar as he will be committed to accomplish the welfare of other societies along with that of his own country, but he would naturally resist any other country harming his own to benefit itself. Bankim described European patriotism as an 'abominable sin': 'The meaning of the European religion of Patriotism is that we should forcibly seize other societies and bring them within our own. We should extend our country, but we should do this by destroying all other societies. Under the influence of this pernicious patriotism, the original people of America have been wiped from the earth. May the Lord free India from such patriotism.'[43]

Many of these treatises, like *Krishna Charitra* and *Dharmatatva* presenting a version of a Hindu world view, do not discard the progressive elements of European positivism. Scholars, although their number is not considerable, have evaluated Bankim's contribution beyond what they have termed as his situational concern for the improvement of Hindu society.[44] In one of his last novels, *Sitaram*, the eponymous Hindu king establishes a Hindu kingdom, but ultimately becomes a debauch and destroys himself, even as both the Hindu and Muslim preceptors in the novel, Chandrachud Thakur and Chand Shah Fakir, finally leave Sitaram's realm for Kashi and Mecca, respectively. Fakir tells Thakur that he 'would not stay any longer in a country which has Hindus. This is the bitter lesson given by Sitaram' (my translation).[45] This sage counsel from Fakir had been blatantly disregarded by Sitaram:

> My child, you want to establish a Hindu Kingdom. But can you achieve that if you are chained to customs. If you do not treat the Hindus and

the Muslims equally you will not be able to protect your Kingdom. What could be a haven of peace will turn into a hell. The same god has created the Hindus and the Muslims. Both are his children. Don't make any distinction between them. That is a sin.[46]

Chand Shah Fakir, through the various editions of the novel, abides as a critic of 'Hindu fanaticism and an apostle of Hindu Muslim unity'.[47] In *Durgeshnandini*, Bankim created Ayesha, 'one of the most memorable characters in the history of Bengali fiction', describing her as *ramani kularatna* (a jewel among women). Similarly, Usman who seeks to marry Ayesha is one of Bankim's finest characters. In *Gaurdas Babajir Bhikshar Jhuli*, the Vaishnav *seer* Gaurdas tells his disciple that 'one who discriminates between a Hindu and a Muslim is not a true worshipper of Visnu'. It is worth mentioning that Bankim regarded himself a Vaishnav in thought and deed. In 1873, Bankim wrote in a book review in *Bangadarshan*:

> Bengal is not a land of Hindus alone. It is a land of the Hindus and the Musalmans. They are now hostile and unsympathetic to one another. But the unity between the two communities is essential for the real progress of Bengal. That unity cannot be achieved so long as the upper class Muslims consider themselves as foreigners, and Bangla not their language and decide to write only in Urdu and Persian. The unity of language is the basis of national unity.[48]

Notwithstanding the inclusivist viewpoint contained in these lines, the problematic of assimilation, however, remains unresolved. As with the identification of the country with the Goddess Durga, the identification of historical movements with primarily Hindu metaphors, however useful as a mobilisational trope in nationalist politics, can hardly be considered as philosophically pragmatic. Perhaps, the inbuilt contradiction in this argument mirrors not only Bankim's own dilemma but also the inherent dilemma of the discourse of identity. At what point of the logic does identity while fashioning itself begin to germinate within its own self, the seeds of irrevocable difference? It is perhaps natural that Bankim did not envisage an exclusively nationalistic programme, and as Clark has said: 'It is doubtful whether he ever conceived the possibility of one, or, for that matter, whether he would have joined it if it had existed.'[49]

When he was writing on polygamy apropos Vidyasagar, Bankim took on for his times a startlingly unusual position with regard to the relation between law and custom. Vidyasagar had called for the eradication of polygamy, on among other grounds that it was against the *Shastras*.

18 ✦ Cuspidal imaginings of political community

Bankim's riposte has been usually interpreted as a churlish rejoinder to a dedicated social reformer. Part of the story regarding a mutual antagonism between them is true. But it might be interesting to explore the point made by Bankim as to whether law should be dictated by custom in a pluralistic society, and to what extent do such codes really affect the practice of society and if they did, what would be the ramification of accepting them as sanctions to create new laws. According to Bankim, the precepts laid down by *Manu Smriti* and other *Dharmashastras* were 'never fully carried out by any society'. They were naturally contradictory and many of them had been spontaneously abandoned. Nevertheless, these precepts were widely believed to have had meticulous adherence in ancient India and that they were only now being lost 'through the influence of the times'. Bankim commented that this belief was not sustainable and now, as in the past, the Dharmashastric provisions were only partly followed. Moreover, even this truncated operation of these provisions was the major reason for 'India's decline'. Bankim believed that the invocation of the *Shastras* was singularly inappropriate in an argument supporting modern legislation against polygamy:

> If a statute is to be drawn up, is it essential that this statute be sanctioned by the Shastras? Or if it were contrary to the Shastras, would this be detrimental? . . . Another point is that in this province half of the people are Hindu, and half are Muslim. If it is proper to enact legislation against polygamy, then it is proper that this law should apply to both Hindu and Muslims. But if we say that polygamy is contrary to the Hindu Shastras, on what grounds can it be made illegal to Muslims.[50]

Although it may sound familiar to the contemporary demand for a uniform civil code with its attendant political logic, the issue before Bankim was quite different. He was essentially considering the foundations of a modern political community and how therein tradition and modernity were to reconcile with each other. It is precisely when he is viewed as part of this project that Bankim, along with his contradictions, appears relevant to the problem of the modality of looking at the past in the imagining of our future aspirations.

Vivekananda: the ethics of responsibility

Vivekananda represents as if the cusp of the Indian imagining of modern India, signifying the trajectory of the nineteenth-century ideas of identity and reform into the twentieth century, wherewith the debate on such ideas acquires a different sharpness. Even if there may be no explicit relation in his thought with the ideas of responsibility and community, this inter-relatedness constitutes a thematic unity in his statements and writings, and this linkage is also manifested in his assessment of the possibility of the emergence, in its historical context, of a liberated and liberal modern Indian nation. The genealogy of his ideas can be traced in his historical situation as well as in his philosophical inheritance: awareness both of nationalistic passions and of the institutional and structural injustices that were also implicated in the otherwise impressive cultural heritage of the country; the colonial experience of the illiberality of government; transactions with Western social thought; appreciation of the knowledge revolution in Europe; perception of the resilience of Indian philosophical traditions and knowledge systems and a sense of human dignity that was based in traditional Indian conceptions; and extensive experience of the West. In the visualising of a future India, his focus is predominantly on the individual as constituent of larger communities and on the making of the ethical individual, which in the Indian context involves also the defining of a modern Indian identity that is not limited by traditional conceptual constraints, although it is fully conversant and identifiable with rejuvenated Indian thought.

It is somewhat of a truism that Vivekananda symbolises the high noon of Hindu revival in modern India. However, his life illustrates more than one dimension of the spiritual consciousness, and as Tapan Raychaudhuri has clearly stated, Vivekananda 'was more than anything else a mystic in the quest of the ultimate reality within a specific Indian tradition'.[51] But this dimension of his mind is not usually accessible, as such experiences are unavailable on a cognitive plane for most of us, and even the very possibility of metaphysics might be rejectable as, in the words of Hume, 'nothing but sophistry and illusion'. Biographers of spiritual personalities have occasionally recorded that the aspect of the mystic remains, for all practical purposes, generally inscrutable.[52] Vivekananda may generally be easily understood as a reconciler and social reformer, in his imagining of India as a people and a common culture, and in his intense idealism regarding the rightful destiny of individuals and communities and the ethical choices that confront communities in the realising of their imagined essential destiny. Compared to Bankim, the case of Vivekananda is relatively uncomplicated, although a perception of the doubtful secularity of his credentials follows from the general idea of the interrelationship of religion and social reform. However, spirituality

20 ❖ Cuspidal imaginings of political community

has many more dimensions than is usually recognised, and the life of Vivekananda is illustrative of a commonality of the 'metaphysical' and the 'social' consciousness.

Renunciation, society and politics

Born, as is well known, to a family of catholic sensibilities and taste – his grandfather and father were affluent, cultured lawyers; his father particularly was a connoisseur of classical music and polyglot with a facility for Persian and Urdu – Vivekananda was occupied with metaphysics from early life. The act of his renunciation, or *sanyas*, freeing him ritually from caste conventions and particularly from the established norms regulating commensality, was the outcome of religious yearning but at the same time, did not entail the abdication of social responsibility. On the contrary, Vivekananda considered *sanyas* as an appropriate condition for serving equally the individual and the social conscience. It is worth mentioning in this connection that on one plane the social consciousness is contained in the religious consciousness, which also seeks to eliminate social mores that impede the realisation of bliss in the lives of the deprived and dispriviledged, and the concept of *seva* (service) thus assumes supreme importance. However, the religious consciousness per se realises the limitations of regarding mere social uplift as a source of bliss, and therefore it is not itself limited by what is generally termed as the purely social consciousness. In this connection, and without thereby forcing an analogy, it may be worthwhile in understanding the history of the tradition of *sanyas* to take note of Govind Chandra Pande's discussion of both the early practice of *sanyas*/mendicancy and the varied perceptions in India regarding renunciation, both as a conformance with and deviancy from the concept of the four *ashrams* of living. 'When towards the close of the later Vedic period Brahmanic values had undergone a great change and some sections at least within the Vedic circle were willing to consider seriously that apparently pessimistic world picture which the doctrine of Samsara entails, more friendly and more fruitful communion with these Munis and Sramanas appears to have taken place.'[53] The vitality as well as the general disruptiveness of Indian society by the sixth-century BC articulated a spiritual quest and disillusionment, in turn leading to a flowering of an earlier ascetic tradition. The nature of this flowering was, however, not unmixed and unrelated to social reality.

'In practice, the ranks of the mendicants are filled not merely by ardent religious souls but in the main by those whom despair and material life has driven into beggary.'[54] This indicates the complicacy of the social dimension of *sanyas*. The core of the 'vows of renunciation' across the different sects typifies the ascetic endeavour in India. It is noteworthy that even with their absolute indifference to worldly possessions in their own individual lives, the renunciants were generally not hostile to the institution of property, although not necessarily ignorant of the social costs of the different social institutions. 'They sought to transcend, not disrupt social life. Indeed, having abandoned secular society, they themselves entered a new society based on spiritual relations.'[55] Pande has further detailed the development of the social dimensions of *sanyas* in his study of the life of Sankaracharya, acknowledging wherein that the act of renunciation entails a formal closing of social linkages for the renunciant, he also at the same time delineates the almost inevitable and continuing social associations of the renunciant. It is interesting that the institutional beginnings of renunciation in India, as in Greece, are almost consistently traceable to social recoil: '[The] concept of *sramanya*, *mauna* or *sannyasa* is reminiscent of the Cynic concept of *apathia* and the associated attitude of withdrawal and protest towards the religious and public life of the *Polis*.'[56] Traversing social and historical stages, it was subsequently conceived by certain religious philosophies, in India and elsewhere, as not simply a preparatory but a final way of living and was even formalised with various codes: 'Although the ideal of mendicancy meant the renunciation of social life, this renunciation itself came to be clearly converted into a social institution.'[57] *The Bhagavadgita* in its eighteenth and final chapter opens with enumerating the definitions of *sanyas* and is especially critical of renunciation for the abandonment of duty. It is relevant to note that in this it categorises as highest that category of renunciation which also entails the dispassionate fulfilment of duties: 'But he who performs a prescribed duty as a thing that ought to be done, renouncing all attachment and also the fruit – his relinquishment is regarded as one of "goodness." '[58]

Renunciation appears generally as an individual-centric action that might germinate in criticism of 'society' and even in social disenchantment, but it may not for that reason be construed also as containing naturally a critique of particular social arrangements. This might possibly explain the absence, in the renunciant, of a theoretical interrogation of the institution of property. This attitude of *sanyas* towards property mirrors

22 ❧ Cuspidal imaginings of political community

its attitude to the institution of family as well.[59] *Sanyas* is not thereby generally indifferent to social injustice. The *Mahayana* rather than the *Hinayana* viewpoint is instructive in this connection. Compared to the *Hinayana* view of *sanyas* being a complete individual striving for personal *moksha* or release from existence in the temporal universe, the *Mahayana* illustrates the praxis of the *Boddhisatva* who opts for repeated births and existence in society till all of humanity is released from suffering. On this plane, *sanyas* instils sensitivity for the suffering of others and *karuna*, or compassion, for the other translates into action for alleviation of general suffering. It may be possible to trace Vivekananda's position on renunciation and his programme of social action to this tradition. Occasionally, Vivekananda has been seen in a certain kinship with the Buddha: 'Vivekananda repeatedly points out that the Buddha had preached the "monastic vow" all over India. He had deeply impressed on the mind of India that ideal of renunciation.'[60]

Even before the arrival of modernity, *sanyas* was, in addition to being an act of faith, occasionally perceived in India as a symbol of social iconoclasm for a Hindu and liberating, and the renunciant's 'unorthodoxy in religious beliefs and behaviour was tolerated – or even revered, if it caught the popular imagination'.[61] Vivekananda considered *sanyas* as being essentially non-sectarian: 'A Sannyasin cannot belong to any religion, for his is a life of independent thought, which draws from all religions; his is a life of realisation, not merely of theory or belief, much less of dogma.'[62] Furthermore, the hermitage was not envisioned as a retreat from the intricacies of living and its responsibility towards society, but as an instrument of cooperation, an institution to 'make men'. In the closing years of his life, Vivekananda continued to emphasise on what could be termed as the social consciousness in the life of the monks: 'Those of you who are Sannyasins must try to do well to others for Sannyas means that.'[63] The monks were to love death, not as in a suicidal desire for martyrdom, but in the effacing of the 'self': 'It is right for you that you should serve your millions of brothers rather than aggrandize this little self. Thus you must die a gradual death.' The monk was visualised not as an individual engrossed in esoteric thinking only, but one who also felt responsible 'for the millions' and yet was 'strong and inflexible', being removed from the pressures of quotidian living.

> In our country the old idea is, to sit in a cave and meditate and die. To go ahead of others in salvation is wrong. One must learn sooner or later,

Cuspidal imaginings of political community ❖ 23

that one cannot get salvation if one does not try to seek the salvation of his brothers. You must try to combine in your life immense idealism with immense practicality. You must be prepared to go into deep meditation now, and the next moment you must be ready to go and cultivate the fields. You must be prepared to explain the difficult intricacies of the Shastras now, and the next moment to go and sell the produce of the fields in the market. You must be prepared for all menial services, not only here, but elsewhere also. . . . The true man is he who is strong as strength itself and yet possesses a woman's heart.[64]

The hermitage of Vivekananda is consciously different from Anandamath; in fact, it is difficult to say whether Vivekananda has on record said anything about the book, but he perhaps never used the evocation of *Vande Mataram*. His primary concern, as he put it, was man-making, and his reasons for accepting the life of a monk to work for national regeneration were embedded in his concept of politics and community in India. He once said: 'I am no politician or political agitator. I care only for the spirit–when that is right everything will be righted by itself.'[65] It was as if he desired to stand outside the political class, while at the same time be a member of the political community and assist in his own way for the general acceptance and observance of ethical politics in the country. Perhaps, naturally for a renunciant, ethics is intrinsically enjoined with religion. He perceived defined national propensities in the exercise of ideas in different nations, and politics was only one plane on which concepts and ideas acquired momentum. The English conceived of religion in terms of politics, Americans expressed their religious attitude through social reform, and in India religion was and would ever be the primary vehicle even of political ideas.[66] He saw it as trying to replace a 'spiritual backbone' by a 'political backbone'. His argued that 'Political ideals, personages representing political ideals, even social ideals, would have no power in India.'[67] This statement was partially accurate, especially of his times and for the following decades, although subsequently men representing socio-political ideals did acquire great power; it is another matter that even some among them acquired a religious halo with time. The ideal religious preceptor would be for him one who inspired perfect religious tolerance and in a way actuated a religious politics capable of pluralistic and ethical aspirations. Personally, he acknowledged his master Ramakrishna Paramhansa as the embodiment of absolute religious harmony. In an age of overriding political and cultural acrimony, Vivekananda appears to be alert to the danger of religious and

24 ❖ Cuspidal imaginings of political community

social discord. Rather than initiate a homogenisation of faiths fraught with danger, spiritual regeneration in India would mainly consist in the reaffirmation of religious toleration. The West was beginning to manifest intolerance: people in India little knew 'how much of intolerance is yet abroad'.[68] His stated mission of *Vedanta* was aimed at the eradication of such dissension and strife. He aspired to 'make this [Ramakrishna] Math a great centre of harmony'.[69] In his famous letter to Sarfaraz Hussain, he placed on record his 'experience' that it was the followers of Islam, and 'Islam alone,' who 'approached' the equality of *Advaita* in 'an appreciable degree in the plane of practical workaday life', which was 'yet to be developed among the Hindus universally'.[70]

Vivekananda may be meaningfully regarded as a significant precursor in the imagining of the Indian political community as primarily dependent on a new vocabulary of entitlement and opportunity. The life of Vivekananda reflected to a great extent, in the Indian context, the essentially moral enquiry of the nineteenth-century Russian thinkers and writers into the human condition that has been described so felicitously by Berlin:

> Their approach seemed to me essentially moral: they were concerned most deeply with what was responsible for injustice, oppression, falsity in human relations, imprisonment whether by stone walls or conformism – unprotesting submission to man-made yokes – moral blindness, egoism, cruelty, humiliation, servitude, poverty, helplessness, bitter indignation, despair, on the part of so many. In short, they were concerned with the nature of these experiences and their roots in the human condition; the condition of Russia in the first place, but, by implication, of all mankind. And conversely they wished to know what would bring about the exact opposite of this, a reign of truth, love, honesty, justice, security, personal relations based on the possibility of human dignity, decency, independence, freedom, spiritual fulfillment.[71]

Admittedly, for Vivekananda, colonial rule was to an extent responsible for degradation and an impediment to material and spiritual progress, but he was equally aware of the deleterious features of the Indian tradition. From the early stages of his work, Vivekananda's stated objective was, unlike the doctrinaire and cultish aims of most religious missions, 'to bring to the door of the meanest, the poorest, the noble ideas that the human race has developed both in and out of India, and let them think for themselves'.[72] Significantly, the religious ideas of Vivekananda were extremely progressive and totally against any privileging of ideas or positions. In this, they indicate both theoretically and practically towards reconciling and egalitarianising possibilities. This recommendation by Vivekananda to the renunciant is relevant for the godmen of our times, as it was also commentary on the existing practices of his times: 'The Sannyasin should have nothing to do with the rich, his duty is with the poor. The Sannyasin should treat the poor with loving care and serve them joyfully with all his might. To pay respects to the rich and hang on them for support has been the bane of all the Sannyasin communities of our country.'[73] Vivekananda was especially harsh on the notions of caste superiority and sacerdotal institutions that propagated the doctrine of *adhikarvada*, which supposed a hierarchy of eligibility along caste lines in higher knowledge, as being 'pernicious to the core': 'With all my respects for the Rishis of yore I cannot but denounce their method in instructing the people.'[74] Vivekananda translated commitment to the deprived to the plane of religious duty, movingly calling them *daridra narayana*, translatable as God the poor. The idea of being conscientious to the deprivation of those who do not normally share our class interests may have interesting theoretical possibilities in the context of recent concerns regarding universal responsibility for the 'other', and how any such responsibility generally operates within, and is limited by, elective affinities or structural commonality of class, race, ability and gender.[75] The idea of the *daridra narayana* exceeds mere sense of obligation in the sense of institutional charity and implies added and crucial responsibility on the part of the benefactor for maintaining the dignity and respect of the beneficiary. Vivekananda's renunciation and sense of social responsibility included both the denying of many prevalent notions of status and privilege and of conversely prioritising the virtue of service to the deprived as being a redemptive duty on the part of the enabled and the provisioned. General benefit and protective discrimination were for him not mutually exclusive, as in his argument that 'a Brahmin is not so much in need of education as a Chandala. If the son of a Brahmin needs one teacher, that of a Chandala needs ten'.[76] This may be relatable to the often fraught relationship between justice and dignity in matters of institutional aid to the dispossessed and the destitute, whether due to the general implication of a slur of inferiority on the part of the recipient or due to an insensitive or callous even if efficient system of distribution of aid, which degrades people, for instance by reducing starving humans to fighting for food thrown from trucks as in famine-stricken Ethiopia.

26 ❄ Cuspidal imaginings of political community

Avishai Margalit mentions this example in his argument that ensuring welfare does not necessarily extend to ensuring dignity and that a just society need not by that quality alone be a decent society. A different level of ethical responsibility and another conception of human life may be a condition for facilitating a merging of social responsibility with the values of kindness and caring. 'There is a suspicion that the just society may become mired in rigid calculations of what is just, which may replace gentleness and humane consideration in simple human relations. The requirements that a just society should also be a decent one means that it is not enough for goods to be distributed justly and efficiently – the style of their distribution must also be taken into account.'[77]

In an increasingly secularising period of history, a purely religious definition of the values of caring could soon become meaningless in modern society. Vivekananda, in acknowledging and analysing the limitations of denominational self-definitions, also indicated at the constructive possibility of pluralistic perceptions. During the building of the Ramakrishna Mission, he continued to work for an accommodation of 'a thousand minds' in its institutions. It was with his particular view of yoga and the *Vedanta* that he welcomed Muslim boys in the institutions run by the Mission and suggested making separate arrangements for them if necessary, yet told the brethren to 'never tamper with their religion'.[78] His stated aspiration for the Mission was 'to lead mankind to the place where there is neither the Vedas, nor the Bible, nor the Koran; yet this has to be done by harmonising the Vedas, the Bible and the Koran'.[79]

Vivekananda was neither a zealot nor a hegemonist. Although his metaphysical vocabulary is predominantly Hindu and he spoke from within a tradition, he employed effectively that tradition against oppression and exploitation, and in matters of social reform, spoke of the advisability of first identifying the 'necessity underlying' an uncivil custom and then by altering the necessity thereby eradicating the custom. Rabindranath Tagore included prominently Vivekananda in the tradition begun by Chaitanya, Nanak, Dadu and Kabir of harmonising the varied communities of India and particularly of building a bridge of ideals across the Hindu and the Muslim character. Of his own times, Tagore remarked: 'It is not as if India is inactive [in this regard] now – Rammohun Roy, Swami Dayananda, Keshabchandra [Sen], Ramakrishna Paramhansa, Vivekananda, Shibnarayan Swami they also have surrendered into India's hands their life's praxis to establish the one in many, the great into the small' (my translation).[80] According to Vivekananda, traditional concepts did not need final excision from contemporary minds as they could even be re-envisioned to serve not only as records of unfairness and inequity but also as conceptual spaces for the institution of rapprochement among historically embittered identities. His criticism of Adhikarvada has been mentioned earlier. He viewed it not only as a shortcoming but also as evidence of malintent on the part of the proponents of the doctrine, since it privileged them directly as custodians of knowledge: 'These advocates of Adhikarvada ignored the tremendous fact of the infinite possibilities of the human soul.'[81]

The responsible nation

The lived experience of the nineteenth century gave to Vivekananda a proximity to the unfolding of the national spirit, and it is undeniable that much of his activity was directed for a resurgent homeland. However, he is powerfully relevant for advocating the values of a responsible nation. On one plane, this advocacy consisted of alerting his countrymen, both to the dangers of the 'huge wave of nationalism' that he had seen sweeping over Europe during his travels in the Continent and to the ill effects of revanchist militarisation. 'But who is to ultimately supply the funds? Consequently the peasants have to put on tattered rags–while in towns you will find soldiers dressed in gorgeous uniforms. Throughout Europe there is a craze for soldiers – soldiers everywhere.'[82] His vision of the future India was totally non-militaristic and non-xenophobic: 'No man, no nation, my son, can hate others and live. India's doom was sealed the very day they invented the word *Mlechchcha* and stopped from communion with others.'[83] On another plane, he was sceptical and dismissive of conventional patriotism: 'Everyone wants me to come over to India. They think we shall be able to do more if I come. They are mistaken my friend. The present enthusiasm is only a little patriotism, it means nothing.'[84] Moreover, he never ceased reminding his compatriots of the institutional and structural injustices that were also implicated in the otherwise impressive cultural heritage of the country. A sense of responsibility for deprivation in society and the undertaking of restitutive acts, at both the individual and collective levels, were considered by him to be crucial for the rectification of these injustices in the future nation. In stating that he was 'no metaphysician' but as one who being poor, loved the poor, he was indicating at an ethics of community.

28 ❖ Cuspidal imaginings of political community

> So long as the millions live in hunger and ignorance, I hold every man a traitor who, having been educated at their expense, pays not the least heed to them! I call those men who strut about in their finery, having got all the money by grinding the poor, wretches, so long as they do not do anything for those two hundred millions who are now no better than hungry savages.[85]

A section of contemporary opinion has, on the contrary, typified these statements as mere piousness or worse, ephemeral propaganda of the ostensible impeccability of his social concerns to obscure the reality of his elitism.[86] During the Indian independence movement, the colonial administration at one point initiated surveillance of the Ramakrishna Mission and eventually took punitive measures including dissolution of the organisation, when it transpired that revolutionaries in Bengal were impressed with the life and thought of Vivekananda, and many of them carried copies of his writings. Public representations in support of the Mission ultimately averted its dissolution by the government. However, this fact in itself does not adequately explain the British government's hostility to the Ramakrishna Mission. The government's unfriendliness to the Ramakrishna Mission can be attributed not so much as to a substantive perception on its part regarding Vivekananda's aggressive nationalistic inclinations and his appeal also among young political extremists, as perhaps more to a residual antagonism of the government towards *sadhus* in general. *Sadhus* were seen wishfully by the government as being overtly and rather violently political and thereupon presented with unsavoury character in police dossiers. There was no doubt quite an enduring political activism in certain monastic orders. In his interesting study of some such 'subaltern' monastic orders, William R. Pinch dismisses British allegations regarding the many moral failings of the *sadhus*. Although the *sanyasis* of the Mission might not be typified under this rubric, they certainly would have received part of the government's general antipathy towards monks as a potentially political group, markedly evident in governmental circles with the later rise of Gandhian mass politics. Pinch says that, for sadhus palpably involved with political programmes, their 'political actions were a function of their religious and philosophical commitment' rather than a personal and ideological failing.[87] It will be crucial to remember that Vivekananda's national sentiment was part of his spiritual-reformist ardour. Amiya Sen illustratively observes a living commitment in Vivekananda's remaining steadfast towards apparently two inconsistent objectives: 'An immensely practical, this-worldly approach and the supra-worldly construct of pure transcendence.'[88] However, the discussion on *sanyas* and the social consciousness, earlier in the study, has perhaps adequately indicated that in the life of an extraordinary individual there need be no inconsistency between spiritual pursuit and amelioration of others' suffering. Differently, Vivekananda has been described as an aggressive nationalist in studies such as that by Bhupendranath Datta.[89] Datta's argument, outlined in the opening two pages of his Foreword to his book, is however not substantiated by references to recorded statements by Vivekananda, and most allusions to his nationalistic intents and programmes in the book are through narrative and largely uncorroborated accounts. Christopher Isherwood states – 'However it is not at all surprising that [Vivekananda] has been much misunderstood; that parts of his message, taken out of context, have been presented as a whole. Even some of his brother monks, at the time of the founding of the Mission, were afraid that he was deviating from Ramakrishna's aims. And there have been some, in much recent times, who have claimed him as a socialist and a nationalist revolutionary. They wish, in all sincerity, to honour Vivekananda as a great Indian patriot, and they are right as far as they go. But their statue of him would have to be a headless torso; Vivekananda without Ramakrishna.'[90] Vivekananda's bitter protestations – which are totally undenotive of any kind of violent nationalism – against missionary propaganda are better understood in the frame of a larger, including European, disgust against the racist core of colonial philosophy. This encapsulates a different nationalist idea. The ethical interrogation by Kant of colonial pretensions and Herder's astringent critique of racist presumptions of European evangelism may indicate such a frame. In his prominent text, discussing the militarist tendencies as commonly pursued in realpolitik, Kant referred to the colonising of India in refuting bluntly any claim of even a mistaken civilising mission in the European marauding of lands across the Old and the New World. 'In East India (Hindustan), under the pretense of establishing economic undertakings, they brought in foreign soldiers and used them to oppress the natives, excited widespread wars among the various states, spread famine, rebellion, perfidy, and the whole litany of evils which afflict mankind.'[91] Berlin refers in a similar context to Herder's mordant portrayal of a cultural situation: ' "Why are you pouring water over my head?" asked a dying slave of a Christian missionary. "So that you can

30 ❖ Cuspidal imaginings of political community

go to heaven." "I do not want to go to a heaven where there are white men," he replied, and turned on his side and died.'[92]

It would involve a detailed discussion in comparing Vivekananda's imagination of India with some of the other colonial imaginings of nationhood, but it might be suitably illustrative for our argument to refer very briefly to some such concerns of reform and change. In traditional societies, such as in Africa, with a different social history than that of India, and without a doctrine of established social exclusivity, anti-colonial writing evidences an uncomplicated defence of traditional social structure apropos the colonising administration. For instance, Aime Cesaire in his *Discourse on Colonialism* defends unqualifiedly the traditional structures and practices of colonised societies.

> Every day that passes, every denial of justice, every beating by the police, every demand of the workers that is drowned in blood, every scandal that is hushed up, every punitive expedition, every police van, every gendarme and every militiaman, brings home to us the value of our old societies. They were communal societies, never societies of the many for the few. They were societies that were not only ante-capitalist, as has been said, but also *anti-capitalist*. They were democratic societies, always. They were cooperative societies, fraternal societies. I make a systematic defense of the societies destroyed by imperialism.[93]

It is quite needless to point out that Vivekananda hardly thought that all traditional Indian social practices were salutary. The Tunisian philosopher and analyser of colonialism, Albert Memmi, described the creation of what he calls a 'countermythology', wherein the colonised turns to an unapologetic defence of native traditions to salvage the image of his country's culture in his own eyes. This unnecessary, and erroneous, glorification indicates as much as to an innate inadequacy on the part of the colonised subject as to reluctance on his part to constructively engage with the issue of rediscovering his tradition. But it most certainly should not be deduced that the distinguished thinker Cesaire can even remotely be comprised in this category. In India, this perhaps happened most uncomplicatedly to some of the young generation, which had taken an unalloyed pleasure in debunking traditional values before they became excessively valiant in their championing of indigenous cultural values and religious principles. Tagore had likened this tendency to a kind of dipsomania. For Memmi, this certainly was a fact in the context of African colonialism. He mentions the trend of reviving old myths initially as resistance to effacement of native identity and progressively as perhaps a fascination for the exoticism of tradition but with inattentiveness to the perils of rationalising of the symbolic. This proceeds to the counter-mythology that is now created by the coloniser. 'Suddenly, exactly to the reverse of the colonialist accusation, the colonized, his culture, his country, everything that belongs to him, everything he represents, becomes perfectly positive elements . . . everything is good, everything must be retained among his customs and traditions, his actions and plans; even the anachronous or disorderly, the immoral or mistaken. Everything is justified because everything can be explained.'[94] The savage fun that Vivekananda made, of those who aspired to preserve unexceptionally all traditional customs and rites in Bengal, is too well known to need further comment. However, the tangible enlargement in the scope and the social possibility of the modern religious consciousness becomes prominently noticeable with Vivekananda. His admiration of tradition is simultaneously fused with incisive criticism of a host of social practices. In his imagination of modern India, he is comparable to the reformer modernist, Rammohun Roy. In spite of his criticism of Roy's approach to religion in matters of reform, Nivedita's account of a conversation with him at Nainital provides an indication of his envisioning himself as continuing with Roy's efforts for a modern Indian consciousness. Speaking in detail of Roy, Vivekananda drew intellectual kinship with him regarding *Vedantism*, patriotism and indiscriminative feeling for Hindu Muslim alike. 'In all these things he claimed himself to have taken up the task that the breadth and foresight of Ram Mohan Roy had mapped out.'[95]

Bernard Williams regards religious ethics as being intrinsically problematic: 'The trouble with religious morality comes not from morality's being inescapably pure, but from religion's being incurably unintelligible.'[96] But a renunciant like Vivekananda could naturally merge the religious and the ethical, even perhaps on the most difficult plane, in sincerely adhering to tradition while being critical of it to a degree that effectively has the potential of recreating that tradition. He might have achieved this to an admirable extent because of his independent exposing of revivalist ambitions. He was acutely aware of the beginning of modern convergence of orthodoxies that had already become noticeable in his time: 'That recently in Eastern Aryavarta, the different caste-people seem to develop a feeling of united sympathy amidst themselves with a view to ameliorate their present social condition – that, in the Mahratta country, the Brahmans have begun to sing paeans in praise of the "Maratha" race – these, the lower castes cannot yet believe to be the outcome of pure disinterestedness.'[97] Vivekananda appreciated the generative impact of

32 ❖ Cuspidal imaginings of political community

ideas borne on political winds from abroad and was rather optimistic of the egalitarian character of English rule:

> The days of exclusive privileges and exclusive claims are gone, gone for ever from the soil of India, and it is one of the great blessings of the British Rule in India. Even to the Mohammedan Rule we owe that great blessing, the destruction of exclusive privilege. That rule was, after all, not all bad; nothing is all bad and nothing is all good. The Mohammedan conquest of India came as a salvation to the down-trodden, to the poor.[98]

He had presciently observed that conflict between nations derives from within intra-national contentions and that countries divert the focus of their communities from domestic disputes through issues of foreign policy.[99] He recognised and welcomed the beginnings of a convergence of civilisations and the inevitable knitting of countries into a global community which would require more reflection and fewer belligerences on the part of nations and also innovative protocols of international understanding.[100] The ideas of Vivekananda regarding the ethics of community and nation offer complex and significant readings in contemporary contexts. Ideologies that are fixative over manipulation and control of community aspirations and effort will be tested through a difficult frame of ethics and decency in the political thought of Bankim and Vivekananda.

To explore a discourse in ideational terms may be sometimes convenient, but it is hardly ever an unproblematic endeavour. The 'real' idea on which the 'real' meaning of the discourse rests or is contained may become severely contested. But I hope that the argument in process can indicate that a discourse, which has so far been largely suspected of subsumed meanings, may convey very different implications for us if the merging of the apparent and the evidential meanings is locatable with fairly reasonable consistency. To do that would, I admit, mean accepting a different relationship of the historical past and the historicised present than say as is contained in Marx's *Eighteenth Brumaire of Louis Bonaparte*. I am aware that viewed in that logic this discourse may seem merely as the weighing of the tradition of all the dead generations, 'like a nightmare on the brain of the living'.[101] Bankim and Vivekananda would then not be seen as proponents of change but rather as protagonists from an epoch which, even when presented with an opportunity of revolutionary change, resurrected 'the old chronology, the old names, the old edicts, which had long become a subject of antiquarian erudition, and the old minions of the law, who had long since decayed'.[102] Marx had written that the 'social revolution of the nineteenth century cannot draw its poetry from the past, but only from the future'. But even critics from within the Marxist tradition of scholarship have occasionally chosen to go beyond this frame. And this seems perfectly consistent to me. In earlier times in India, the identificational Hindu or Muslim did not in the political community approximate to *Hindutva* or its Islamic variant of today. Writing of the different paths opted for by Maulana Azad and M. A. Jinnah in their imagining of a political community from a religious community, Aijaz Ahmed has stated: 'It is one of the great paradoxes of modern Indian history that traditions of Islamic piety, from Azad to the Deoband *ulema*, eventually found their way into composite cultural and political nationalism; theories of modernization, as taught in the British and proto-British institutions, from Lincoln's inn to Aligarh, begat, on the other hand, communal separatism.'[103] Confining myself to the first half of his statement, I would mention that Ahmed consciously did not extend this thesis to the period under discussion. It is our contention that it could be profitable to do so with regard to the two gentlemen who are mainly the subjects of the present discussion.

Notes

1. Sudhir Chandra, *Dependence and Disillusionment: Emergence of National Consciousness in Later Nineteenth Century India* (New Delhi: Oxford University Press, 2011), xxv.
2. Charles L. Griswold, *Forgiveness: A Philosophical Exploration* (New York: Cambridge University Press, 2007), 209.
3. Michael O. Hardimon, *Hegel's Social Philosophy: The Project of Reconciliation* (Cambridge: Cambridge University Press, 1994), 17–18.
4. Hardimon, *Hegel's Social Philosophy*, 19.
5. Hardimon, *Hegel's Social Philosophy*, 258.
6. Jotirao Phule, 'Slavery', trans. Maya Pandit in ed. G. P. Deshpande, *Selected Writings of Jotirao Phule* (New Delhi: LeftWord Books, 2002), 89. In a way commenting on the historical attitude of the leading political parties to the issue, Ambedkar, speaking on 25 November 1949, to the Constituent Assembly, warned of the disastrous consequences of an abiding disillusionment of the suppressed classes with constitutional processes: 'These are my

34 ❖ Cuspidal imaginings of political community

reflections about the tasks that lie ahead of us. They may not be very pleasant to some. But there can be no gainsaying that political power in this country has too long been the monopoly of a few and the many are not only beasts of burden, but also beasts of prey. This monopoly has not merely deprived them of their chance of betterment, it has sapped them of what may be called the significance of life. These down-trodden classes are tired of being governed. They are impatient to govern themselves. This urge for self-realization in the down-trodden classes must not be allowed to devolve into a class struggle or class war. It would lead to a division of the House. That would indeed be a day of disaster.' *Constituent Assembly Debates: Official Report*, 5 Books (New Delhi: Lok Sabha Secretariat, 1950; rpt. 1999), 5: 980.

7. *Congress Presidential Addresses*, ed. A. M. Zaidi, 5 vols. (New Delhi: Indian Institute of Applied Political Research, 1986–1989), 1: 28.

8. *Congress Presidential Addresses*, 1: 47–48.

9. *Congress Presidential Addresses*, 1: 128.

10. Gopal Krishna Gokhale, *Speeches and Writings of Gopal Krishna Gokhale*, 2 vols. (Delhi: Anmol Publications, 1987 [hereafter *Speeches and Writings*]), 2: 743.

11. *Speeches and Writings*, 2: 744.

12. *Speeches and Writings*, 2: 745.

13. Jean Améry, *At the Mind's Limits: Contemplations by a Survivor on Auschwitz and Its Realities*, trans. Sidney Rosenfeld and Stella P. Rosenfeld (Bloomington: Indiana University Press, 1980), 76.

14. Nikos Kazantzakis, *Report to Greco*, trans. P. A. Bien (London: Faber and Faber Limited, 1973), 176–177.

15. Tapan Raychaudhuri, *Europe Reconsidered: Perceptions of the West in Nineteenth-Century Bengal* (Delhi: Oxford University Press, 2006), 360.

16. S. N. Mukherjee refers to the prevalence of this perception: 'It is often suggested that Bankim Chandra was a counter-reformist, a Bengali Loyola in relation to Rammohun Roy, a Bengali Luther.' S. N. Mukherjee, 'Introduction', in trans. and ed. S. N. Mukherjee and Marian Maddern, *Bankim Chandra Chatterjee – Sociological Essays: Utilitarianism and Positivism in Bengal* (Calcutta: Rddhi-India, 1986), 14.

17. For a subtle analysis of such modernity, see Sudipta Kaviraj, *The Unhappy Consciousness: Bankimchandra and the Formation of Nationalist Discourse in India* (Delhi: Oxford University Press, 1995), 158–168.

18. S. N. Mukherjee, 'Introduction', 14.

19. Rachel Van M. Baumer, 'The Reinterpretation of Dharma in Nineteenth-Century Bengal: Righteous Conduct for Man in the Modern World', in ed. Rachel Van M. Baumer, *Aspects of Bengali History and Society* (New Delhi: Vikas Publishing House, 1976), 96. In an early study of modern Indian political thought, Bimanbehari Majumdar wrote of Bankim in

perhaps slightly emotional appreciation: 'In the history of western political thought, Machiavelli is regarded as the prophet and preacher of the principles of nationalism and patriotism. In the history of the political thought of Modern India, Bankimchandra holds a position analogous to that of Machiavelli. Like the great Florentine statesman, Bankimchandra too held patriotism as the first principle of political philosophy. But Bankimchandra's political philosophy is based on such high ethical conceptions that it would be nothing less than sacrilege to utter his name in the same breath with that of Machiavelli.' Bimanbehari Majumdar, *History of Political Thought from Rammohun Roy to Dayananda*, vol. I (Calcutta: University of Calcutta, 1934), 402.

20. Bankim Chandra Chatterjee, *Essays & Letters*, eds. Brajendranath Nath Banerji and Sajani Kant Das (New Delhi: Rupa, 2010), 117.

21. Chatterjee, *Essays & Letters*, 117–118.

22. Majumdar, *History of Political Thought from Rammohun Roy to Dayananda*, 404.

23. Hayden White, *Metahistory: The Historical Imagination in Nineteenth Century Europe* (Baltimore: The Johns Hopkins University Press, 1975), 213.

24. Hugh Seton-Watson, *Nations and States: An Enquiry into the Origins of Nations and the Politics of Nationalism* (London: Methuen & Co., 1977), 463.

25. Kedourie gives the originary definition of the nation as in Europe: '*Natio* in ordinary speech originally meant a group of men belonging together by similarity of birth, larger than a family, but smaller than a clan of people.' Elie Kedourie, *Nationalism* (Malden, MA: Blackwell Publishing, 1993), 5.

26. I am grateful to Murali Manohar Dwivedi for references, interpretation and the translation of the relevant Sanskrit verses.

27. '*Atvaharshamantaredhi dhruvastishthavichachalih / Vishastva sarva vanchhantu matvad rashtramadhibhrashat.*' *Rigveda* (Poona: Vaidik Sanshodhan Mandal, 1946), 10/173/1.

28. For details, see *Yajurveda* (Delhi: Motilal Banarsidass, 1978), 22/22; and generally *Atharvaveda* (Pardi, Valsad: Svadhyaya Mandal, 4th edition, not dated), 1/29/1; 1/29/4.

29. For details, see *Rigveda*, 10/12/3.

30. '*Na hi tad bhavita rashtram yatra ramo na bhupati / tad vanam bhavita rashtram yatra ramo nivatsyati.*' Valmiki, *Ramayana* (Gorakhpur: Gita Press, 1976 [2033 Vikram Era]), 2/37/29.

31. Raychaudhuri, *Europe Reconsidered*, 135–136.

32. '*Vajasyemam prasavah sushuvegre somam rajanamoshadhishvapsu / ta asmabhyam madhumatirbhavantu vayam rashtre jagryama purohitah*'. – *Yajurveda* 9/23. For a comprehensive analysis of the essential qualities, in Sanskrit literature, of the preceptor who normally functioned as both priest and counselor, see Jan Gonda, *Change and Continuity in Indian Religion* (1965; rpt Delhi: Munshiram Manoharlal Publishers, 1997), 229–283.

33. Chatterjee, *Sociological Essays: Utilitarianism and Positivism in Bengal,* trans. and ed. S.N. Mukherjee and Marian Maddern (Calcutta: Rddhi-India, 1986), 55.
34. Chatterjee, *Sociological Essays,* 56.
35. Chatterjee, *Sociological Essays,* 56.
36. Chatterjee, *Sociological Essays,* 58.
37. Chatterjee, *Sociological Essays,* 60.
38. Chatterjee, *Sociological Essays,* 117.
39. This attitude towards ancient kingship as being somewhat benevolent was not entirely uncommon in the early days of Western-educated Indians responding to sweeping critiques of traditional Indian polity by English historians. Perhaps, the earliest such riposte was a thoughtful paper presented by a twenty-two-year-old student of the Hindu College, Kashi Prasad Ghosh, during his annual examination in 1828. Ghosh defended Brahmins and kings from Mill's charge of perpetuating an arcane and retrogressive social system. According to Ghosh, the traditional Brahmin pundit was respected not as a priest but as a scholar and drew his resilience from his complete devotion to learning as well as the traditional prohibition for Brahmins from acquiring wealth. The authority of the Hindu monarch was never unrestrained from law and a kind of public opinion: 'The allurement of wealth and power on one side, and the terror of religion and law on the other, secured the peace of the kingdom.' C. Ghosh, 'Essay on Mill's British India', quoted in David Kopf, *British Orientalism and the Bengal Renaissance: The Dynamics of Indian Modernization 1773–1835* (Berkeley: University of California Press, 1969), 263–264.
40. Bankimchandra Chatterjee, *Prabandha o Onnanya Rachana* (Kolkata: Sahityam, 2007), 536.
41. Chatterjee, *Prabandha o Onnanya Rachana,* 561.
42. B.N. Ganguli, *Concept of Equality: The Nineteenth Century Indian Debate* (Simla: Indian Institute of Advanced Study, 1975), 104.
43. Chatterjee, *Sociological Essays,* 197–198.
44. Rezaul Karim, 'In the Eyes of a Non-Hindu', trans. William Radice, in ed. Bhabatosh Chatterjee, *Bankimchandra Chatterjee: Essays in Perspective* (New Delhi: Sahitya Akademi, 1994), 177–181.
45. Chatterjee, *Bankim Rachanabali: Upannyas Samagra* (Kolkata: Shubham, 2009), 998.
46. Sisir Kumar Das, *The Artist in Chains* (Delhi: New Statesman Publishing Company, 1984), 239.
47. Das, *The Artist in Chains,* 239.
48. Das, *The Artist in Chains,* 236.
49. T.W. Clark, 'The Role of Bankimcandra in the Development of Nationalism', in ed. C.H. Phillips, *Historians of India, Pakistan and Ceylon* (London: Oxford University Press, 1961), 445.

Cuspidal imaginings of political community   ❖   37

50. Chatterjee, *Sociological Essays*, 76.
51. Raychaudhuri, *Europe Reconsidered*, 230.
52. Peter Heehs discusses in his biography of Aurobindo the difficulties of a biographer in making a study of the 'spiritual life' of a subject. Hees states: 'It is one thing to scrutinize descriptions of spiritual experiences, quite another to interpret them. Unlike such disciplines as history and literary criticism, the study of spirituality has no generally accepted hermeneutic framework. Spiritual experiences are not available on demand, nor do they lend themselves well to intellectual systematizing.' For details, see Peter Heehs, *Sri Aurobindo: A Brief Biography* (Delhi: Oxford University Press, 2003), 85–87.
53. G. C. Pande, *Studies in the Origins of Buddhism* (Delhi: Motilal Banarsidass, 1995), 326.
54. Pande, *Studies in the Origins of Buddhism*, 327–328.
55. Pande, *Studies in the Origins of Buddhism*, 332.
56. G. C. Pande, *Life and Thought of Sankaracharya* (Delhi: Motilal Banarsidass, 2004), 246.
57. Pande, *Life and Thought of Sankaracharya*, 246.
58. '*Karyam ity eva yat karma/niyatam kriyate 'rjuna/sangatam tyaktava phalam cati 'va/sa tyagah sattviko matah*'. S. Radhakrishnan, *The Bhagavadgita* (Bombay: Blackie & Son, 1982), verse 8, chapter xviii.
59. I am grateful to Sibesh Chandra Bhattacharya for this interpretation of the relationship between *sanyas* and the social consciousness.
60. Lal Mani Joshi, *Discerning the Buddha: A Study of Buddhism and of the Brahmanical Hindu Attitude to It* (Delhi: Munshiram Manoharlal Publishers, 1983), 210.
61. Charles H. Heimsath, *Indian Nationalism and Hindu Social Reform* (Princeton: Princeton University Press, 1964), 9.
62. Swami Vivekananda, *The Complete Works of Swami Vivekananda*, 9 vols. (Mayavati/Kolkata: Advaita Ashram, 1948–1997 [hereafter *Complete Works*]), 5: 187.
63. *Complete Works*, 3: 446.
64. *Complete Works*, 3: 447.
65. *Complete Works*, 5: 35–36.
66. *Complete Works*, 3: 314. This view was shared by many of his contemporaries. For instance, Tagore opined: 'We will surely have to remember this doctrine that if any effort in our country aspires to help the people of the country then it cannot by any means be successful if it does not take recourse to religion. No countrywide opportunity, no temptation of the accomplishment of national self-interest has ever generated vigour in the mind of our common people' (my translation). Rabindranath Tagore, *Rabindra Rachanabali* (125th anniversary edition), 15 vols. (Kolkata: Visva-Bharati, 1986–1992 [1393–1398 Bengali era]), 5: 789.

38 ❖ Cuspidal imaginings of political community

67. *Complete Works*, 3: 32.
68. *Complete Works*, 3: 187.
69. *Complete Works*, 7: 160.
70. *Complete Works*, 4: 375.
71. Isaiah Berlin, *The Crooked Timber of Humanity: Chapters in the History of Ideas*, ed. Henry Hardy (Princeton, NJ: Princeton University Press, 1990), 3.
72. *Complete Works*, 5: 25.
73. *Complete Works*, 5: 188.
74. *Complete Works*, 5: 190.
75. Iris Marion Young, *Responsibility for Justice* (New York: Oxford University Press, Inc., 2011), which discusses responses to, among others, Derrida, Sartre and Levinas can be one reference on the topic.
76. *Complete Works*, 6: 287.
77. Avishai Margalit, *The Decent Society*, trans. Naomi Goldblum (Cambridge, MA: Harvard University Press, 1998), 280–281.
78. *Complete Works*, 6: 370.
79. *Complete Works*, 6: 376. Peter Van der Veer finds Vivekananda's view of yoga distinctive in the context of a pluralistic vision of religion: 'What I find important in Vivekananda's construction of yoga as the core of Hindu "spirituality" is that it is devoid of any specific devotional content that would involve, for example, temple worship and thus a theological and ritual position in sectarian debates.' Peter Van der Veer, 'Colonial Cosmopolitanism', in ed. Steven Vertovec and Robin Cohen, *Conceiving Cosmopolitanism: Theory, Context, and Practice* (New York: Oxford University Press, 2002), 177.
80. Rabindranath Tagore, *Rabindra Rachanabali*, 5: 763.
81. *Complete Works*, 5: 190.
82. *Complete Works*, 3: 374.
83. *Complete Works*, 5: 40.
84. *Complete Works*, 5: 39.
85. *Complete Works*, 5: 45.
86. One such highly critical, if equally polemical and schematic, study in this regard has been authored by Narasingha P. Sil. This comment by Sil is representative of his critique: 'All this dithyramb for the downtrodden was in fact simply wishy-washy fashionable humanitarianism of a Bengali *bhadralok*'. Narasingha P. Sil, *Swami Vivekananda: A Reassessment* (Selinsgrove: Susquehanna University Press, 1997), 76.
87. William R. Pinch, *Peasants and Monks in British India* (Delhi: Oxford University Press, 1996), 9.
88. Amiya P. Sen, *Swami Vivekananda* (Delhi: Oxford University Press, 2013), 101.
89. For details, see Bhupendranath Datta, *Swami Vivekananda: Patriot – Prophet* (Calcutta: Nababharat Publishers, 1993).

90. Christopher Isherwood, *Ramakrishna and His Disciples* (Kolkata: Advaita Ashram, 2007), 326. Peter Heehs, a veteran scholar who has observed in detail the nuances of the nationalistic idea in Bengal, similarly agrees: 'It is possible, by taking passages from Vivekananda's writings out of context, to make him look like a consciously nationalistic figure. But if one goes through the *Complete Works* dispassionately, one is forced to conclude that Vivekananda never ceased to regard his mission as a spiritual one.' Peter Heehs, *The Bomb in Bengal: The Rise of Revolutionary Terrorism in India 1900–1910* (Delhi: Oxford University Press, 2004), 25.

91. Immanuel Kant, *Perpetual Peace* (Minneapolis: Filiquarian Publishing, LLC, [1795] 2007), 22.

92. Isaiah Berlin, *Three Critics of the Enlightenment: Vico, Hamann, Herder*, ed. Henry Hardy (Princeton, NJ: Princeton University Press, 2000), 185.

93. Aime Cesaire, *Discourse on Colonialism*, trans. Joan Pinkham (Delhi: Aakar Books, 2010), 44.

94. Albert Memmi, *The Colonizer and the Colonized*, trans. Howard Greenfeld (Boston: Beacon Press, 1967), 138–139.

95. *Complete Works*, 9: 341.

96. Bernard Williams, *Morality: An Introduction to Ethics* (Cambridge: Cambridge University Press, 1993), 72.

97. *Complete Works*, 4: 407.

98. *Complete Works*, 3: 294.

99. *Complete Works*, 3: 316.

100. *Complete Works*, 3: 241.

101. Karl Marx, *The Eighteenth Brumaire of Louis Bonaparte* (Moscow: Progress Publishers, 1967), 10.

102. Marx, *The Eighteenth Brumaire*, 12.

103. Aijaz Ahmed, 'Azad's Careers: Roads Taken and Not Taken', in Aijaz Ahmed, *Lineages of the Present* (Delhi: Tulika, 1996), 189.

II ❂
Politics

Truth and non-violence

Non-violence and truth might provide the finest definition and the axis of the political principles of Gandhi and Tagore. Their ethical operability can be evaluated by a theoretical discussion that fleshes the first principles of their political thought in difficult, even inhospitable, contexts. Michael Walzer has pointed out that issues involving practical morality are better understood casuistically and suitably illustrated through historical cases paying attention to the 'nuances and details of historical reality'. He also admits that these cases can be frequently controversial. But it was at the same time important to him that he could in all justification believe that he was 'reporting on experiences that men and women have really had and on arguments that they have really made'.[1] I have according to this frame, attempted to study the ethical politics of Gandhi and Tagore in the context of historical experience. The following discussion of the essential principles of their politics, perhaps best describable in terms of conscionableness, truth and non-violence, situates these virtues as political values in the ambiance of protest, resistance and tragic despair.

Tagore: freedom of conscience and ethics of community

It will be interesting to explore translation of Rabindranath Tagore's ideas on the ethics of community and, what perhaps is for many of us somewhat paradoxical for Tagore, the ethics of nation. The ground for these ideas is traceable in his historical situation and his philosophical inheritance, including the awareness of nationalistic passion; experience of illiberal colonial government; interaction with the West and other cultures of what can now be called as the global South; and a sense of

Politics: truth and non-violence   41

human dignity in traditional Indian concepts, and its playing out, with its possible and attendant complications, in some of his major writings such as *Atmashakti, Samuha* and *Kalantar*. These writings are still untranslated and also largely under-analysed on the plane of a conversation among the established and the alternative ideas of political action. The vision of Tagore also, in a way, explores the ways to reconciliation between opposing historical inheritances. In this, Tagore's focus is predominantly on the individual as constituent of larger communities, and his ideas on social responsibility deliberate on the making of the ethical individual. It may prove interesting to detect the development and interplay of these ideas in a still later text of Tagore's, and I attempt to bring particular focus on a controversial novel by him – *Char Adhyaya* (*Four Chapters*, 1934). *Char Adhyaya* has been seen mainly as his response to a political situation, but his deliberate choice, regarding form, of a novel over a political essay may imply an engagement with the human condition which permits of a more nuanced representation of a theme that had in a sense engaged Tagore all his life. This was regarding the ethical choices confronting communities during difficult times, as also the negotiating of the issue of 'freedom' – whether the acquiring of the freedom of political intervention was, for even the briefest moment and at whatever point, prioritisable over the freedom of conscience, and how could an ethics of a community render that prioritisation adverse in the perception of the community. The presuppositions which Tagore brought to his political experience also helped to form that experience. Although not grounded on the plane of the merely political, this transition from the metaphysical to the political-plus, if one can call it such, was conducive for creating a space for historical imagination and insight, and crucially, involving an insistent ethics in his political writings. Early in his mid-twenties, on the death of his sister-in-law Kadambari Devi, an experience of the metaphysical foundations of living reinforced his faith, which had been formed in childhood in nearness to his father. 'Yet amid unbearable grief, flashes of joy sparkled in my mind on and off in a way which quite surprised me. The idea that life is not a fixture came as tidings that helped to lighten my mind. That we are not forever prisoners behind a wall of stony-hearted facts was the thought that kept unconsciously rising uppermost in rushes of gladness.'[2] This inspirational awareness remained both a source of puzzlement and resilience in his dealings with the political world; his puzzlement remained, paradoxically, even with the political positions of, arguably the supreme practitioner of ethical politics, Mahatma Gandhi.

42 ❋ Politics: truth and non-violence

As Tagore wrote to Rolland: 'It is the moral loneliness which is a constant and invisible burden that oppresses me the most.'[3] A poignant instance is Tagore's agonising in a letter to C. F. Andrews over Gandhi's position on the Hunter Commission:

> And for this, all the moral fervour which the life of Gandhi represents, and which he, of all other men in the world, can call up, is needed. That such a precious treasure of power should be put into the mean and frail vessel of our politics allowing it to sail across endless waves of angry recrimination is terribly unfortunate for our country where our mission is to revive the dead with the fire of soul. The external waste of our resources of life is great owing to external circumstances – but [that] the waste of our spiritual resources should be allowed to happen on adventures that are wrong from the point of view of moral truth is heartbreaking. It is criminal to turn moral force into a blind force.[4]

I

It may appear to be a simplification to argue especially given Tagore's vocabulary that the major concern in his thinking is with freedom, both from the fetters of the intellectual orthodoxies as well as from the fetish of total revolution. But it may not be impossible to attempt transactions between the modern terminologies of participation and democracy and the early indigenous concepts of knowledge and liberty.[5] Tagore's pervasive regard for freedom inhabits his prioritisation of the ethical and is intrinsically related to his defining the scope and validity of human goals. On the plane of constitutive principle, Tagore's idea of the just society is sustained by the concept of such a freedom, as was later defined by Hannah Arendt: 'Freedom, moreover is not only one among the many problems and phenomena of the political realm properly speaking, such as justice, or power, or equality; freedom, which only seldom – in times of crisis or revolution – becomes the direct aim of political action, is actually the reason that men live together in political organization at all. Without it, political life as such would be meaningless. The *raison d'être* of politics is freedom, and its field of experience is action.'[6] However, Tagore extends his idea of freedom forward from the point of a basic convergence with Arendt's concept. For Tagore, freedom did translate into a societal virtue, but it was embodied in the individual and it was as an individual attribute and aspiration that it was primarily valuable and most worth cherishing. The freedom of the individual was crucially reflected not in autonomy of consumption and leisure, but in the individual's courage to act according to his conscience. On this plane of practice, the freedom of conscience would be best sustained by the abiding philosophical principles and the example of historical personalities who symbolised this courage. This faith, on Tagore's part, in the value of philosophical/historical inheritance, as also his insistence on such freedom which, even as it was political it had, at the same time, distinctly non-political origins, is radically different from Arendt's basic premise. It needs to be mentioned that Arendt's view on the metaphysical concepts of living, located as they are in a specific epistemological tradition, are so very different from those of Tagore. Although Tagore too regards modernity, with its discounting of reflective modes and of the ideas of the sanctity of virtue, as inhospitable to individual freedom, the sequential divergence between their ideas is markedly apparent in this statement by Arendt: 'Obviously, this notion of an interdependence of freedom and politics stands in contradiction to the social theories of the modern age. Unfortunately it does not allow that we need only to revert to older, pre-modern traditions and theories. Indeed, the greatest difficulty in reaching an understanding of what freedom is arises from the fact that a simple return to tradition, and especially what we are wont to call the great tradition, does not help us.'[7] Tagore, while not favouring a return to the past, would place the highest value on many ideals from past traditions, which he believed would help in the living of a life of integrity.

Tagore would not have subscribed ultimately to Arendt's discrimination, which she has outlined in another essay by her on 'Truth and Politics', between the philosophical and the political: 'Since philosophical truth concerns man in his singularity, it is unpolitical by nature.'[8] As we shall subsequently see, Tagore refused to accept a concept of politics, which he acknowledged that contemporary Western political practices had made appear the sole mode of politics, which was only strategy without any ethical principle: 'This statement is no doubt correct that in the modern scripture of western civilisation, politics is at the highest, dharma is below it.'[9] The emphasis on the 'modern' is not merely incidental; Tagore venerated the foundational ideals of civilisations. Arendt refers to Plato on the virtue of truth telling: 'In other words, since man contains within himself a partner from whom he can never win release, he will be better off not to live in company with a murderer or a liar. Or, since thought is the silent dialogue carried on between me and myself, I must be careful

44 ❖ Politics: truth and non-violence

to keep the integrity of this partner intact; for otherwise I shall surely lose the capacity for thought altogether.'[10] This would be for Tagore the core principle of ethical living. Unlike Arendt, who regarded those principles as being in actual practice largely peripheral to the conduct of the individual as the citizen, Tagore would have acknowledged the platonic dialogues on the intrinsic and instrumental virtue of justice as similar to the *Upanishadic* dialogues on conduct and ethics, and both of them as extremely relevant for ethical living for the individual as human being as well as for the individual in his role as a political agent and constituent unit of the community.

A probable thematic axis in Tagore's political writings is the relation between truthfulness and politics. The definition of 'truthfulness' as offered by Bernard Williams maybe apposite to the discussion: 'While truthfulness has to be grounded in, and revealed in, one's dealings with everyday truths, it must go beyond truth as displayed in everyday truths.'[11] It was not an easy proposition for a writer also addressing the topic of decolonisation and self-government, and relatedly the somewhat extended issue of the defining of emergent communitarian identities in a land with a history of fractious difference among communities, to locate the centre of gravity of his writings on such metaphysical grounds. In the face of painful everyday truths regarding racial discrimination by colonial government and its affront to native sensibilities, Tagore persistently highlighted before his compatriots, the many unjust social practices that were still largely appreciated as forming the cultural heritage of the country. In addition to remonstrating against the inherent injustices of colonial governance, he engaged in the complicated exercise of indicating and discussing the disturbing truths regarding Indian society; this also extended the definitions of dominance and exploitation and pointed at the ethical unsustainability of Indian claims for equality and autonomy before the colonial government, when many Indians denied in practice such claims to large sections of their own countrymen. Admittedly for him, the truth of India's history was not limited by the evidence of retrogressive and unjust practice. Appreciative of the egalitarianising impulse of modern, and in part Western, thinking, he at the same time considered it both feasible and advisable to negotiate the issues of structural and institutional injustice within Indian society within the framework of the Indian philosophical heritage and its intellectual tradition. Throughout his life, Tagore spoke glowingly of the austerity and self-sacrifice of the *seers* of India who were ever absorbed in the pursuit of the realising of truth. This, for him, was the essential truth of India, and he evoked the image of Shiva, the eternal yogi, as a metaphor for the Indian spirit. A pride in the philosophical traditions of India was vital to Tagore's understanding of Indian history and culture. In an essay written in 1930 and entitled 'Rabindranather Rashtranaitik Moth' ('Rabindranath's Political Theory'), Tagore stated that he believed that the compulsory delinking of his Brahmo family from the ritualistic associations of Hindu society had created in his elders an 'extremely powerful reverence for the ages-old community ideals of India':

> That sense of pride that day has occupied in many shapes the inner nature and outer behaviour of our home. During the days of that time those whose faith towards a ritualistic Hindu religion wavered, their minds were beset either by an atheism of the particular mould of that of eighteenth century Europe or by an inclination to the Christian religion. But this account is known to everyone that, in that time our family was always conscious in its zeal to reclaim India's religion by following the best ideals of India. Needless to say, that zeal naturally has in childhood in a particular essence initiated my mind.[12]

Tagore identified that essence in the recognition of the fact that the most sublime gift of our life can only culminate through our own inner nature, and we cannot receive for ourselves the alluring elements that exist outside the limits of our innate nature unless we misappropriate them into our innateness. This qualification was for him a crucial condition in the growth of both the individual as well as the community, and he also transposed this argument to the plane of national regeneration. 'We will surely have to remember this doctrine that if any effort in our country aspires to help the people of the country then it cannot by any means be successful if it does not take recourse to religion. No countrywide opportunity, no temptation of the accomplishment of national self-interest has ever generated vigour in the mind of our common people.'[13] This is not to simplify the complexity of the issues of discrimination and dishonour in Indian society and to gloss over the problem of scriptural endorsement of many discriminative practices of the past. Tagore himself was highly aware of such sanction of social inequity on the part of religion. But he used the term religion without any connotation of sacerdotal authority, of which he remained extremely critical throughout his life. However, he did not subscribe to the customary notion that representational empowerment and the consequent enablement regarding political intervention would by itself alleviate the distress of the deprived. He was equally uninterested in the pretensions of the affluent leadership of the Congress concerning the welfare of the masses, as he considered them to be wholly elitist and motivated by selfish political interests. 'Nobody can completely usurp our country, and nobody has such power to bestow this country to us from the outside from kindness. It is to the proportion in which we have relinquished our natural right over the country that the other has occupied it.'[14] The rule of India by the West had hurt the country's soul, which has hitherto existed in dissemination in the ubiquitous social matrix of its people. The state's taking over the traditional social arrangements had only served it ill. 'Ever since this occupation [by the state] became permanent, the ponds dried up in villages; ruined temples and guest houses grew peepul trees, their remained nothing to deter deception-fraud, untruth-perjury; the entire country sank to hell due to disease, affliction, helplessness, ignorance and unrighteousness.'[15] It is of course undeniable that his portrayal of the traditional structure of social responsibility in India was fairly idealised. The significance of his argument, however, lies in the strong advocacy of an ethics of responsibility, and the imagining of an ideal society that can only reside on the ground of such an ethics. The refurbishment of the structural fissures in the Indian nation was indicated in a sense of responsibility for social deprivation and in ideas of restitution at both the individual and collective levels.

A central question that derives from much of his writings is the question which has been described elsewhere and in another context by Williams as, 'What does truthfulness in politics matter?'[16] For Tagore, truth was intrinsically linked to freedom of conscience, and this question for him vitally affected the centre of man's individual and corporate consciousness. In the sphere of governance, Tagore would be directly opposed to the view which Williams describes as a 'moderate version of Machiavelli's thesis', 'the responsibilities of government are different enough from those of private individuals to make governmental virtue a rather different matter from the virtue of individuals'.[17] This translated into the essential need for defining truth, and not only philosophically, as a supreme virtue; truth and justice also needed to be defined as the effective restraint to the tyranny not only of the government, but also to the tyranny of amoral politics, and thereby as the basis for working towards establishing as public principle, such restraint to the tyranny of the merely political. Tagore discussed the consistency of this principle in the context of the public restlessness and governmental repression that had beset Bengal during the closing years of the first decade of the twentieth century, in a way trying the argument in a most unfavourable political climate, when the general public opinion and government policy alike seemed to relegate the qualities of community ethics and justice as being irrelevant and unpractical. 'In the times that have set in now it is meaningless to make an appeal for ethics. The reason for this is that the person who expresses with complete faith the doctrine that there is a place for ethics in state policy is disregarded by people as either being devoid of common sense or being neurotically obsessed with ethics.'[18] Tagore described that to proclaim 'Martial Law' meant to exile the sense of justice by calling it a hindrance, and on that occasion to declare that the uncontrolled brutality of revengeful human nature was the prime resource of fulfilling requirements. The conscienceless brutality of using the 'punitive police' to oppress with force all the helpless village people also fell in the same category. The use of all these methods conveyed to people that 'pure ethics was not enough for fulfilling the requirements of state policy'. Tagore stated that this perfidious statecraft of Europe was vitiating conscientiousness everywhere in the world today. Hence, it will be of no avail to revile all those people in the country who have decided on the clandestine path as the only way of accomplishing the welfare of the nation and who will laugh away any sermonising on righteousness. Therefore, in the present condition, if the agitated people of the country are to be told an opinion, then it will have to be said only from the angle of necessity. It will have to be well explained to them that even the gravest need should be fulfilled through a commendable path; if we attempt to accomplish any task in short and by a parochial path, we shall one day lose direction and in the end we shall not find the path and destroy the work we set out to do. No path in the world will reduce itself for us because of our ardour to attain the goal, and neither will time shorten itself.[19] Tagore warned that the path of truth brooked no lapses. He reminded his fellow citizens that duty towards the nation could on no account be taken to operate independently of the duty to the individual conscience; purporting to serve the interests of the nation by contravening the ethical code would inflict irreparable damage to the community/nation. Enduring hardship was infinitely more worthwhile for the community than to opt for political strategies that were ethically unsure:

> Enduring sorrow is not so difficult, but to apply restraint in the face of false thought is extremely difficult for the mind. If we once consider injustice and tyranny as executive resources then the entire innate strength

48 ❖ Politics: truth and non-violence

for protecting the mind from perversion is lost; wavering for once from the fixed centre of truth is enough to ruin our sagacity, there is no longer any resoluteness in our action, and then a terrible collision becomes unavoidable to effect a symmetry between the universal law of truth and this corruption in our lives.[20]

Tagore would have been in complete agreement with Arendt's definition of the quality of truth: 'Conceptually, we may call truth what we cannot change; metaphorically it is the ground on which we stand and the sky that stretches above us.'[21]

The thematic axis, mentioned earlier regarding Tagore's writings, resides largely in his philosophical inheritance. The term home was perhaps more of a connotation for Tagore. He laid greater emphasis on concepts like 'atmosphere', 'associations' and especially 'milieu'. This last can be construed as the defining constituent of the individual rather than mere geographical location. Milieu was also a growing idea being formed through a variety of ethnic and cultural participations. In 1921, when Tagore was dissenting from Gandhi's idea of non-cooperation, he also wrote to the educationist and philosopher Brajendranath Seal against the idea of 'fragmenting of education' that he considered particularly inappropriate at a time when 'the different peoples of the world are coming within each other's purview'. Attempting to 'block their vision with a screen of partisanship is to flout God's purpose'. Significantly, he did not envision a colourless cosmopolitanism. 'To sacrifice the diverse forms of goodness on the altar of mere necessity is not good. But for which form am I particularly responsible? Questions of this kind churn constantly in my mind when I feel weary.' The idea of his heritage is clearly conveyed in his complaint in the letter against his latest biography by Edward Thompson, which he felt had 'firmly detached me from my atmosphere'. 'But a cutout is an incomplete picture of a man, who is not a mere individual but relates to his milieu; and this relationship is far reaching and ill-defined.' His own mental climate had been formed by a mingling of 'Vaishnava literature and the Upanishads', as his father's had been by the *Upanishads* and Hafiz. 'In my father's heart Hafiz and the *Upanishads* were in confluence, a union of two opposed elements, as is necessary for the creation of beauty.'[22] He never advocated returning to a pristine culture, and this was in fact very significant for a society aspiring to outlive historical and acrimonious contestation between its communities; in fact, he strongly refuted the possibility of such a return in the career of nations/civilisations, not least because he disbelieved in the historical existence of such pristine cultures. He stated that the main problem before India was unique, and for which no precedent existed in the history of other nations. The problem, 'extending from the mountain regions to the borders of the sea, and plainly visible to the eye, was that, so many different races, so many different languages, different habits as in India are found in any one country of the world'.[23] Throughout his writings, he has consistently argued that there existed no real communitarian kinship between the Hindus and the Muslims, and even though it might suit nationalistic propaganda to blame the British for this divide, the roots of suspicion between the two communities lay much deeper, particularly in the indifference of the majority Hindu community, on the plane of everyday living, including commensality, to create enduring bonds with their Muslim neighbours. He observed that 'It is because that no all-inclusive and real unity has been generated between Hindu and Muslim, that suspicion and scepticism has originated regarding the effort to unite them in the area of politics'.[24] He was so very mindful of the dangers of imagining histories among contested ideas of the past, a risk ever present during efforts at crafting national communities. Naturally, truthfulness regarding history is crucial, and as Williams indicates: 'Notoriously, the politics of identity is not necessarily a friend of plain truthfulness. It breeds, almost inevitably, its own myths or, not to put too fine a point on it, lies. It may be very important to rescue from the authenticity of communal attachment the more elementary virtues of truth.'[25] Notably, Tagore venerated the saints from the *Bhakti* tradition, like Chaitanya, Nanak, Dadu, Kabir also for having, in the different regions of India, tried to bring about the unity of *bhakti* in the plurality of races and scriptures by 'showering ambrosia of devotion' on them, and especially, as earlier mentioned, for being engaged in forming 'a bridge of ideals between the natural qualities of Hindu and Muslim'.[26]

Tagore's stand on the national question examines the position of individual conscience within the majority principle. His idea of the nation may also indicate theoretical possibilities; the hypothesis that every liberation/egalitarianising movement, at least theoretically, begins as individual dissent on matters of conscience, but in course of time, it may come to confront an individual conscience which opposes the dynamics of the movement while remaining in sympathy with its broad objectives. The sustainability and significance of such movements may depend in substantial measure on the successful negotiation of such dissents. During

50 ❄ Politics: truth and non-violence

the Indian national movement, Tagore argued against the idea of fixative nationalism and the principle of non-cooperation. Mindless opposition to progressive Western ideas and superstitious reliance on tradition would smother the tradition that was being extolled. His idea of India's supreme achievement – even when it was being denied its political freedom – was not the mere fact of self-rule, but its role in facilitating through becoming an ideal, the cooperation and accord between nations. He felt that 'the true India is an idea and not a mere geographical fact': 'The idea of India is against the intense consciousness of the separateness of one's own people from others, and which inevitably leads to ceaseless conflicts. Therefore my one prayer is: let India stand for the *cooperation* of all peoples of the world. The spirit of rejection finds its support in the consciousness of separateness, the spirit of acceptance in the consciousness of unity.'[27] It was this faith in a common human destiny which led to his complete rejection of violence as an instrument of protest. However, even while speaking of Tagore's opposition to nationalism, his universalism ought not to be confused with mere cosmopolitanism. His was more a faith in the harmony of influences and traditions. He spoke of the 'web of unity' in Indian culture, 'which binds all of us' without our 'knowing or not knowing it', and the 'truth of which was not contingent on our knowledge and acknowledgement of it'. In 1915, drawing an outline of his own identity, he emphasised on retaining the distinctiveness of traditions in building bridges between cultures. 'One who makes himself an outsider can never make an outsider his own, it never happens that the world agrees to partake the hospitality of a home that has been disowned by its owner; the position that it is only through giving up one's own foothold that one can occupy the vast space of the universe can never be an honourable one.'[28]

Largely because of, as yet, a very incomplete translation of his prose writings, which comprise almost two-thirds of his complete oeuvre, Tagore is persistently perceived as an impractical dreamer. Along with his poems, which are of course central to an understanding of his vision, his prose exhaustively explains his idea of the human destiny. Tagore had an abiding commitment towards the socially disprivileged groups. But while acknowledging exploitation and criticising it, he did not subscribe to water-tight identities; for him, human relations were in a fluid state and class/caste categories did not perpetually obtrude upon individual emotions. As Isaiah Berlin says of many of the leading Russian thinkers and writers, Tagore, too, consistently 'saw tendencies, political attitudes, as functions of human beings, not human beings as functions of social tendencies. Acts, ideas, art and literature were expressions of individuals, not of objective forces of which the actors or thinkers were merely embodiments'.[29]

Tagore believed that the country/nation was only as sound as its citizens. Along with Gandhi, he represents a different philosophy of decolonisation, wherein the means are equally important as the ends and which thus puts equal premium on reconciliation as it does on political liberation. Within the Indian context, this also emphases on ideas which have the potential of providing intellectual rigour to the exercise begun slightly earlier, of facilitating, not so much as a command effort but as a free and honest exercise, the even participation of the religious and social groups of the Indian political community, in the transactions which had commenced for achieving the idea of the future Indian nation. Relatedly, Tagore strove to articulate an abiding intellectual justification to the cause of a harmonious world order. He conceived, and expressed through intellectual argument, the idea of a reality transcending a strictly empirical verification, the 'Eternal Spirit of human unity', which inspires humans towards 'disinterested works, in science and philosophy, in literature and arts, in service and worship'. He indicated at the unknown power of the ideals of that 'Universal Spirit' at whose 'call we hasten to dedicate our lives to the cause of truth and beauty, to unrewarded service of others, in spite of our lack of faith in the positive reality of the ideal values'.[30]

Tagore also confronted the contemporary philosophies of social revolution, which believed the institution of private property to be primarily exploitative and redundant. The programme of arbitrary restructuring of economic relationship contained portents of the still more dangerous restructuring of social – intellectual relationships. Different to this idea was a kind of composite rural reconstruction. Economic cooperation was integral to the idea of Santiniketan, which would 'not only instruct, but live; not only think but produce'. Tagore valued the economic aspect of life, as its 'necessities are the simplest and the most universal'. This motivated his initiative at Sriniketan, where he institutionalised his ideas regarding 'complete education'. Health, education, social awareness and economic advancement were some of the prominent components in his scheme of rural reconstruction. He engaged with most of the crucial sociocultural and political issues of his times, and this engagement largely reflects his idealism with regard to the possible imaginary of an individual as well as of a community pertaining to its innate qualities as also to its

52 ❖ Politics: truth and non-violence

accomplished past and aspired future. Isaiah Berlin's remark on social idealism and the ethics of political philosophy is also very appropriate in the context of the political writings of Tagore:

> Ethical thought consists of the systematic examination of the relations of human beings to each other, the conceptions, interests and ideals from which human ways of treating one another spring, and the systems of value on which such ends of life are based. These beliefs about how life should be lived, what men and women should be and do, are objects of moral enquiry; and when applied to groups and nations, and, indeed, mankind as a whole, are called political philosophy, which is but ethics applied to society.[31]

II

Before moving to discuss Tagore's response to revolutionary violence in Bengal, which eventually crystallised in *Char Adhyaya*, a prefatory mention of Tagore's well-known meeting with Mussolini in 1926 may indicate his commitment to the idea of freedom and in remarking on the occasion when his instinct failed him, one also specifies his characteristic caution against 'strong men' with visions of the future as with Indranath in *Char Adhyaya*. Alex Aronson, a sympathetic scholar-critic, inferred that Tagore succumbed to a poet's natural approval for vigour when he met and admired Mussolini, and Tagore went wrong in not looking, as it must be mentioned he generally did in matters relating to all else, at Italy 'in terms of human criteria and experience' and indulged in 'wishful thinking, self-deception, and an unjustifiable optimism'.[32] However, his mistaken impression apart, there was no deviation by Tagore from his essential idea of freedom, and his unfortunate appreciation of Mussolini was given on the basis of Tagore's ideals, as in this remark to Mussolini.

> Perhaps a new Rome is being created. I see signs of a new creative activity. There is need of harsh discipline before one can attain true freedom. But such discipline is negative, it merely removes obstacles, it cannot of itself create. A great vision is necessary for a new synthesis. I believe I see signs of this masterful vision in Italy. We are waiting for this freedom of the spirit without which all discipline is meaningless. I hope there will be a great future for Italy. Material wealth and power cannot make a country immortal. She must contribute something which is great and which is for everybody, and which does not merely glorify herself.[33]

Tagore withdrew his approval of Mussolini when he was informed of the facts of fascist Italy, precisely on the grounds that he had extended his approval in the first place. This foregrounds his unvarying concern with truth and freedom and obviously, violent political strategy, for whatever end and on whatsoever provocation, was entirely unacceptable, not least because it destroyed the *svabhava* of the perpetrator and rendered him unfit for *dharma*. His major statements on this theme were articulated around the years immediately following the Muzaffarpur bombing by Prafulla Chaki and Khudiram Bose, in which two English ladies, Grace Kennedy and her mother were killed instead of the target, Douglas Kingsford, an unpopular English magistrate who was known for giving harsh punishments to political offenders. Chaki committed suicide and Khudiram was hanged. They became martyrs in public perception. Tagore was disturbed both at the public approbation for conspiracy and political assassination as well as at the ethical perils of such thinking. Shortly after, he wrote that those who knew that any kind of welfare, whether of the individual or the community or the country, could be accomplished only by the courageous, the self-abnegating and the ascetic, could never even momentarily countenance putting up with the robbery and unjust persecution that were circulating around the country in the guise of accomplishing the country's welfare. He asserted that he who surely knew that virtue was the only power would never for a moment entertain this terribly mistaken idea in his mind, that one could build up one's community by destroying the character of the community.[34] He continued to hone this argument in essay after essay, even as he accepted the charge that almost everyone in Bengal, tacitly, including himself, had contributed towards the current spirit of militancy, which was quite easily translating itself as downright political violence, including acts of terror. He affirmed that even without minutely judging and thereby ascribing the proportionate responsibility that each among the Bengalis had towards the assemblage of whatever had been lately happening in Bengal, this could be said with certainty that every one of them, whether in body, mind or words, had supplied fodder to this volatile situation in some kind or the other.[35] He rued that in the inflamed political climate, no one even wished to reflect on the incontrovertible human truth of the universe that 'it can never be possible that we can – by oppressing welfare obtain welfare, by striking at the very foundation of freedom achieve freedom'.[36] This is the core of the argument that we obtain also in *Char Adhyaya*.

54 ❖ Politics: truth and non-violence

The ideas possibly emerging from a discussion of Tagore's position on, and his relationship with, the revolutionary violence of his times in Bengal need to be perhaps discussed generally, and even if tangentially, with some of the prominent voices which argue in favour of violence as a means to achieve 'legitimate' political ends – what they invariably term as the 'legitimacy of violence' against 'illegitimate orders'. Although such 'violently revolutionary' activity may seek to draw its legitimacy from the logic of history, should the present forever attempt to transfer its burden on to the past/history and can the sanction to 'burn', as is the urge in the poet Majaz, be ever taken to have been given?

The voices which are represented, besides being very evocative, possess a dialectical power contained in the anguish and despair, which perhaps essentially constitute the urgings to take to violence as an act of political /social remedy. However, the proponents here appear to generally agree that violence is in principle the last resort and that it is never the revolutionary but always the unjust and the oppressor that are responsible for the act of political violence – persecution forces the revolutionary into violence. Issues of ethics and morality are irrelevant, and even deceptive, for those who are engaged in combating an unequal and cruel socio-political order. Malcolm X had stated:

We want freedom by any means necessary. We want justice by any means necessary. We want equality by any means necessary . . . we want it now or we don't think anybody should have it. . . . If they don't want you and me to get violent, then stop the racists from being violent. Don't teach us non-violence while those crackers are violent. Those days are over. Tactics based solely on morality can only succeed when you are dealing with people who are moral or a system that is normal.[37]

In this connection, it is worth mentioning, as a point of reference, Wolfenstein's comment on Malcolm X and on violence, which in a sense sums up from his point of view, the argument regarding means and ends.

Finally, although 'freedom by any means necessary' is a morally justified conception of the relationship between political means and ends, it does not follow that the end of human freedom is historically realizable, and therefore situationally rational. But speculation about whether or not class-racial struggle can lead to a society in which the 'free development of each is the condition for the free development of all' is quite beside the point. We are not interested in a metaphysical or contemplative conception of historical truths but, rather, in its production: given that can be no apodeictic certainty concerning the future except that it will not be the past; that all knowledge must be constituted in the light of a projected future if it is to be historical at all; and that history itself must be viewed as nothing more or less than the process of human self-production . . . . The truth of the ethic of revolutionary responsibility can only be proven in practice.[38]

Frantz Fanon, a theoretician of political violence, and whose influence is evident in the writings of Malcom X and other Black Panther leaders, uses in his book, *A Dying Colonialism*, the fifth year of the Algerian revolution as a 'point of departure' to offer a *post facto* explication of the legitimacy of violent means and to ruminate on the way forward for revolutionary violence in a state where the revolutionaries had come into a reasonable position of assurance and influence. It is with a sense of accomplishment that Fanon discusses the path of liberation as 'revealed in a number of its particular aspects' and which indicate that a 'fundamental, irreversible, ever more far-reaching' revolution has occurred 'strictly on the level of the individual and his tremendous dynamism'.[39] He praises the 'resistance of the masses' in a 'thousand ways, not only with arms at hand', and then proceeds to offer the classic argument for political violence as 'oppression is maintained by violence from above, it is only possible to liquidate it with violence from below. Ultimately, once the struggle reaches a certain point, arms in hand are indispensable'.[40] The statement that 'Having a gun, being a member of the National Army of Liberation is the only chance the Algerian still has of giving a meaning to his death. Life under the domination has long been devoid of meaning . . . ', and Fanon's comment on it that such statements 'were not the error of judgement or of a "to-the-bitter-end" attitude, but an acceptance of indisputable fact, are significantly similar to the sentiments expressed by the members of the terrorist underground during the Indian freedom movement. There is a very slight caveat in the argument of Fanon. Fanon triumphantly proclaims even while the Algerian war of liberation remains unfinished, that: 'The old Algeria is dead. All the innocent blood that has flowed onto the national soil has produced a new humanity and no one must fail to recognize this fact'.[41] However, there is a prefatory acknowledgement of revolutionary infallibility, although these seemingly illegal acts are deemed as a necessary corollary to wars of social change, and never as occasion to rethink the principle and strategy of violent means of achieving political ends. 'It has in fact happened that Algerian citizens have violated the directives of the commanding bodies and that things that should have been avoided have transpired on the national soil . . . [but what could be] psychologically more understandable than these sudden acts of violence against traitors and war criminals?'[42] Significantly, Fanon states that even though revolutionary violence is justified, it must abide by the 'international laws of war', and ironically declares that the European nation 'that practices torture is a blighted nation, unfaithful to its history'. Thus, for Fanon, it is a historical fact that certain wars in European history have abided by the rules governing combat, and perhaps his implication is that by so doing they demonstrate a redeeming virtue. It is equally significant that without mentioning reconciliation explicitly and even while placing the onus of the unsaid but expectedly future effort of reconciliation on France, Fanon recognises the psychologically lasting and deleterious consequences of revolutionary violence, exhorting an 'underdeveloped people [to] prove', even while fighting a revolutionary war, 'by the purity of every one of its acts, that it is, even to the smallest detail, the most lucid, the most self-controlled people'.[43] He states: 'Because we want a democratic and a renovated Algeria, because we believe one cannot rise and liberate oneself in one area and sink in another, we condemn, with pains in our hearts, those brothers who have flung themselves into revolutionary action with the almost physiological brutality that centuries of oppression give rise to and feed.'[44] It need hardly be said that Fanon feels that it is oppression that drives the oppressed to brutality, but revolutionary violence is in fact the only agency that can cleanse, notwithstanding the occasional slips into inhumanity, the feeling of stony submission on the part of the oppressed, and provide them with a sense of 'purity' of mission. The question of an error of perception, therefore, cannot simply enter the discourse in the face of such unequal positions and grave provocation as from an unjust oppressive order.

Wolfenstein has referred to the tendency prevalent among the oppressed, when confronted with various stages of despair, to 'mistake a good front for substantial strength, machismo for manhood, and restless action for self-conscious activity'.[45] Despair is known to produce not only 'restless action', but restlessness in poetic sensibility as well, where restlessness is manifested in a tragic aspiration to destroy indiscriminately the surrounding world. The reference is to the revolutionary poet Asrar-ul-Haq, better known by his pseudonym Majaz Lakhnavi or simply

Majaz, who was a poet of an altogether different calling from Tagore. The overwhelming passion almost an angst that beset Majaz produced at times an aspiration, expressed through his verses, to destroy and 'burn' along with symbols of despotism, altogether innocent objects of nature such as the 'moon and the stars'. In the closing lines of his famous Nazm, *Awara* (*The Wanderer*), the poet, as a restless youth with a heart laden with sorrow, fear and helplessness, gives vent to his anger and to his desire to indiscriminately destroy the objects, which he realises embody and reflect despotism and exploitation.

III

The temptation to refer to Berlin yet again is irresistible, mainly because of the acuity of this observation on Alexander Herzen which is so strikingly reminiscent of Tagore, and also because Herzen is a representative of a society in decisive times; if roads that then were not taken had been explored for passage, a different outlook for ideas of politics may have become achievable. Rabindranath, we need hardly remind, was a seminal exponent of exploring such alternative ideas of the enlargement of human destiny. Berlin states:

> Herzen's most constant goal is the preservation of individual liberty. That is the purpose of the guerrilla war which, as he once wrote to Mazzini, he had fought from his earliest youth. What made him unique in the nineteenth century is the complexity of his vision, the degree to which he understood the causes and nature of conflicting ideas simpler and more fundamental than his own. He understood what made – and what in a measure justified radicals and revolutionaries: and at the same time he grasped the frightening consequences of their doctrines.[46]

Something very much to this effect can be said of Tagore. At this stage of the argument, it may be relevant to mention the theme of perception or attitude which is constitutive of the responses to the question of 'legitimate' violence. In specific philosophical traditions, even the concept of a just war is attitudinally denied, although the tradition may acknowledge its inevitability under certain conditions. G. C. Pande has offered a nuanced reading of Jaina political thought on the paradox of violence, on both the individual as well as the societal plane:

58 ❖ Politics: truth and non-violence

The definition of *himsa* [violence] the root evil, has two parts, viz., the presence of *pramada* or wrong attitude, and the infliction of injury to life. Egoistic passions are inherently other-disregarding and constitute *bhava-himsa* [sentiment of violence]. The infliction of injury positively as *aghata* [strike] or negatively as *pratibandha* [alternatively, retaliation/ the fending off the blow/defence/counterblow] on any aspect of vital activity physical, vocal or mental, or breathing etc., constitutes *dravya himsa* [materialized violence]. It will be obvious that a limited acceptance of such *himsa* is inevitable in social life. The rules of such limitation take into account the connection of eternal behaviour with internal motivation. While they arise from moral consciousness or *bhava-ahimsa* insofar as they apply to dravya-himsa especially *sthula dravya himsa* they become susceptible of behavioural definition and theoretically at least, of sanction by the state.[47]

The style of writing coupled with references to Jain Prakrit terminology (with its specific connotations) has perhaps made this statement slightly dense, but it reflects an essential position on violence/non-violence, involving a statement of wider scope – not only should the unmanifested violent sentiments be abjured but also that the violence that occurs while fending off a blow is also deemed to be a violent activity and is as condemnable as primary violence. Jain philosophy also calls into question the policy of deterrence adopted by the state, and enunciates, as in early Jaina cannon, that 'policemen and executioners [were] parallel to the robbers and murders', and that 'war [was] mere brigandage, only more organized and on a larger scale'. However, Pande does not describe the unambiguity of such a position as constituting an inherently unpragmatic approach to politics, but as an ideal that is simultaneously valuable and sustainable:

The question may be raised that such moral advice cannot be regarded as political thinking which ought to be concerned with devising impersonal and institutional ways of improving the laws and regulating political behaviour. This objection has force only in a very narrow and trivial sense of politics. Fundamentally, one may argue that there are no non-moral solutions of political questions which arise from the conflict of interests. Like Plato and Confucius, Buddha and Mahavira also hoped for an ideal society through the agency of enlightened rulers. Their political thinking, therefore, has a broad moral, not a narrow technical orientation. The unity of ethics and politics follows from the fact that the psychic and physical components of behaviour have to be coordinated and regulated together.[48]

It has been stated that Tagore had a 'duality' in his feeling and approach to the terrorist groups of Bengal, and that this duality is evidenced, on the one hand, in his poetry and fiction, and notably in his essays, letters and speeches, and on the other, his conversations on the subject within his intimate circle and with revolutionaries and in his personal relations with them, which included helping them in many ways and even on occasions extending shelter to them.[49] Notwithstanding such assertions, Tagore never compromised on his disapproval and opposition to the 'path of horror', as he called the way of revolutionary violence – as hopefully adequately discussed in the earlier sections of this chapter, even though he was appreciative of the self-sacrifice of the protagonists and acutely sensitive and sympathetic to their predicament, and to the tragedy of their lives. Moreover, he did not in the least absolve the colonial regime of the injustice of its rule and its insensitivity and harshness to the revolutionaries in particular, and to Indians in general. Tagore's single-most powerful statement against revolutionary violence is contained in his novel *Char Adhyaya* (*Four Chapters*), the third and final novel in the trilogy of *Gora* (1908), *Ghaire Baire* (1916) and *Char Adhyaya* (1934), which engage with issues including national identity, cultural chauvinism and of course the relationship of the self with political experience. Of the three, *Char Adhyaya*, perhaps differently from the others, was written in times more complex and hence more restless than was the case with the earlier novels. Even when his stand on violence remained very clearly undivided, Tagore was undeniably disturbed at the torture being undergone by the young revolutionaries and the 'extremism of the government' and what he bitterly called the 'evil touch of the secret police'. An uncharacteristic bitterness infuses his poem entitled *Prasna* (*Question*, 1932) commenting on the evil of police persecution and perhaps also on those whom Tagore held responsible for spreading the doctrine of revolutionary terrorism and instigating the atmosphere of mistrust and brutality that we see described in *Char Adhyaya*. This short poem is illustrative for our purpose, and the complete text is reproduced in translation:

> God, age after age, you sent messengers over and over again
> To the merciless world,
> They have said: 'Forgive everyone', have said 'Love –
> Obliterate from within the poison of hatred.'
> Venerable are they, memorable are they, even then at the doorstep

60 ❖ Politics: truth and non-violence

At the hour of darkness today I have turned them away with barren greeting.
I that have seen secret violence in the sham shadow of night
Fell the helpless,
I that have seen the voice of justice weeping in lonely silence
At the un-redressed crimes of the powerful.
I have seen a young boy rush in mad excitement
Die in what agony bursting his head against a stone in vain.
My voice is choked today, the flute has lost its music.
The prison of dark night
Has made my world disappear under nightmare,
That is why I ask you over tears –
'Those who your air have poisoned, extinguished your light,
Have you forgiven them, have you given them your love'.[50]

The certitude of Nikhilesh is absent from *Char Adhyaya*, and the novel, in reflecting on the tension between the conflicting values in one consciousness, represents the general mood of the times. The challenge before Tagore was to refute the way of violence and to foreground the sovereign virtues of truth and freedom, and this was more difficult in the bitter atmosphere of the times. Tagore, it can be conjectured, deliberately chose the novel over the political treatise, and in the novel itself he deployed a montage of characters and dialogue to represent the narrative; this enabled him not to speak in the first person and effectively translate the argument onto the plain of philosophical questions regarding good and evil and of means and ends. What Bernard Williams says of Plato, in another context, is relevant in analysing Tagore's present choice of form. 'The dialogue form is not meant to give an historical record; it is a style of writing that enables Plato to explore philosophical questions in ways more vivid, and more intellectually flexible than are available to a treatise.'[51]

The narrative of *Char Adhyaya* details a chapter in the career of a revolutionary group, in a way foregrounding Ela the heroine, whose story comes to an end with that of the novel, as misguided nationalism and violence vitiate human relationship, and ultimately claim the life of Ela, who has played her part in the terrorist enterprise by inflaming the boys by marking their foreheads with 'drop[s] of blood-red sandalpaste' and bringing them to the group in an act of unconsciously semi-erotic invitation. It was written in the closing years of Tagore's life, also as a conscious protest against Sharat Chandra Chatterjee's provocative novel

Pather Dabi (1926), espousing the cause of revolutionary terrorism.[52] Tagore's earlier novel *Ghare Bhaire*, portraying Sandip as the callous, amoral revolutionary, was severely criticised across Bengali readership. Bhupendra Nath Datta, the younger brother of Vivekananda and himself a Marxist revolutionary, protested that he had not encountered a single person like Sandip among the revolutionaries of Bengal. This protest, articulated in Datta's book on the extremist movement, is however ironically preceded by an acknowledgment of the truth of Tagore's charge in his portrayal of Sandip:

> Punjabi revolutionaries say that in their revolutionary endeavours during the war Punjabis had laid down their lives, and among the Bengali's some had misappropriated money. This statement cannot be rejected. But if an evaluation based on the qualities of the [revolutionary] group as such is conducted, barring stray individual examples, the good qualities will outnumber the defects.[53] (my translation)

Tagore, however, retained great affection for the revolutionaries and was in turn revered by them, although they were hurt and bewildered by *Four Chapters*. Chinmohon Sehanobis, in *Rabindranath o Biplabi Samaj* (1998), documents and analyses Tagore's relationship with the votaries of change the world over and his support for aspirations of social change. Tagore expressed warm regard for the fervour and selflessness of the young revolutionaries, who cheerfully underwent torture and death.

> They were born with the fire. But alas! the fire that should have lit the lamps and given us light was used to burn and destroy. They paid dearly for their mistake. They themselves were consumed by the flames and after the conflagration was over, there remained no light to guide the benighted. But misguided though it was, the heroism that they showed even in the tragic futility of their blunder was something which I did not see anywhere else in India at that time.[54]

The essay 'Chhoto o Boro' ('Small and Big'), published in 1917, is a cogent analysis and an explanation of Tagore's opposition to revolutionary terrorism.[55] Tagore argued that wrong means ultimately vitiated the end, however noble that end might be. 'Extremism' in government policy was also a crime, even though the West believed that untruth was essential to politics, as alloy was to gold. Indians had also begun to think that the 'placing of the welfare of the individual above the interests of the

62 ❋ Politics: truth and non-violence

nation, while continuing to harp on dharma is foolishness, weakness; it is sentimentalism'.[56] He was troubled by the country's misfortune that revolutionary violence was casting its dark shadow on the glow being ushered in by patriotism: 'The light of patriotism is glowing, but what sight do we see in this light – this thievery, brigandage and secret killing? . . . The paths of the thief and the brave will never meet at any crossroads.'[57]

Tagore's definition of the brave had altogether different meanings, and the 'brigandage' that he mentions is brutally depicted in *Ghaire Baire* and especially in *Char Adhyaya*. It is a fact that all types of revolutionary violence against the oppressors of a community inevitably begin at an early stage to strike terror in the oppressed community itself, initiated in the name of eliminating collaborators, deviants, informers and the like. We have seen Fanon terming this as unfortunate, even while acknowledging its inevitability. Tagore came out very strongly against violence, not only because it violated rules of human living but also because of what violence does to the perpetrator of that violence and also what it does to the oppressed community's life and psyche, in whose name recourse is taken to such activity. It is worth mentioning that for Tagore, political freedom, as this was understood in the West, was of secondary importance, being mostly understood there in a half-baked sense, and substantially responsible for conflicts. It was coveted as an object that had to be taken, wrested even, and thus in need of being defended with vigilance and aggression. Tagore valued dharma as something highly superior to political freedom, dharma being the inner strength of humans independent of any external agency, therefore self-validating and self-supporting. Dharma was vastly different from religious norms; it was the essence of life, the life giving equanimity that finds expression in so many of Tagore's writings. Here, Tagore was at one with Gandhi.

Given his relationship with the extremists, the question may naturally be asked why Tagore felt compelled to write in *Char Adhyaya* in 1934, almost twenty years after *Ghare Baire*, a novel that was even more critical of extremism than *Ghare Baire*. Tagore had been tirelessly petitioning the government for the release of those detained on charges of extremist activities and was at the same time scathingly critical of the policy of government repression and its horrific effects on the young men and women of the community and was anguished at the suicides committed by youth who had broken down under the stress of constant surveillance and house arrest and who had recorded and conveyed their agony in the suicide notes written to their family members. He had responded to every

Politics: truth and non-violence ❖ 63

such incident by sending messages of condolence, throbbing with pain at a tragedy he felt he was a hopeless spectator to; importantly, he had protested against the tyranny of the state in public, putting on record that such rule was evil and that in such circumstances as prevailed the very touch of the police was horrific to the lives of men and women. The revolutionaries in turn revered him. There are many instances of extremists, such as Surya Sen, quoting Tagore's songs in their last letters written from their 'condemned cells' while awaiting execution.

Now, having seen the acts of revolutionary violence and their reprisal, and knowing the minds of the terrorists and their sympathisers through his close and frequent encounters with them, he felt compelled to once again starkly explain the ethical and psychological ramifications of violence on the country and its perpetrators, even that violence which was being portrayed as sublime by its own ideologues. He was shaken by the course of events, and also by the way in which many men and women, many of them students of Shantiniketan, were thinking. This is illustrated by a conversation that Gopal Haldar had with Tagore in the presence of the eminent linguist Suniti Kumar Chatterjee in Tagore's residence at Jorasanko, in 1931, a few days after prison guards had killed young political prisoners in Hijli jail, an incident which Tagore denounced as the main speaker at a mammoth public meeting in Calcutta. On coming to know that Haldar was associated with extremist politics he said, 'I do not know what you people think, but the solution to the problem does not lie in anger and anguish. Only energy is wasted in this. Power must be established on truth only. But freedom cannot come through man's sudden ignition, the secret killings of the rulers'[58] (my translation). Haldar explained that in spite of their acknowledging this truth, many revolutionaries also believed in the dictum that the maximum sacrifice by the minimum would rouse the maximum for minimum sacrifices. Tagore dismissed this idea. He explained that such sacrifice could momentarily dazzle people but eventually the majority would recoil, thinking themselves incapable of such sacrifices. The need of the times was to inspire them along a path of constructive endeavour, which might appear unattractive in the short term but would ultimately be proven to be the right course of action. Haldar did not disagree. However, he further said that the revolutionaries perceived the situation somewhat differently:

> There are some who say – ours is such a vast country, with a legacy of such an ancient civilization. Men from an ordinary, distant country sit as rulers

64 ❋ Politics: truth and non-violence

and wield the rod in such a manner as if it were a challenge against our humanity and a personal insult for everybody. I become untrue to myself if I am unable to answer this.[59] (my translation)

Tagore fell silent for a moment. Then, as if 'removing the shadow from the brow', he replied in a calm tone:

I have understood your pain, but look, it will not do to see the issue in this way. It is an extraordinary problem in our country – it is a huge question, possibly linked to the greater problem of the earth. And we shall have to find a solution in our country that will be acceptable to the entire world. There can be no short answer to this – a big problem will have to be answered in a big way.[60] (my translation)

The views expressed by Tagore in this conversation find complete expression in *Char Adyaya*. That he understood the 'inner pain' of the revolutionaries is evident in his treatment of the characters. Indranath, the leader of the terrorists, is not a flat character; some of his views are strikingly similar to Rabindranath. Indranath's assessment of the English character, as well as the contemporary Indian mind, echoes Tagore's thinking.[61] But Indranath appears to be blinded by a sense of insult and injustice, lapsing into cynicism even while claiming to be clear sighted: 'I do not believe blindly Kanai. I have abandoned all thoughts of either victory or defeat. I am here because it is meet that I should be the master of such a grand affair. The stakes are high either way, whether or not it ends in victory or defeat. They tried to shut all the doors on my face, to belittle me. I want to prove that I am greater than they are even as I die.'[62] Tagore portrays Indranath as a person who has become primarily the representative of politics and for whom politics is both the means as well as the end. Further, through his character, the danger of being haunted by a sense of personal and communitarian hurt, as expressed by Haldar, is seen in the novel as real and exacting were one to succumb to it. However, it is necessary to mention that the kind of political strategy which Indranath represents remains implacably unaware of what Arendt, like Tagore, so evocatively describes 'as the actual content of political life': 'The joy and the gratification that arise out of being in company with our peers, out of acting together and appearing in public, out of inserting ourselves into the world by word and deed, thus acquiring and sustaining our personal identity and beginning something entirely new.'[63]

Kanai tells Indranath what is in fact Tagore's apprehension regarding strategies focussed on manipulation and abhorrence: 'The business that you've got into brother – that is bound to go bankrupt sooner or later.'[64] Similarly, towards the close of the novel, Antu expresses Tagore's views of the tragedy of the lives of young terrorists. His reiteration that there is 'something bigger than patriotism', and that being patriotic resembles riding a crocodile across the river, echoes sentiments that are repeatedly expressed in Tagore's writings. 'Deception, pettiness, mutual suspicions, conspiracies for power and spying will one day pull them down into cesspools. I see this clearly. In the ugly world inside the pit, the poisonous air engulfs them by day and night. They will never be able to defend the *paurush* in themselves, without which no great work is ever achieved in this world.'[65]

The world of *Char Adhyaya* is a world of futile endeavour. The group of young men seems unconnected to the larger world of ordinary people. Atindra lives without warmth in the vicinity of poor jute mill workers; men of the group rob an old woman benefactor and kill her; it is hardly incidental that there are no Muslim characters in the novel. Ela sounds the ominous note of foreboding to Indranath very early in the novel – 'I shall remember your words Master-moshai. I will be prepared. Perhaps a time will come to remove me: I shall disappear without a trace, silently.'[66] The English are, at the same time, 'struck by a terminal disease, their insides hollowed out through years of ruling people and other lands'.[67] Indranath explains to Kanai – 'No race carries on its shoulders the burden of so many nations, and that eats into their swabhava, their very nature.'[68] Tagore had said as much in so many contexts. Ironically, Indranath fails to realise that, in ruling over the personal lives of his disciples, he too tries to carry the burden of other lives, which eats into his *svabhava*. Correspondingly, he is insensitive to the toll that a ruthless campaign takes on the lives of the helpless sufferers of hatred and violence. *Char Adhyaya* appears more or less to be Tagore's full statement on violent paths of political liberation. One is led to believe that he had consciously intended the novel to carry his message on this contentious and painful issue. It is hardly incidental that the dialogue largely reflects his own views and that of his interlocutors. In his essay 'Ladaiyer Mool' ('The Origins of War'),[69] Tagore refused to buy into mere political rhetoric and said that World War I was a conflict between capitalist countries to seize more markets, although he used the word *jati prem* (nationalism) in place of imperialism. Locating, as ever, his position on the plane of the philosophy of life

66 ❋ Politics: truth and non-violence

and its human dimensions rather than on that of a political discourse of identity and rights, he felt that in most cases imperialism masqueraded as nationalism in the theatre of war. He had earlier commented presciently in his 'Desher Katha' ('Country's Tale):

> To sell humanity at every step in the interest of nationalism, to shelter falsehood, to shelter deception, to shelter cruelty, is in reality to be deceived. If we continue to deceive ourselves in this manner, it shall be seen one day that nationalism is on the verge of bankruptcy . . . If nationalism sells off the welfare of mankind, then one day the welfare of nationalism itself will begin to be sold into the hands of individual, selfish interests. There can be no other outcome but this.[70]

At the close of the novel, its hero Atindra laments:

> All over the world there are nationalists who have begun to announce in bestial voices the terrible lie that you may save the country only after you have killed its spirit. I protest this in my mind, racked by an unbearable pain. I might have enunciated my protest with integrity: it would have been a universal truth far greater than playing hide and seek inside tunnels and trying to save the nation. But there will be no time to say so in this life time.[71]

The metamorphosis that violent political activity for 'higher causes' brings to the lives of its protagonists, like Atindra, is somewhat similar to the transformation of the diligent, diffident, quiet school teacher Pasha Antipov to the feared Soviet Commissar Strelnikov in *Dr. Zhivago*. Strelnikov's nostalgic yearning for his early life with his wife and daughter is reminiscent to Atindra's longing for a return to being the young man he thinks he once was; Strelnikov sits in his compartment on the train berthed at a station close to where his home used to be, in a place called Yuratin:

> Suppose his wife and daughter were still there! Couldn't he go to them? Why not now, this very minute? Yes, but how could he? They belonged to another life. First he must see this one through, this new life, then he could go back to the one that had been interrupted. Some day he would do just that. Someday. But when, when?[72]

The interruption in his life turns out to be permanent. Soon after, Strelnikov shoots himself.

In *Char Adhyaya*, Kanai, a very astute reader of situations and men, represents a kind of ideal, the sense of loyalty to a cause, the limitations of which he understands but is by nature disinclined to interrogate to a point of irrevocable rupture. Ela and Atindra begin their career in the novel as political characters, but beyond a point transcend their political role and become human. Ela recoils from the sordidness of violence and realises instinctively that to love and share was a rightful human destiny, howsoever paltry Indranath may make it appear to be in his scheme of things. She is the only one of his group who speaks her mind to him. A critic has commented: 'No other heroine of Rabindranath is so outspoken and analytical as Ela.'[73]

Atindra is seemingly indifferent to sharing his thoughts with Indranath who knows that Atindra is not a camp follower. Atindra is the complicit dissenter, unbelieving of the ideals of the group, but bound by his own sense of downfall and unworthiness to living out the life of a conspiratorial violence that he detests.

> Like Dante, Atin too had leapt into the turbulence of a national revolt, but for him where was the truth? courage? glory? In a short while he had been sucked into the mire, into an infernal darkness of masked banditry and murder from which no radiant pillar of light would ever rise in history. At the cost of degrading his spirit he now found no worthy realisation in this path, only an unequivocal submission. There is value in submission, but not in the submission of spirit that is dragged out from furtive secret terrors – that has no meaning and no end.[74]

The tragedy of Atindra and Ela is on one plane a perennial tragedy – of the human being trapped in the fate of the mundane world and by having lost the freedom of conscience also losing the means which can redeem the life lived out in the mundane world. Atindra laments that 'the very boys who were the most outstanding and had the highest ideals, were gradually losing their humanity. There is no greater loss than this'.[75] For Tagore, the loss of truth and conscience constituted the highest tragedy. This loss represented the destruction of something even higher than *dharma*; it was the subversion of *rita*, which was the sustaining principle of the universe. The noblest characters in the novel, Ela and Atindra, suffer the most; Atindra's suffering is even more brutal, and the suffering of an individual of his sensitivity can only be imagined after he has killed Ela. The only path of redemption could have been

68 ❋ Politics: truth and non-violence

through love, but Atindra's unflinching adherence to what he feels is the truth of his unworthiness effectively closes that path to him. He declines Ela's appeal to him to leave it all: 'Make me your wedded companion and take me on your path'. 'Had it been a path of danger I would have. But where Dharma itself has been destroyed, I cannot make you a companion.'[76] The novel begins as a political novel but ends as a metaphysical novel – ruminating on the human possibilities of redemption and belief and faith. Tagore's vision on this issue can be termed as being profoundly non-historicist, in a sense. Revolutionary violence in seeking to change society, because of the means it adopts, remains a prisoner of a limitation which it sees as imposed on it by history. This is often due to the analysis of the past performed almost solely through the terms of the present, wherein even the historical instances of the transcendence of those limitations are very often overlooked. There is, perhaps, an existential responsibility upon the present to fashion its own terms of existence and of engagement with the germinal issues of its day. Instances of this effort, even when instituted in spheres of thought and activity customarily deemed as non-political, are often obscured in the question regarding the means of protest against unjust regimes. It is puzzling as to why the political writings of Tagore should remain untranslated for so long, given that they so unambiguously speak his conscience and his thought, and that he himself never considered them to have engaged with only contemporary and temporary issues. One might ask in a lighter vein – it is widely known and equally widely circulated that Surya Sen mused on Tagore's songs till his last day; why is there no proportionate curiosity as to whether Sen read Tagore's prose writings, or if at all he did, what did he think about them?

I have, in the above discussion, attempted to set up conversations between voices which, for chronological and other reasons, did not engage in conversation, and I have, perhaps too rashly, reached out at a merging of philosophical and historical categories.

This attempt had also begun from a wondering at the protocols of certain contemporary debates, insofar as it concerns the representation of certain voices that have been so far generally absent in these debates. Adrian Moore described the contribution of Bernard Williams to the history of philosophy in such words: 'This contribution was not, as philosophers in the analytic tradition used to think, to indicate voices of yore which could be heard as participating in contemporary debates: precisely not. It was to indicate voices of yore which could not be heard as participating in contemporary debates, and which thereby called into question whatever assumptions made contemporary debates possible.'[77]

This discussion of Tagore's political writings is a humble attempt at also calling into question the assumptions that make certain contemporary debates possible.

Gandhi: the limit and pragmatism of non-violence

This section seeks to explore Gandhi's concept of political non-violence, which had been originally given shape in *Hind Swaraj* the text to which Gandhi can be said to have adhered till the last day of his life, barring perhaps one exception, which however could be read in accordance to what he had theorised in *Hind Swaraj*. The statement of his ideas occasionally invited critical comment, and perhaps none more so than when he advised Jews living in Germany to offer non-violent resistance in the face of Nazi persecution. This discussion will focus on the significant aspects that can be culled over from this episode regarding the centrality of non-violence to Gandhi's politics.

This episode is significant for a number of reasons. The Holocaust constitutes one of the most horrific chapters of human history and Gandhi's suggestion that the Jews offer their lives to awaken world opinion was greeted in most quarters with incredulity and derision. This episode embodies to a great degree not only the question of the ultimate validity of Gandhian non-violence, but it also holds within itself the contours of the debate as to whether non-violent protest can succeed against despotic regimes, and therefore provides an opportunity to examine its relevance for our times.

Is non-violence endowed with an abiding intrinsic validity existent only on its own set of conditions on the plane of praxis or is it perpetually dependent upon its other to whom it is directed? Is the source of its validity intrinsic or will it be perpetually understood to subsist within a set of extraneous factors? These will be the questions that this study of the details of this episode will try to look into.

It was 'not without hesitation' that Gandhi ventured to offer his views on the 'Arab–Jew question in Palestine' and on the 'persecution of Jews in Germany' through an article written in the *Harijan* on 26 November 1938, in response to letters that he had been receiving which

70 ☀ Politics: truth and non-violence

solicited his opinion on these issues. It would be relevant to quote in some detail from his response:

> My sympathies are all with the Jews. I have known them intimately in South Africa. Some of them became life long companions. Through these friends I came to learn much of their age long persecution. They have been the Untouchables of Christianity. The parallel between their treatment by Christians and the treatment of untouchables by Hindus is very close. Religious sanction has been invoked in both cases for the justification of the inhuman treatment meted out to them. Apart from the friendships, therefore, there is the more common universal reason for my sympathy for the Jews.[78]

He then stated that his sympathy for them was, however, tempered with the untenability of the demand for a Jewish homeland and that he wished that the Jews should make their native lands their home. To restore Palestine 'partly or wholly' to the Jews would be a 'crime against humanity', as it would reduce greatly the position of the Arab population which had been living there for centuries. Gandhi's remark on the persecution of Jews, as we shall see, reflects on larger philosophical and moral questions. Since the responses to Gandhi's statement are generally quoted in greater detail than as to what Gandhi actually stated in this case, I would rather than summarising it prefer to quote his statement in substantial measure. He stated:

> The nobler cause would be to insist on a just treatment of the Jews wherever they are born and bred. The Jews born in France are French in precisely the same sense that Christians born in France are French. If the Jews have no home but Palestine, will they relish the idea of being forced to leave the other parts of the world in which they are settled? Or do they want a double home where they remain at will? This cry for the national home affords a colourable justification for the German expulsion of Jews. But the German persecution of the Jews seems to have no parallel in history. The tyrants of old never went so mad as Hitler seems to have gone. And he is doing it with religious zeal. For, he is propounding a new religion of exclusive and militant nationalism in the name of which any inhumanity becomes an act of humanity to be rewarded here and hereafter. The crime of an obviously mad but intrepid youth is being visited upon this whole race with unbelievable ferocity. If there ever could be a justifiable war in the name of humanity, a war against Germany, to prevent the wanton persecution of a whole race, would be completely justified. But I do not

Politics: truth and non-violence　❁　71

believe in any war. A discussion of the pros and cons of such a war is, therefore, outside my horizon or province. . . . Germany is showing to the world how efficiently violence can be worked when it is not hampered by any hypocrisy or weakness masquerading as humanitarianism. It is also showing how hideous, terrible and terrifying it looks in its nakedness.

Can the Jews resist this organized and shameless persecution? Is there a way to preserve their self-respect and not to feel helpless, neglected and forlorn? I submit there is. If I were a Jew and were born in Germany and earned my livelihood there, I would claim Germany as my home even as the tallest gentile German might, and challenge him to shoot me or cast me in the dungeon; I would refuse to be expelled or to submit to discriminating treatment. And for doing this I should not wait for the fellow Jews to join me in civil resistance, but would have confidence that in the end the rest were bound to follow my example. If one Jew or all the Jews were to accept the prescription here offered, he or they cannot be worse off than now. And suffering voluntarily undergone will bring them an inner strength and joy which no number of resolutions of sympathy passed in the world outside Germany can. Indeed, even if Britain, France and America were to declare hostilities against Germany, they can bring no inner joy, no inner strength. The calculated violence of Hitler may even result in a general massacre of the Jews by way of his first answer to the declaration of such hostilities. But if the Jewish mind could be prepared for voluntary suffering, even the massacre I have imagined could be turned into a day of thanksgiving and joy that Jehovah had wrought deliverance of the race even at the hands of the tyrant.[79]

Gandhi went on to say that *Satyagraha* in South Africa had been practiced by a 'handful of Indians', who attracted no sympathy to their cause from any quarter, and 'world opinion and the Indian Government came to their aid after eight years of fighting'. The Jews in Germany were 'far more gifted' than the Indians in South Africa, and were a compact, homogeneous community, and therefore 'infinitely' better placed to offer *Satyagraha*. Were they to turn to non-violent resistance, they would be able to turn a 'degrading manhunt' into a calm and determined stand against the 'godless fury of dehumanized man'. They would be able to render 'service to fellow-Germans' and to 'prove their title to be the real Germans as against those who are today dragging, however unknowingly, the German name into the mire'.[80]

This statement aroused a storm of controversy, not only among Jews around the world but among non-Jewish Germans also. The Germans alleged that Gandhi had indulged in slander against their nation, while

72 ❖ Politics: truth and non-violence

Jew opinion expressed outrage and anguish at Gandhi's ignorance of the situation and his insensitivity to the horrors that the Jews in Nazi Germany were experiencing. Non-violence has been a debated issue even within the Indian national movement. There is an effective critique of extremism and revolutionary terrorism, notably by Gandhi and Tagore. In turn, there are critiques of Gandhi and Tagore by thinker activists such as M. N. Roy. These centre around Gandhi's allegedly ambivalent attitude towards the relationship of non-violence and religion and non-violence and state formation; Tagore's 'upper class' outlook on questions of social change/tradition; and analyses particularly of the 'innate violence' in much of 'tradition'. Gramsci understood Gandhi's movement of political liberation of India, as in many ways possessing the same features as Germany's political struggle against France in 1923 and that of Hungary against the Little Entente and described the stages of the Indian freedom movement in terms of a war: 'War of movement, war of position, and underground warfare.' 'Gandhi's passive resistance is a war of position, which at certain moments becomes a war of movement, and at others underground warfare. Boycotts are a form of war of position, strikes of war of movement, the secret preparation of weapons and combat troops belongs to underground warfare.'[81] Apart from misunderstanding, the revolutionary violence in India to be part of Gandhi's movement, this simplistic view thwarts the understanding of either the nuances or the ethics of Gandhi's philosophy of non-violence.

A set of three letters – Gandhi's open letter of 26 November 1938 to the Jews in Germany suggesting *Satyagraha* against Hitler's inhuman treatment of Jews[82] and responses to him from two highly distinguished Jewish scholars, Martin Buber's letter of 24 February 1939[83] and the letter of 26 February 1939 from Judah L. Magnes[84] – contain a difficult and remarkable debate on non-violence. Buber and Magnes, while placing on record their great appreciation of Gandhi, make an impassioned protest against Gandhi's advocating non-violence as a form of resistance/protest by the Jews against genocide. It is open to deduction as to whether Buber and Magnes seek to limit the scope of non-violence and also whether there was a subtle truth in their critique of Gandhi. Their letters, confronting the issue of the practicability of non-violent protest against a despotic regime, carry a larger philosophical load as well. They question the ultimate validity of Gandhian non-violence and posit a major argument of the religious traditions regarding justice and non-violence, on the possibility of non-violence and justice becoming contradictory in certain specific situations, as in the 'evil' regime of Hitler. In that case, war becomes necessary, neither as a 'righteous war' nor as a 'justifiable war', but a 'necessary war against the greater evil'. It is greatly unfortunate that Gandhi never received these two letters and therefore did not get to respond to them. It is said that there is no record in Jerusalem of the letters having been posted to Gandhi.[85]

These two letters to Gandhi are exceptional in their thoughtfulness and tone. Buber and Magnes both appear disappointed that even with his moral genius, Gandhi could have so misread the situation and recommend a noble general principle, which was wholly unsuitable in the face of an evil regime. All three of them draw on the ancient traditions of the Jews. Gandhi refers to the Jewish conceptions of Godhead to indicate Jew resilience in suffering which is basic to non-violence, while Buber and Magnes invoke tradition to argue the position that not only the efficacy but also the justification of pacifism is not universal but determined by its context. Jews are burdened by the tragedy of their pacifism and their self-restraint expressed in the term *Havlaga*. This also serves as an interrogation of the normative capacity of traditions. Instances of Jewish testimony and martyrdom have been ineffective and unmemorialised in Germany. Even noble deeds of individuals are not axiomatically emulative in situations of collective suffering. Both Buber and Magnes mention the ethics of war which while limiting non-violence is not anti-thetical to it. In an agonised response written on 24 February 1939, from Jerusalem, Martin Buber, confessed to 'having been very slow in writing this letter to you, Mahatma . . . to have made repeated pauses – sometimes days elapsing between short paragraphs – in order to test my knowledge and my way of thinking. . . . searching whether I had not in any one point over stepped the measure of self-preservation allotted and even prescribed by God to a human community and whether I had not fallen into the grievous error of collective egoism'.[86] Recollecting the 'many instances of genuine Satyagraha' he had seen among Jews, where 'force nor cunning was used to escape the consequences of their behaviour', but which 'apparently exerted not the slightest influence on their opponents', Buber stated that non-violence may harbour the hope of gradually bringing unfeeling human beings to their senses, but a 'diabolic universal steam-roller cannot thus be withstood':

> There is a certain situation in which from the 'Satyagraha' of the strength of the spirit no 'Satyagraha' of the power of truth can result. 'Satyagraha'

74 ❖ Politics: truth and non-violence

means testimony. Testimony without acknowledgement, ineffective, unobserved martyrdom, a martyrdom cast to the winds – that is the fate of innumerable Jews in Germany. God alone accepts their testimony, and God 'seals' it, as is said in our prayers. But no maxim for suitable behaviour can be deduced there from. Such martyrdom is a deed – but who would venture to demand it.[87]

Buber stated directly that he would not have been a 'supporter' of Jesus:

For I cannot help withstanding evil when I see that it is about to destroy the good. I am forced to withstand the evil in the world just as the evil within myself. I can only strive not to have to do so by force. I do not want force. But if there is no other way of preventing the evil destroying the good, I trust I shall use force and give myself up into God's hands.[88]

He alluded to the *Mahabharata* and particularly to the *Bhagavadgita* in its similar position on this issue, which placed the highest value on justice for which all striving is right, and in its stating that in this only the heart needed to be freed of hatred.

Another prominent critic of Gandhi's position, Rabbi Judah L. Magnes thought that the possibility of Jews offering 'civil resistance' in Germany did not exist as the protagonists of such action were either killed or sent to concentration camps in the 'dead of night', without 'even a ripple' being produced on the 'surface of German life', in contrast to Gandhi's actions like the salt march 'when the whole world is permitted to hang upon your words and be witness to your acts'.[89]

Magnes was agonised at his moral dilemma between the philosophical and the political. War cannot be righteous even against the 'ghastly Hitler savagery', which itself has been the consequence of the sins of the 'conquerors and conquered alike' of the last war; it is 'because of our lack of generosity and the spirit of conciliation and renunciation that the Hitler beast has been enabled to raise its head'. It is humbling to see such adherence to principles even at an hour of supreme disillusionment, when natural instinct dictates a bitter apportioning of blame to other communities, which so clearly were responsible in varying degrees for a human catastrophe. But Magnes could not bring himself to abandon his lifelong beliefs at the point of cruel choice. The Evian conference might compel the Jewish world to cooperate financially with Nazi Germany and to deal 'in Jewish flesh and blood in a most modern and up-to-date slave market' for saving lives: 'Have you an answer'. He seeks Gandhi's guidance on the 'pros and cons' of a war against Germany as well as on 'practical technique of satygraha' against Nazis: 'But we have no one comparable to you as religious and political leader.' Jews may not be the fit subjects of *Satyagraha* as the Biblical injunction is to live not to die, and *Satyagraha* required also non-cooperation and 'renunciation of property and the disdain of death'.

I will be overreaching myself in attempting to surmise Gandhi's responses to questions of such integrity. It may be, however, possible to indicate some basic premises in Gandhi's position. Gandhi seems to have refrained from absolutising the question of war in stating that as he did not believe in any war, it was outside his province to discuss the pros and cons of a justifiable war such as seemed so needful against Germany 'in the name of and for humanity'. The caveat is closer to the position of the religious traditions, in this respect. Markedly, he does not discuss the cons of war. In fact, within days of this letter, he clarified that his advice to Jews did not by inference suggest non-interference by the democratic nations on behalf of the Jews. 'They will, they are bound to, do all they can to free the Jews from the inhuman persecution.'[90] Nonetheless, this cannot mean undeniably that this is endorsement for military intervention. Around this time, particularly in his writings on the Czech predicament before German aggression, Gandhi appears to interlink terms such as honour, life, freedom, soul, non-violence, the science of non-violence and democracy, as existing in coherence. Ideally, Czech's should free other nations from the obligation to defend their country with war as it 'can only mean bloodshed and destruction such as has never seen before'. Yet, they 'must live' with complete independence 'or perish'. Instead of the 'pure bravado' of seeking to win in a clash of arms, they should refuse the aggressor his will, even though thereby they perish unarmed. 'In so doing, though I lose the body, I save my soul, i.e. my honour.'[91] Living can, thus, only be possible with freedom. Gandhi is perhaps suggesting the principle that 'I live even without *the* body if I retain *my* soul that is *my* honour'. Soul and honour, herein, are translated into ethical qualities as opposed to the body which represents the appetent not only materially, but also socially and historically. Significantly, honour is at this point being delinked by Gandhi from its general association with hierarchy and violence. Gandhi appears to postulate that the principle of non-violent living remains uncontroverted by historical factuality since its validation transcends material achievements.

76 ☀ Politics: truth and non-violence

History has no record of a nation having adopted non-violent resistance.[92] If Hitler is unaffected by my suffering, it does not matter. For I shall have lost nothing worth (*sic*). My honour is the only thing worth preserving. That is independent of Hitler's pity. But as a believer in non-violence I may not limit its possibilities.[93]

Non-violence is primarily a matter concerning man's own soul.[94] As had been evident in his position on the Jallianwala Bagh massacre, to be discussed in detail in the subsequent chapter, Gandhi saw martyrdom as the affirmation of non-violence in a conscious act of suffering. Voluntary suffering would be a source of greater 'inner strength and joy' for Jews than expressions of solidarity by others, even war in their cause 'can bring no inner joy, no inner strength'. The philosophical emphasis of Gandhi is different from that of Buber and Magnes. Rather than indicating success and failure in objective terms, Gandhi perceives non-violence on a mainly psychological plane. Practice of non-violence, particularly in extremely adverse circumstances, is only possible with the conviction that it is essentially an individual virtue. It is significant that for many survivors, one of the central deductions drawn from their experience of the Nazi concentration camps concerns the idea that 'acts of courage and virtue are irreplaceably individual'.[95] Events in Jewish history show that both the evil of the Nazi state and the degradation in the life of those who moved from hopelessness and passivity to become well-meaning and deceived collaborators in the extermination of their own community, followed from the abdication of individual responsibility for protest against evil. Sensitive individuals like Adam Czerniakow, an official of the Warsaw ghetto, committed suicide at the brink of crossing the ultimate boundary of human conduct.[96]

A powerful stream of Holocaust literature is inhabited by thinking which approximates to Gandhi's position. The entire Nazi exercise at the same time was inhered in and aimed at reducing Jew agency to levels lower than what are commonly known as human standards of behaviour. Such reduction affirmed theories of racial inferiority and justified animal torture. The preservation of sanity seemed to depend on remaining human. It is not possible to say with absolute certainty that Gandhi had foreseen such attempts at degradation. But it can be argued reasonably that the idea of living, which was carried in his suggestion of non-violent resistance, could have constituted an important source of resilience and dignity which was so essential to Jews in their hour of inhuman suffering.

The supremely nuanced and sensitive portrayal of the Jewish experience of the Holocaust in the writings of Elie Wiesel and Primo Levi affirms in many ways Gandhi's position. Wiesel's response to the violence of Nazism, contained in the following description of a metaphorical (?) photograph of the last moments of a father and his little boy – in what was, going by an identical description in the Nuremberg court, probably a scene near the execution pits at Dubno in the Ukraine – seems to immortalise the tragedy of human reasoning confronting wanton cruelty.

> It [photograph] shows a father and his son, in the middle of a human herd, moving toward the ditch where, a moment later they will be shot. The father, his left hand on the boy's shoulder, speaks to him gently while his right hand points to the sky. He is explaining the battle between love and hatred: 'You see, my child, we are right now losing the battle.' And since the boy does not answer, his father continues: 'Know, my son, if gratuitous suffering exists, it is ordained by divine will. Whoever kills, becomes God. Whoever kills, kills God. Each murder is a suicide, with the Eternal eternally the victim.'[97]

Recalling the horror of Auschwitz, Levi has stated that while he never forgave 'our enemies' nor 'their imitators in Algeria, Vietnam, the Soviet Union, Chile, Cambodia, or South Africa', his demand for justice excluded retributive violence. The intransigence of violent ideologies deprives life of the vital capacity of 'finding joy in life, indeed of living'. 'Those who "trade blows" with the entire world achieve dignity but pay a very high price for it because they are sure to be defeated.'[98]

In *Dawn*, Weisel portrays the dilemma of a Holocaust survivor turned fighter of the Jewish underground in Palestine, who agonises over questions of memory and revenge when he is ordered to kill for the cause a British officer who has been taken hostage. The arguments advanced for killing are the standard ideological arguments conflating violence and justice. Tragically, he kills. The abiding theme is what refuses to leave his mind as he wrestles within himself before the killing. 'There are not a thousand ways of being a killer; either a man is or he isn't . . . He who has killed one man alone is a killer for life.'[99]

Ironically, most of the analyses, specifically of Gandhi's position on Jewish responses to Nazi persecution, appear to concur with the view that his statements on the Holocaust brought discredit on Gandhi. Joan Bondurant, to whom we shall return later, is arguably the major exception,

78 ❖ Politics: truth and non-violence

who argues in favour of Gandhi's stand, but her analysis confines itself to the general principle of struggle against totalitarian systems, without going into the specifics of the case at hand. Dennis Dalton, one of the few scholars who have examined this episode in a slightly more detailed fashion, wondered: 'Where is his compassionate understanding for the oppressed or even a hint of practical programme of action? He seemed unable at this time to grasp the enormity of the Holocaust. Yet the differences between Nazi Germany and British India were evident then as now.'[100] However, it is rather puzzling to find Dalton's counter assertion in the relevant end note that 'Gandhi was unusually well informed during the 1930s and 1940s about the plight of Jews in Europe in the face of Nazi persecution'.[101]

Ronald Terchek, arguing, on another plane and in a slightly different mode, against Gandhi's position has reasoned that Gandhian non-violence was not an autonomous principle but was effectually dependent on the context of its application. The cost of non-violent resistance against individuals and regimes that are inured to appeals of truth and justice will not only be excessive but in fact also prohibitive. In a fairly common analogy on the topic, Terchek compares the totalitarian Nazi state to the comparatively much more democratic and humane British regime which had rendered success to Gandhi's *Satyagraha*. Gandhi, according to Terchek, obscured this crucial difference in the character and ethos of these two political systems when he advocated *Satyagraha* against Hitler's Germany.[102] It is important to mention here that Terchek has further speculated on the possibilities of the epistemic extensibility of non-violence in case Gandhi had enlarged his argument to include 'justifiable violence' in his position on Jew resistance to persecution in Germany.

> A problematized reading of Gandhi invites a different recommendation to German Jews than the one Gandhi himself gives. It moves away from a position that always denies the applicability of violence and invites a dialogue about specific, limited cases where violence may be appropriate to protect autonomy. Any conclusion about exceptions to non-violence reached in such a dialogue does not falsify the theory but recognizes there are exceptional circumstances where violence might be appropriate.[103]

The sheer inhumanity of the Nazi state has understandably obscured the nuances of Gandhi's position regarding non-violent resistance to Hitler's regime. Unfortunately, this has relatively proceeded to conceal the potential of the ideas that are encapsulated in the debate which is still being carried on different planes, between different interlocutors over the times.

In a study unallied to Gandhi and the Jews, Hannah Arendt similarly, and famously, stated:

> In a head-on clash between violence and power, the outcome is hardly in doubt. If Gandhi's enormously powerful and successful strategy of non-violent resistance had met with a different enemy – Stalin's Russia, Hitler's Germany, even pre-war Japan, instead of England – the outcome would not have been decolonization, but massacre and submission. However, England in India and France in Algeria had good reasons for their restraint. Rule by sheer violence comes into play where power is being lost . . . [104]

She went on to say that power and violence were opposites, 'where the one rules absolutely, the other is absent', and that unchecked violence ensures the disappearance of its power. Strangely, she is led to the conclusion that 'This implies that it is not correct to think of the opposite of violence as non-violence; to speak of non-violent power is actually redundant'.[105] But the statement that can be said to emerge from her study is that violence will hardly be 'effective with respect to the relatively long-term objective of structural change'[106] and that 'much of the present glorification of violence is caused by severe frustration of the faculty of action in the modern world'.[107]

Gandhi was in fact trying to revitalise the faculty of action among Indians through his movements in India and suggested the same to Jews in Germany. However, in a study on Gandhi, while discussing 'Hitler, Jews, Palestine', Rajmohan Gandhi writes:

> There is no way of knowing how, if born a Jew in Germany, Gandhi would have organized non-violent resistance there. In him we have seen a calling to present non-violence joined by strong pragmatism. He never asked Indians to invite a massacre from the British, or Hindus, Muslims or 'Untouchables' to invite a massacre from their Indian foes. The real commander of a non-violent battle was very different from the professor of a remorseless non-violent ethic.[108]

This statement is extremely significant because unlike most of the other statements on this issue, it has perhaps inadvertently let in a suggestion

80 ❋ Politics: truth and non-violence

of uncertainty into Gandhi's stand and put to question Gandhi's repeated assertion made right from the days of writing *Hind Swaraj* till the last day of his life that presented with an irremediably unjust situation he would opt for non-violent protest, irrespective of the cost such a course of action entailed. Rajmohan Gandhi's statement seems to imply that in extreme cases, even with Gandhi, the pragmatic could become opposed to the ethical. I would like to argue that Gandhi's position on the issue of Jews in Nazi Germany illuminates the point that Gandhi's pragmatism is a different pragmatism: it is the ethical as pragmatic, an unshakeable conviction that the ethical was the pragmatic. To delineate the 'why' and the 'how' of this premise, let us go back to our different interlocutors and in due course contemplate on the two different scenarios that might possibly seem to emerge from this debate.

For a few months after his initial statement of November 1938, Gandhi was engaged in a written dialogue with people who responded to his suggestion and his responses to the reservations of his interlocutors through the pages of the *Harijan* to clarify his stand. In his first reply to his German critics, he refuted the allegation that as he was ignorant about the real situation his intervention was misinformed and inaccurate. Admitting his 'ignorance about European politics', he spoke of the 'main facts about the atrocities' being 'beyond dispute'. He stated that non-violence was a sovereign remedy, and that 'to commend my prescription to the Jews for the removal of their many ills, I did not need to have an accurate knowledge of European politics'. He wondered whether his 'remedy was after all not so indecorous as it may appear, but that it was eminently practical if only the beauty of suffering without retaliation was realized'.[109] His subsequent statement is a cogent exposition of the ethical as pragmatic:

> To say that my writing has rendered neither myself, my movement, nor German-Indian relations any service, is surely irrelevant, if not also unworthy, implying as it does a threat; and I should rank myself a coward if, for fear of my country or myself or Indo-German relations being harmed, I hesitated to give what I felt in the innermost recess of my heart to be cent per cent sound advice.[110]

It would be interesting to compare this with what his disciple, Jawaharlal Nehru, was to say on the Tibetan issue while replying to a non-official resolution, which was moved in the Lok Sabha on 4 September 1959

Politics: truth and non-violence ❖ 81

seeking to enjoin the Indian government to raising in the United Nations the question of Chinese aggression on Tibet. Nehru mentioned that his government's approach was governed mainly by 'sympathy for the Tibetan people' and the 'desire to maintain friendly relations with China', and that the 'slight contradiction' between the two was the 'difficulty of the situation'. Any step, therefore, could not be taken 'in a huff, regardless of the consequences', as it was 'essential' that India and China 'should have friendly and as far as possible, cooperative relations'. His summing up of the situation was in a sense a classic display of diplomacy:

> Looking at it from this point of view, the United Nations may come into the picture for two reasons: one, violation of human rights and two, aggression. Now, violation of human rights applies to those who have accepted the charter of the United Nations; in other words, the members of the United Nations. You cannot apply the charter to people who have not accepted the charter, who have not been allowed to come into the United Nations.
>
> Secondly, if you talk about aggression by one sovereign independent state on another, as I told you, in so far as world affairs are concerned, Tibet had not been acknowledged as an independent state for a considerable time. Suppose we get over the legal quibbles and legal difficulties. What good will it achieve? It may lead to a debate in the General assembly or the Security Council which will be after the fashion of the cold war. Having had the debate what will the promoters of the motion do? Nothing more. They will return home. Obviously, nobody is going to send an army to Tibet and China, for that was not done in the case of Hungary which is a part of Europe and which is more allied to European nations. It is fantastic to think they will move in that way in Tibet.
>
> All that will happen is an expression of strong opinion by some and denials by others. The matter will be raised to the level of the cold war and will probably produce reactions on the Chinese Government which will be more adverse to Tibet and the Tibetan people then even now.[111]

It hardly needs to be pointed out that there is no mention of the moral issues at stake: the suppression of the voice of a people and of the need to protest against such repression. We witness in these lines the pragmatism of the state, where the pragmatic is opposed to the ethical. One wonders what Gandhi would have said to Nehru or perhaps one need not; one can perhaps accurately conjecture what counsel he would have offered to Nehru as also to the Dalai Lama. It is said that when Gandhi was proposing non-violent resistance to the Jews, he was unaware that

82 ❖ Politics: truth and non-violence

Hitler in November 1937 had offered a simple suggestion regarding the Indian political movement to Lord Halifax: 'All you have to do is to shoot Gandhi. If necessary, shoot more leaders of Congress. You will be surprised how quickly the trouble will die down.'[112] It has been narrated elsewhere as to how Hitler had similarly remarked in January 1942: 'If we took India, the Indians would certainly not be enthusiastic, and they'd not be slow to regret the good old days of English rule.'[113] Goebbels, on another occasion, is said to have called Gandhi 'a fool whose policies (of 'passive resistance') seem merely calculated to drag India further and further into misfortune'.[114]

Gandhi would have been hardly disconcerted by the prospects of his likely reception in Germany. In one of his comments on the supposed cruciality of the receptivity of the object of non-violent protest, he drew a distinction between the 'passive resistance of the weak and active non-violent resistance of the strong', which 'can and does work in the teeth of the fiercest opposition'. He clarified that by advising non-violent resistance against Nazi persecution he had not thereby logically advised the 'democratic powers' to refrain from appropriate action on their part; on the contrary, he expected them to come to the rescue of the Jews since they were duty bound to do so. He, however, was convinced that the any such help would be largely ineffective, and to all intents and purposes the Jews would have to fashion their own resistance, for which he felt his prescription to be infallible when taken recourse to in the correct manner. Gandhi also acknowledged the criticism that he had not been able to gain universal acceptance to his remedy even within India, and that even where he was the 'self-appointed General', his own country had been unable to imbibe non-violence in its right spirit. He, however, said that it would be unethical on his part to refrain from advising non-violence to situations which required it and that he believed without doubt in the necessity and effectivity of non-violence in Germany. Moreover, he counted himself among the blessed, who expected nothing from others, not least in the realm of non-violent movements. Subsequently, during a speech to the *Gandhi Seva Sangh* at Wardha in 1940, in outlining a frame of reference for the practice of *ahimsa*, Gandhi had drawn attention to the fact that notwithstanding his own imperfections and of which he said he was fully aware, 'what little power [he possessed] is derived from [his] ahimsa', and made a comment on the need for unremitting cultivation of *ahimsa* in the mind of aspiring *satyagrahis*. The comment might be highly significant for our discussion.

Politics: truth and non-violence ❊ 83

But neither you nor I can trade on our capital. We have to be up and doing every moment of our lives and go forward in our *sadhana*. We have to live and move and have our being in ahimsa, even as Hitler does in *himsa*. It is the faith and perseverance and single-mindedness with which he has perfected his weapons of destruction that commands my admiration. That he uses it as a monster is immaterial to our purpose. We have to bring to bear the same single-mindedness and perseverance in evolving our ahimsa. Hitler is awake all the 24 hours of the day in perfection of his *sadhana*. He wins because he pays the price. His inventions surprise his enemies. But it is his single-minded devotion to his purpose that should be the object of our admiration and emulation. Although he works all the waking hours, his intellect is unclouded and unerring. Are our intellects unclouded and unerring? A mere belief in ahimsa or the charkha will not do. It should be intelligent and creative. If our intellect plays a large part in the field of violence, I hold that it plays a larger part in the field of non-violence.[115]

It ought to be underlined at this point that there is a noticeable similarity in the conditions which had, in 1909, engendered the writing of *Hind Swaraj* and Gandhi's statement in 1938 on the possible options of non-violent resistance open to Jews in Nazi Germany. Although *Hind Swaraj* contains the much more elaborate treatment of non-violence, his statement to the Jews introduced dramatically, and in a trying context, the concept of non-violence to the Western world in general, whose ethos he deemed to be broadly anti-thetical to the concept and its practice. Germany, in particular, had the most adverse conditions imaginable for the practice of non-violent resistance. The similarity of origin between *Hind Swaraj* and his statement of 1938 lies in the apprehension of violence being acknowledged as the viable expression of protest under inhospitable conditions. *Hind Swaraj* was the rebuttal of the growing ideas of political violence within the Indian freedom movement, demonstrated in the assassination of Curzon-Wyllie by Madan Lal Dhingra.[116] It is highly significant that Gandhi understood the undercurrent of violence in the Jewish psyche of the 1930s, which led to the predominance of David Ben Gurion over Chaim Weizmann in the Zionist movement and which has come to represent a major stream of thought in modern Israel. It is another matter that the Jews were helpless before Nazi persecution; indeed, their very passivity could be said to have been channelised later into the violent assertion that we witness today. The greater meaning, in human terms, of the suffering of their community, appears to have been unfortunately lost on many of them. Even before Nazi persecution began, a strong

84 ❖ Politics: truth and non-violence

Jewish opinion had begun to build up against the 'assimilationists', the Jews who favoured assimilation in the culture and society of the land of their domicile. The opponents of assimilation within the Jewish community felt that assimilatory aspirations were diluting the movement for a separate Jewish homeland through the emphasis that the 'fight against anti-Semitism' was the need of the hour rather than the assertion of a separate, exclusive identity. Curiously, a pro-Zionist attitude had characterised the first stages of the Jewish policy of the National Socialists. On the other hand, the polemical Jewish slogan 'Wear it with pride, the yellow star', given in response to the Boycott Day of 1 April 1933, was also directed at the assimilationists for whom it was said among the community that they 'were always behind the times'. It was only six years later that the Nazi state would actually compel the Jews to wear the Star of David as a mark of inferiority. The evolving of the militaristic psyche in European Jewry is not entirely unprofitable in a discussion of the efficacy of political non-violence against a diabolical Nazi machine, which it is widely believed would have anyway not been dissuaded from its course of state terrorism. However, the degree of its success would have to depend also on the state of the Jewish mind, as in turn it would be the state of the Jewish mind which would opt on the subsequent course of Jewish action, on which arguably would rest substantially the subsequent course of world history. Robert Weltsch, who had coined in 1933 the slogan of displaying publicly the Star of David, was to say later that he 'would never have issued his slogan if he had been able to foresee developments'.[117] In October 1938, Zindel Grynszpan, a German Jew of Polish descent, along with thousands like him, was brutally evicted from Germany. On 7 November 1938, his seventeen-year-old son Herschel Grynszpan, living in Paris, shot and killed a young German diplomat posted in Paris named Ernst Vom Rath. The assassination was the immediate provocation for the 'Kristallnacht' or the 'night of the broken glass' of 9 November, when 'seventy five hundred Jewish shop windows were broken, all synagogues went up in flames, and twenty thousand Jewish men were taken off to concentration camps'.[118]

On 26 November, Gandhi wrote his first statement on the issue of Jewish persecution, referring to Herschel Grynszpan as an 'obviously mad, but intrepid youth'. However, Gandhi's recommendation of an altogether different intrepidity for the Jews continues to be misunderstood, with the resultant denial of its relevance in human history. Gandhi accepted the probability expressed by one of his correspondents that 'a Jewish Gandhi in Germany, should one arise, could "function" for about five minutes – until the first Gestapo agent would lead him, not to a concentration camp, but directly to the Guillotine'.[119] But for Gandhi that did not disprove the 'efficacy of Ahimsa'. He could imagine the suffering and death of many more in such a course of action: 'Sufferers need not see the result during their lifetimes. They must have faith that, if their cult survives, the result is certainty. The method of violence gives no greater guarantee than that of non-violence.'[120]

There can conceivably be two possible scenarios which can be offered to what might still be an abiding question as to what could have possibly happened if German Jewry could have followed Gandhi's advice.

Two scenarios

Scenario 1

There is unified non-violent resistance movement by Jews in Germany, in which they come out openly against the decree of wearing the Yellow Star, refuse to leave Germany when given expulsion orders, refuse to report when served summons from the Gestapo offices. There are public demonstrations all over Germany, as in 1938, World War II has not yet commenced, and Nazi's are in control only in Germany and Austria. Jews in the rest of Europe and America begin protests against the Nazi regime.

Hitler diverts the war machine he had been assembling for the future war, from preparing for a state of war readiness, against the Jews. Most of them are mercilessly killed and the survivors taken to incipient concentration camps, such as Dachau, as systemised extermination camps like Auschwitz have not yet begun operating, where they also die. Most of these operations against the Jews are public knowledge, as the world press still has access to public events in Germany since Hitler is still negotiating with the major European powers and wartime restrictions are not in place, as it is not yet wartime in 1938. However, there is no effect on German public opinion. The major powers ignore this massacre or pass resolutions against it, all the while engaging diplomatically with Hitler to further goals and aims of real politic. Hitler goes ahead with his plans of aggrandisement. The World War takes place with more or less the same results. The Jews are almost decimated. Only the comment of Gandhi regarding non-violent resistance/Holocaust would have changed. Or would it?

86 ❋ Politics: truth and non-violence

But this scenario seems rather implausible, simply because too many imponderables are involved. This will be borne out from the obsessive secrecy that shrouded the details of the infamous 'final solution' throughout the war. It is indicative of the power of reality, which even in the harshest of times outrages opinion and also that the possibility of such outrage deters flagrant transgression, at least till the complete domination of opinion can be ensured by the aggressor. Even when the scheme of extermination of Jews began to be implemented well into the war, with the concomitant dispensing of all international norms of war on the part of Germany, the perpetrators of the horrible crimes were immensely anxious to obliterate all traces and evidence of their infamy. In his documented study of the Hitler rule, Shirer describes the methodical camouflage and the subsequent attempt at denial of the existence of such a programme. 'What became known in Nazi circles as the "Fuehrer Order on the Final Solution" apparently was never committed to paper – at least no copy of it has yet been unearthed in the captured Nazi documents. All the evidence shows that it was most probably given verbally to Goering, Himmler and Heydrich, who passed it down during the summer and fall of 1941.'[121] Similarly, in what is regarded as the standard text on the Nazi extermination of European Jewry, Raul Hilberg has recorded the process in German bureaucracy of 'an atrophy of laws and a multiplication of measures for which the sources of authority were more and more ethereal'.[122] On the field, the German army had to confront the psychological repercussions for soldiers who were participating or witnessing mass executions in Eastern Europe. The army command regarded this issue as a substantial threat for German society after the end of the war and felt constrained to issue a number of directives to rationalise, with racial theories of inadequacy and deviance, the mass executions and to prevent soldiers participating in executions from graduating to what were termed as wanton killers, especially with a view towards post-war German society. There were instances of soldiers and high-ranking officers having to submit for medical treatment for suffering from hallucinations and other psychosomatic disorders. The killings were ordered to be conducted away from the city and preferably at night, and involved units were ordered to prevent strictly other soldiers watching as spectators. On one occasion, even Himmler in a speech to troops responsible for mass killings had to claim that he personally hated the slaughter and had on witnessing them 'been aroused to the depth of his soul' but that he was only 'obeying the highest law by doing his duty'. He reiterated that combat and a hierarchy of survival was a law reflected and established in nature and that he undertook sole responsibility 'before God and Hitler'. The soldiers persisted in watching, taking photographs and writing letters describing them, and consequently information began to stealthily disseminate into Germany. Notwithstanding the systematic attempts to control these repercussions, nervous breakdowns and subsequent persistent alcoholism spread into the units that were connected with the extermination of Jews.[123] The visual and public effect of a *Satyagraha* by the Jews, with the ensuing of a possible turbulence in opinion on the part of the German public, even if flowing from a stampeding desire to be spared the overt but unavoidable knowledge of the details of the persecution, can well be imagined. Logically, therefore, global quietude in the face of Jew resistance and its described possible reprisals seems inconceivable, and as evidenced earlier, the possibility of such quietude had not been expected by the Nazi state either.

Describing the Holocaust as the 'greatest crime of our time', Gandhi reiterated in 1946 what he had said in 1938 that a Jewish resistance would have had definitely other consequences than those which had occurred without such a movement: 'They should have thrown themselves into the sea from cliffs . . . It would have aroused the world and the people of Germany . . . As it is they succumbed anyway in their millions.'[124] A section of opinion still holds this statement to be typical of Gandhi's lack of sensitivity and understanding of the Holocaust, where he offered prescription without offering a practical programme.[125] But it is a fact that Gandhi's contemporary interlocutors on this issue did not ask for practical suggestions. They were simply incensed that he had linked Nazi persecution with the Jew–Arab dispute in Palestine. They normally stated as fact that non-violent resistance was simply not possible in Nazi Germany, and Gandhi's unflinching stand that it was almost never provoked them to ask of him as to how precisely could it be organised. They stopped with censuring him. There was no effort to explore the moral issues Gandhi had raised: individual responsibility to protest against inhuman regimes; the preparation of the self for undertaking such a protest; that passivity before oppression was doubly unethical inasmuch as it violated the principle of individual responsibility and frequently, if not always, allowed passivity to depict itself as non-violence.[126]

Hayem Greenburg's allegation (made out in his article published in the *Jewish Frontier* and sent to Gandhi) that Gandhi had been misled because of his proclivity for Muslim appeasement is cited in detail in most

88 ❖ Politics: truth and non-violence

studies, but the infinitely more significant portion of his article is not so often quoted. It is another matter that Greenburg did not recognise that appeasement is built into pragmatism of a kind which was entirely alien to Gandhi, and which would make appeasement of a person or a principle impossible for him. However, it was perhaps only Greenburg, of all the distinguished correspondents of Gandhi on this issue, who understood and acknowledged the subtle point which Gandhi had made on the virtue of non-violence, more clearly in a subsequent statement on the debate: 'I hold that non-violence is not merely a personal virtue. It is also a social virtue to be cultivated like the other virtues. Surely society is largely regulated by the expression of non-violence in its mutual dealings. What I ask for is an extension of it on a larger, national and international scale.'[127]

Greenburg saw no schism in Gandhi's thinking and accepted that his suggestion of non-violence was 'quite natural' and in 'complete harmony with his entire outlook' and that 'his ethical-religious convictions dictate to him the duty of heroic and active resistance', the truth of which was to Greenburg 'as self-evident as a mathematical axiom'. Noting at the same time that Gandhi had since years advocated *Satyagraha* 'as a universal ideal which could be applied by all the oppressed and injured everywhere and independent of the specific historical situation' and that it had 'proved to be practical and effective', Greenburg expressed his doubts as to whether *Satyagraha* would succeed among the Jews of Germany, not only because of the adverse situation in Nazi Germany but also much more so because the German Jews were psychologically not equipped for such a movement given that it was not in keeping with the ethos and character of the Western world.

> But I admit to myself that in order to apply Gandhi's method of struggle it is necessary to accept it not only on a purely intellectual plane; it is also imperative that it be assimilated emotionally, that it should be believed in with all the force of one's being. Such faith the Jews of Germany do not possess. Faith in the principle of Satyagraha is a matter of special predisposition which, for numerous reasons, the German Jews have not developed. The civilization in which German Jews have lived for so many generations, and to the creation of which they have so energetically and ably contributed, has not prepared them for the "pathos" of Satyagraha.... They cannot resort to passive resistance because they lack the heroism, the faith and the specific imaginative powers which alone can stimulate such heroism.[128]

Greenburg's analysis of *ahimsa*, as being anti-thetical with the predominant ethos of the Western world, came quite close to what Gandhi himself had said in *Hind Swaraj*. But Greenburg's highlighting of the brutality of the Nazi regime was coupled with a hint that even though the hope of a passive resistance from the German Jews could be to some extent nurtured, the expectations of that hope being fulfilled would be unrealistic as it would require a near enormous change in the psyche of Jews living in Germany.

This brings us to the second scenario. Could passive resistance have been successful in Germany, and if so what would be the time frame in which the success or failure of such resistance be judged? The second scenario can be envisaged through the examination of some of the major trends of the Holocaust. It would be useful to have a sense of what had actually occurred, and thus to know what ought not to have happened for a non-violent resistance of some magnitude to have been born in Nazi Germany itself.

Scenario 2

This scenario is recreated from Hannah Arendt's interrogation of the cast of characters in her report on the investigation of the Holocaust, at the trial of Adolf Eichmann in Jerusalem. Arendt's book, which upset Jew opinion, justifies Gandhi's analysis of the situation without her knowing it. This is especially noteworthy in the light of her comments, mentioned earlier, on Gandhian techniques. It also illustrates how some of Gandhi's forebodings regarding the perils of not protesting against injustice were proved accurate in the context of the Holocaust.

First, the ironical dimensions of the killing of Vom Rath by Herschel Grynszpan. Vom Rath was 'a singularly inadequate victim', who far from being a Nazi fanatic was known for his 'openly anti-Nazi views' and was, in fact, being kept under surveillance by the Gestapo because of his sympathy for Jews. Grynszpan was probably a 'psychopath' who had been unable to finish school, having been expelled in Brussels and Paris. The German government had him extradited, although he was never put under trial, and it is said that he survived the war. It was the 'paradox of Aushwitz' that Jews who had committed criminal offences were allowed to live. The Gestapo encouraged a theory of homosexuality to explain Vom Rath's murder. Arendt has speculated that the story of his homosexuality might

90 ❖ Politics: truth and non-violence

have been a fabrication by the Gestapo: 'Grynszpan might have acted as an unwilling tool of Gestapo agents in Paris, who could have wanted to kill two birds with one stone – create a pretext for pogroms in Germany and get rid of an opponent to the Nazi regime.'[129]

Arendt wrote about the collusion of some Jewish leaders with the Nazis during the Holocaust, basing her comments on the Holocaust largely on the depositions in the court in Jerusalem and on various highly respected investigative studies on the subject, prominently Hilberg's *The Destruction of the European Jews*.[130] Emissaries from Palestine approached the Gestapo and the Schutzstaffel, or the SS, on their own initiative in the early stages of the Nazi regime, to 'enlist help for immigration of Jews' into Palestine, which was promptly rendered. The emissaries were not interested in rescue operations: 'They wanted to select "suitable material", and their chief enemy, prior to the extermination program, was not those who made life impossible for Jews in the old countries, Germany and Austria, but those who barred access to the new homeland, that enemy was definitely Britain, not Germany.'[131]

We may recall Gandhi's relating of the issues of militant Zionism in Palestine with that of civil resistance of Jews in Germany in 1938. Some of the overzealous proponents of a Jewish Palestine had begun to operate in Nazi Germany around this time, of course without a foreknowledge of the sinister plans the Nazi's harboured for future implementation. Unfortunately, the Zionists thought that the Jews themselves should extricate the 'best biological material' for survival away from a hostile situation. The obsession with the 'best biological material' was also common to the Nazis. Gandhi's worst apprehensions, regarding the consequences of a combination of passivity on the one hand and militant Zionism on the other, seem to be completely realised in this comment of Arendt on the activities of the Zionists in Germany: 'It was this fundamental error in judgment that eventually led to a situation in which the non-selected majority of Jews inevitably found themselves confronted with two enemies – the Nazi authorities and the Jewish authorities.'[132] Gandhi had refused to believe that the 'Germans as a nation have no heart or markedly less than the other nations of the earth'. Hitler would have been forced to take cognizance of German opinion as he 'would be a spent force if he had not the backing of his people'.[133] He wrote that an armed conflict would entail widespread destruction and may even terminate the present regime in Germany. but it would fail to produce a general change in human heart and might ultimately serve to produce another Hitler as after the last war. Referring to the continuing incarceration of Pastor Niemoller and of other protestors against Nazi militarism, Gandhi believed that actions such as theirs would, as would a protest by the Jews, never be in vain. It was a scientific principle that energy was never wasted, it was only that the mechanical forces were less abstract. Human actions resulting from a concurrence of forces albeit invisible had a similar power; the only thing required was to keep faith. Individual human responsibility was thus of utmost importance.

Joan Bondurant has doubted the power of any totalitarian system, 'however effective in its policing', to 'prevent word-of-mouth propaganda of an idea, or even of an understanding of a technique if there had been some previous understanding of its meaning and effectiveness'. In her opinion, '[H]ad the Jews of Germany been schooled in satyagraha, an organized satyagraha could have got under way.'[134]

The trial of Eichmann demonstrated how the mistaken notions of the leaders of the German Jews had made collaborators out of them, and how anxious the Nazis had been to secure their collaboration to ensure the secrecy and continuity of their operations. An authoritative account of those years unambiguously states that 'without the cooperation of the victims, it would hardly had been possible for a few thousand people, most of whom moreover, worked in offices, to liquidate many hundreds of thousands of people'.[135] It is ironical that Arendt stated in a later work that a Gandhian movement in Germany would have resulted in massacre and submission. In her earlier report on Eichmann's trial, she had raised those very questions which are central to Gandhi's argument, and her documentation supports with empirical data Gandhi's claim that non-violence would not have been entirely unsuccessful in Germany as Hitler would not have been able to dispense with the veil of secrecy and the semblance of order in the fulfilling of his evil design. In a different, somewhat non-judgemental manner, Elie Wiesel had in the beginning of *Night*, his famous account first published in 1958 of life in the extermination camps and predating Arendt's work, described the reluctance of the Hungarian Jewish community of Sighet, in as late as 1944, to believe itinerant informants describing the extermination of Jews deported from Hungary and scepticism regarding Hitler's plans to exterminate the entire race: 'Yes, we even doubted his resolve to exterminate us. Annihilate an entire people? Wipe out a population dispersed throughout so many nations? So many millions of people! By what means? In the middle of the twentieth century!'[136] Even after accounts from Budapest conveyed

92 ❖ Politics: truth and non-violence

that Jews there lived 'in an atmosphere of fear and terror', the initial foreboding changed very quickly to one of 'optimism': 'And thus my elders concerned themselves with all manner of things – strategy, diplomacy, politics, and Zionism – but not with their own fate.'[137]

Hilberg has adeptly conflated his knowledge of Jew history with that of the German state in analysing the response of the Jews of Europe to the Nazi state. Both historical and psychological factors created the attitude of the victims in a traditional combination of what Hilberg describes as resistance, alleviation, evasion, paralysis and compliance. The Jews adopted mainly a policy of complying with all orders aimed at their own destruction from their historical knowledge of pogroms, when the fury of the attackers would gradually abate and the community could somehow recover from their emotional and material debris the means of proceeding with its life. Thus, for them, the German state resembled a wild beast, which would at some point satiate its rapacity and violence, and Jews would, as in the past, turn to rebuilding a broken life. Moreover, many in the community relied on their own recognition that Jews were not economically useless – 'one does not kill the cow one wants to milk' – and additionally, in Central and Eastern Europe, Germany was generally regarded as a traditional place of refuge as compared to Russia. As stated by Hilberg, 'We see, therefore, that both perpetrators and victims drew upon their age-old experience in dealing with each other. The Germans did it with success. The Jews did it with disaster.'[138]

At the same time, it cannot but be obvious that consenting to the death of oneself and one's own should naturally be difficult, and the attempt to escape or, as happened in many cases, to actually only postpone destruction, through petitions, cooperation, even bribery, were the acts of a consumed and abandoned people. However, in spite of the extreme circumstances, Jewish resistance organisations at places did make an attempt 'to reverse the mass inertia' and exhorted their community to deny to their being 'led like sheep to slaughter'.[139] It is concurrently remarkable that Gandhi addressed himself principally to both the naturality and the liability of psychological crisis in victims, as well as to the possibility and complicacy of resistance in the harshest of conditions.

The numbing and silential descriptions of life under the shadow of deportation and death convey a kind of coherence to the seeming willingness of the community to be deceived by the false assurances of their torturers. It is grievous reading of accounts of how the Jews, being human, were perhaps compelled to endeavour to maintain continuity in their lives, even when they were confronted with almost incontrovertible indicatives against any possibility of survival.[140] Even at points, when in the minds of Jewry the consequences of resistance and compliance were on balance and equitable, the futility of the situation rendered a kind of paralysis. What is, however, more crucial and less understandable is the widespread phenomenon of 'institutional compliance by Jewish councils employing assistants and clerks, experts and specialists.'[141] The Germans did not have the resources to run the Ghetto administration and whenever required, the Jew councils provided their German supervisors information, money, labour and police. Although this was done primarily to ward off punishment, this was of vital assistance to their persecutors, and for this reason, the German administration both maintained and exploited the ghetto councils. Arendt more or less similarly concludes: 'Without Jewish help in administrative and police work – the final rounding up of Jews in Berlin was, as I have mentioned, done entirely by the Jewish police – there would have been either complete chaos or an impossibly severe drain on German power.'[142] It needs to be mentioned that Hilberg differs pointedly with the counterfactual proposed by Arendt that, without the leadership as was, the Jews would have been nevertheless reduced to great misery in the Holocaust, but the disruptive absence of a cooperative leadership would have made it impossible for the German administration to annihilate six million Jews. In a later assessment of her argument, Hilberg, offering a historic explanation for the compliance of the Jew leadership with German directives, did not agree to the postulate of a disjunction between the Jew leadership and the community.[143] Arendt, however, maintains that 'this role of the Jewish leaders in the destruction of their own people is undoubtedly the darkest chapter of the whole dark story'.[144] She spoke of the absurdity of presuming either the collective guilt of the German people on an 'ad-hoc interpretation of history' or 'a kind of collective innocence of the Jewish people', and criticised the 'reluctance evident everywhere to make judgments in terms of individual moral responsibility'.[145] In his statement regarding Jew resistance in Germany, Gandhi had said much the same in evoking the centrality of the moral responsibility of resistance on the part of the victims. It is pertinent to recall his definition, given during his trial in an Ahmadabad court in 1922 for leading a non-cooperation movement in India, of the ethics of protest as also of its undeniability even in extreme situations: 'I am endeavouring to show to my countrymen that violent non-co-operation only multiplies evil, and that as evil can only be sustained by violence, withdrawal of support from evil requires complete abstention from violence. Non-violence implies voluntary submission to the penalty for non-co-operation with evil.'[146] Is, thereby, the sufferer, even the vulnerable and infirm, never exempt from the responsibility to resist injustice? Do truth and non-violence admit no exemption, and are therefore for their practice never conditional to memorialisation? The depictions by Holocaust survivors, of the horrific life in the camps housing the gas chambers, also contain tragic accounts of the inevitable dehumanisation of not only the perpetrators but also of many of the victims trying to survive the hellish torture of the situation.[147] Levy, in particular, agonises over the general inability of the victims to 'acquire an overall vision of their universe'. The sheer pressure of survival forced them into an attitude that relinquished scrupulousness. 'Every victim is to be mourned, and every survivor is to be helped and pitied, but not all their acts should be set forth as examples.'[148]

The scenario that we have been discussing raises in Arendt's evocative words 'one of the central moral questions of all time, namely upon the nature and function of human judgment. . . . that human beings be capable of telling right from wrong even when all they have to guide them is their own judgment, which moreover, happens to be completely at odds with what they regard as the unanimous opinion of all those around them'.[149] Gandhi unfailingly recognised and sustained the centrality of this principle, particularly important during times of peril when suffering could be borne and redeemed; only possible, perhaps, with the sufferer realising that individual, moral responsibility was a non-modifiable virtue.

All the same, one must acknowledge at this point that *post facto* evaluation, such as the present discussion, of a situation which involved cruel choices must inevitably and perhaps correctly, begin to seem to a degree insensitive and even sanctimonious. However, my endeavour is hopefully far from being judgemental. This consideration of the historical hypothetical is motivated by the possibility of an indication of the historical alternative.

The possible historical

In the history of Nazi persecution of Jews, there are indeed some stray stories of individuals reclaiming a sense of responsibility along with a moral, human space for themselves. The story of Anton Schmidt was told at the trial of Eichmann. He was a sergeant in the German Army,

Politics: truth and non-violence   95

assigned to a patrol in Poland, who in the course of his duties came across members of the Jewish underground, whom be helped with forged papers and trucks, without taking any money. He did it for five months from October 1941 to March 1942, when he was caught and executed. Arendt wondered how 'utterly different everything would be' not only in Israel, but also in the entire world, 'if only more such stories could have been told'. Peter Bamm, a German Army physician had, in his account of the killings of Jews in Sevastopol, acknowledged that he and others like him knew of the extermination units but did nothing because any protestor would have summarily disappeared, as totalitarian regimes 'don't permit their opponents to die a great, dramatic martyr's death for their convictions'. 'A great many of us might have accepted such a death,' he says, if only totalitarian states let them do so. Any sacrifice in anonymity would have been futile. However, he had the courage to say, 'This is not to say that such a sacrifice would have been morally meaningless. If would only have been practically useless. None of us had a conviction so deeply rooted that we could have taken upon ourselves a practically useless sacrifice for the sake of a higher moral meaning.'[150] This is obviously the kind of utilitarian ethics, where ethics dilutes its essence and loses its way into becoming a pragmatism shorn of value.

Contra Bamm, the German bureaucracy, faced as it was with an unprecedented 'chasm between moral precept and administrative action' did take resort, in albeit a very limited way, to some criticism if not protest and in the deliberate delaying of the executing of a few orders relating to the Final Solution, reflected what has been termed by Hilberg as 'the lingering effect of two thousand years of Western morality and ethics'. They either conducted themselves with suitable discretion in this or due to the abovementioned problematic consequences for the entire system that were anticipated by Nazi state; very few of them were actually penalised. In a speech in 1943, Himmler referred to the extermination of Jews as a 'particularly difficult chapter', which he was thankful to God for being accomplished smoothly and without being talked about openly in Germany. His view was that although everyone, including himself, of the performers of the difficult task had been 'horrified', all of them knew that they would not hesitate to do it again if necessary. In one case of true public protest – one which Gandhi would have wholeheartedly endorsed – involving the Catholic Church in Germany, a priest named Bernhard Lichtenberg continued to offer public prayers at St. Hedgwig's Cathedral in Berlin for victims of the ongoing Holocaust and was ultimately

96 ❄ Politics: truth and non-violence

arrested. Subsequently, he denounced National Socialism and wished to go to Eastern Europe to pray for, and suffer along with, the Jews who were being massacred there. He died en route to a concentration camp. In a more dramatic, if much less valid, protest involving close proximity with Hitler, the wife of a hardened Nazi functionary, Gauleiter Schirach, on the advice of her husband, mentioned to Hitler during a visit to him an instance of rounding up of Jews at night in Amsterdam. The screaming of the women had disturbed her, and assured in the belief that the Fuehrer would naturally be ignorant of such activity and would order stopping any recurrence of it, she described the incident to him. Hitler listened rudely, repeatedly interrupted her and told her not be 'sentimental'. The couple withdrew from the by now thoroughly embarrassed gathering and while leaving the next morning were unable to present their farewell greetings to Hitler.[151]

Another question which arises from the second scenario is why in the face of such odds, as are characteristic of totalitarian regimes, did Gandhi continue to emphasise on the validity of suffering for ones convictions? This is contained in the obviously larger question: Why is the ethical also the pragmatic? An answer to this must negotiate through Gandhi's very occasional statements to the effect that he preferred people to die 'fighting violently than become helpless witnesses', with its inference that he could have, in certain eventualities, legitimised violence. This statement of 1945, with regard to protecting women against rape, however did not specifically entail men to take to violence, but declared Gandhi's belief that rather than becoming merely a 'helpless witness' to such heinous crimes, the 'truly non-violent man would never live to tell the tale of such atrocities. He would have laid down his life on the spot in non-violent resistance'.[152] In this, Gandhi thus reiterates the sovereignty of non-violence rather than suggest a caveat.

In a broad overview of Gandhi's statements on non-violent protest, the year 1920 is significant, particularly regarding Gandhi's public definitions of bravery, sacrifice, resistance and chiefly, his exhortations, on a couple of occasions, against the cowardice of the community during pillage and molestation by the police on 30 November that year, in a village near Bettiah in Champaran. Occasionally, extracts from the speech given at Bettiah and at Dacca, and from an essay entitled 'Dyerism in Champaran' published in the *Young India* and all occurring in the course of December in 1920, are assumed to be evidential of Gandhi's endorsement of violent resistance in extreme situations. Following the popular foiling of the arrest of an influential local in connexion with a village dispute near Bettiah, the police organised in the village a spree of loot and molestation by some men from the neighbouring village. Gandhi mentioned that 'houses were denuded of their contents – grain and ornaments', and women were molested, including cases of public stripping. Gandhi was incensed that the villagers had in fear abandoned their homes and the womenfolk to depredation and abuse. On his visit to the village, women narrated their torture, and broken bins and boxes in the plundered houses were shown to him. He had since long regarded the peasantry in Champaran as 'the most helpless and the most terror-stricken of all [Gandhi] had seen', who dreaded the police and fled on the merest sign of their approach. On their part, the local police had become grossly corrupt and demoralised, who did not know and did not care about the intervallic reprimands from the magistracy: '[a] system of terrorism continues and flourishes'.[153] Since Gandhi believed that the government had not connived at the incident, he felt one possible solution would be for a delegation to reason with the police that they were bound to protect the people and hence restore the loot. He was particularly angry that the villagers with their 'long sticks' had shown their 'heels' while the women were being dishonoured and clearly stated that cowardice was not *Satyagraha*. 'Our dharma does not teach us to be cowards, to submit to tyranny. What it teaches is that, instead of taking the life of the tyrant, it is better to lay down one's own. If we could do this, we would be as gods; should we, however, run away from the scene of oppression, we would have behaved worse than beasts.'[154] But fleeing from persecution to save one's life was being akin to 'neither beasts nor men' but plain cowards. Gandhi had always believed that delivering the people of India from cowardice was central to his duty to his country, since truth and cowardice were simply incompatible, and the fact that people had run away at the sight of the police was intolerable for him. Lacing his speech with sarcasm he now observed, 'If the people of India cannot display their humanity, they can certainly show that they are animals.'[155] He said that he would laud them for laying down their lives, even for having 'fought [the police] hard', but it was abominable for him to countenance their timidity; even the law permitted the employment of force for defending life and property. He then stated what has since become controversial: 'Hereafter, every inhabitant of Champaran will fight back on such occasions and kill or be killed. I cannot bear to hear what I heard today.'[156] He added that only the resistance must be proportional to the attack on oneself. Almost immediately, however,

98 ❖ Politics: truth and non-violence

Gandhi cautioned that he might be misunderstood and urged that the 'sober' among those present must continue to repeat exactly to others his advice on this occasion. 'I want that you should never behave as cowards, and yet not take anyone's life.'[157] Gandhi returned publicly to the issue a week hence, through the pages of the *Young India*. He said that Congress workers needed to be careful while motivating 'a people so fallen as in Champaran' and that any resistance to the lawful activity of the police, such as resisting any arrest made with a warrant – even if the arrest were to appear and proven unlawful – would be wrong. Reiterating his earlier criticism of the villagers for fleeing in terror from a persecution which could have been warded off by organised resistance, he provided his definition of bravery. 'A brave man does not kill a thief but arrests him and hands him to the police. A braver man uses just enough force to drive him out and thinks no more about it. The bravest realises that the thief knows no better, reasons with him, risks being thrashed and even killed, but does not retaliate.'[158]

Gandhi's position regarding violent resistance in this episode is obviously not entirely uncomplicated in the tracing of his idea of non-violent resistance. It might appear ironical that within a year of this incident, a village mob attacked and killed nineteen constables after some of the villagers were killed in unprovoked police firing on a peaceful demonstration in Chauri Chaura. Yet, however striking it might appear to be, the linkage is tenuous between Gandhi's exhortation in Bettiah against cowardice and the killing of policemen who were begging for mercy. Along with almost all parametres of ethics and non-violence in Gandhi's concept of protest, which clearly deny any justification to the action of the protestors in Chauri Chaura, even the most mundane clause of proportionate response stands violated in this context. While calling off the civil disobedience movement in the aftermath of Chauri Chaura, Gandhi announced a personal penance for himself in the form of a public fast to arouse the conscience of his co-workers. We will return in greater detail to this incident in the subsequent chapter, but a reference to Gandhi's statement on the linkage between all actions is markedly relevant to the present discussion. Gandhi felt that the repression by the police and the violent response by Congress volunteers signified the corruption of standards that had become widely prevalent in the polity of the nation. Volunteers were either ignorant of his ideals or, still worse, were participating in the movement wilfully sceptical of the principles of truth and non-violence. The symptom of the malady, expressed in the violence of the protestors, also provided an opportunity for atonement and purification. 'They and we must suffer for the crime of Chauri Chaura. The incident proves, whether we wish it or no, the unity of life. All, including even the administrators, must suffer. Chauri Chaura must stiffen the Government, must still further corrupt the police, and the reprisals that will follow must further demoralize the people. The suspension and the penance will take us back to the position we occupied before the tragedy . . . If we learn the full lesson of the tragedy, we can turn the curse into a blessing.'[159]

Twenty years later, during the closing stages of the national movement, in a letter to Reginald Maxwell in 1943, answering Maxwell's criticism of his fast, Gandhi said – 'I have stated times without number that I detest violence in any shape or form.' He then asked a rhetorical question: 'Which is better, to take the opponent's life secretly or openly or to credit him with finer feelings and evoke them by fasting and the like? Again which is better, to trifle with one's own life by fasting or some other way of self-immolation, or to trifle with it by engaging in an attempt to compass the destruction of the opponent and his dependents?'[160]

For the practice of such means of protest, Gandhi relied on the inter-related ideas of faith and the conservation of all human acts. In 1928, he had asserted that non-violence was a practicable 'religious ideal', even as it was not fully realisable 'in the flesh'. Such ideals as this derived their energy from the 'ceaseless quest' they involved. The impossibility of a 'cut-and- dry model' was thus not an impediment; it was, on the contrary, a positive quality.

> The virtue of an ideal consists in its boundlessness. But although religious ideals must thus from their very nature remain unattainable by imperfect human beings, although by virtue of their boundlessness they may seem ever to recede farther away from us, the nearer we go to them, still they are closer to us than our very hands and feet because we are more certain of their reality and truth than even of our own physical being. This faith in one's ideals alone constitutes true life, in fact it is man's all in all.[161]

Relatedly, the ethical is thus proven to be the pragmatic, insofar as the belief in certain ideas is beneficent because of their inspirational value along with their practical efficacy. This also transforms the plane of their practicability. This position is not similar to Pascal's wager and not exceptionable, since belief in truth and non-violence is not subject to a narrowing, as may otherwise be the case with a sectarian belief. The

100 ❋ Politics: truth and non-violence

admission of the ethical in the sphere of pragmatism regarding communal choices is indicated as well in Arendt's poignant comment on Peter Bamm's reference to the futility of a sacrifice consigned to oblivion:

> The holes of oblivion do not exist. Nothing human is that perfect, and there are simply too many people in the world to make oblivion possible. One man will always be left alive to tell the story. Hence, nothing can ever be 'practically useless', at least, not in the long run. It would be of great practical usefulness for Germany today, not merely for her prestige abroad but for her sadly confused inner condition, if there were more such stories to be told. For the lesson of such stories is simple and within everybody's grasp. Politically speaking, it is that under conditions of terror most people will comply but some people will not, just as the lesson of the countries to which the final solution was proposed is that 'it could happen' in most places but it did not happen everywhere. Humanly speaking, no more is required, and no more can reasonably be asked, for this planet to remain a place fit for human habitation.[162]

Conversations on the Holocaust (*Shoah*) between the Church and the Synagogue have been persistently dominated by the general silence on the part of the Vatican during the Nazi persecution of Jews.[163] One response of the Catholic Church to the accusations relates to the futility of any intervention in Nazi Germany and to the fact that a concerted response on its part would have endangered whatever little it otherwise was able to accomplish for Jews through scattered initiatives. Lately, in an interesting shift for the issue of human agency, the traditional question regarding the absence of God has been subtly replaced by an emphasis on the absence of human action. In a recent conversation with Pope Francis, Rabbi Skorka incisively brings the question centrestage with the comment that human society occasionally eschews its consistent claim on free will for the purpose of abdicating responsibility for action in certain crucial periods of history. Skorka proceeds to inquire into the ramifications of the acceptance of a state of general helplessness in a theatre of injustice: 'There are things that we will never be able to understand, but it is clear that before we ask God where He was during the Holocaust, we should ask where the people were, both those who took action as well as those who mercilessly and cruelly failed to act – those who murdered and those that looked the other way.'[164] For Skorka, the patrician Pius XII had believed in diplomacy as the only instrument of redressal – 'that if a solution could not be found through diplomacy,

Politics: truth and non-violence ❖ 101

there was no solution' – as opposed to the activist practicality of John XXIII with his roots in the peasantry which inculcated a kind of care ethics which was the 'complete opposite of diplomacy'.[165] It needs to be recalled that in situations of injustice, Gandhi's prioritisation of the ethical imperative made avoidance of individual resistance impossible. Skorka's position approximates to that of Gandhi, and in speculating on the relationship of resistance and the human conscience, Skorka underlines the significance of Gandhi's faith in ethical action and in a way historicises the centrality of this faith in the ethics of resistance. It can be drawn that like Arendt, Skorka perceives that protest, by non-Jews as well, would not only have been a saving grace in a period of agential atrophy, but also, while problematising the acknowledged sequence of injustice and revenge, would have perhaps constituted an insight into the possible equation of politics and truth.

> The great existential doubt that I have is how could [Pius XII] have kept quiet when he came to learn about the Shoah? What kept him from shouting about it in anger from the rooftops? Prophets cry out against the smallest injustice. What could have happened if he had cried out? Would consciences have been awakened? Would more German soldiers have rebelled? I am not saying that these things would have happened, I am just trying to put myself in the place of those who suffered, those that do not have a voice anymore, as if I were talking to them and sharing their pain. Should some be saved if it means others will be abandoned? According to Jewish law, when an enemy army surrounds a city and declares that they will murder everyone in town if an innocent person is not handed over to them to be killed, the whole town should let themselves be killed. No one has the right to choose who is saved and who is not.[166]

In arguably his last major statement on this issue made during the last months of his life, Gandhi lamented that the heartless persecution of Jews had driven them to Palestine, but it also grieved him that they sought to impose themselves on an 'unwelcome land' with the 'aid of naked terrorism', and 'American money' and 'British arms'. He hoped a universally gifted race such as theirs would 'adopt the matchless weapon of non-violence whose use their best prophets have taught and which Jesus the Jew who wore the crown of thorns bequeathed to a groaning world'. It would be a 'soothing balm to the aching world', and their case would then become the world's case.[167]

The Gandhian path of non-violence may not be entirely irrelevant in the way forward in one of the most intractable conflicts of our times, which has so far failed all attempt at a rapprochement. Tagore had written to Gandhi in 1919 at the commencement of his first nationwide *Satyagraha* that 'Those who believe in spiritual life know that to stand against wrong which has overwhelming material power behind it is victory itself, – it is the victory of the active faith in the teeth of evident defeat'.[168] Gandhi provides in this, perhaps, a philosophical guarantee that it is possible to accomplish moral resistance in spite of its apparent remoteness from our immediate capabilities. The examination of the two foci of non-violence and truth in the political thought of Tagore and Gandhi see a further play with issues of nation and community in the ensuing discussion.

Notes

1. Michael Walzer, *Just and Unjust Wars: A Moral Argument with Historical Illustrations* (New York: Basic Books, 2006), xxiv.
2. Rabindranath Tagore, *Selected Letters of Rabindranath Tagore*, eds. Krishna Dutta and Andrew Robinson (Cambridge: Cambridge University Press, 1997), 83.
3. Tagore, *Selected Letters*, 322.
4. Tagore, *Selected Letters*, 237.
5. Sudipta Kaviraj and Sunil Khilnani, among others, refer to the possibility of this transaction: 'Many non-Western societies have intellectual cultures of great antiquity and sophistication. Often, however, these intellectual traditions did not have a pronounced attention to the sphere of 'politics' in the modern sense and therefore do not have a highly developed vernacular tradition to draw upon and develop. As a result, their historical entanglement with the modern state – the expression of its entirely novel structure of historical experience, dealing with its concentrated power, its ability to affect people's lives on an unprecedentedly large scale – has to rely at least initially on the language that comes from the West, the habitual, standard language of conveying and reflecting on this experience. However, over the longer historical term, as these historical state trajectories and the human experiences associated with them come to diverge from Western forms, inevitably new elements emerge.' Sudipta Kaviraj and Sunil Khilnani, 'Introduction', in eds. Sudipta Kaviraj and Sunil Khilnani,

Civil Society: History and Possibilities (Delhi: Cambridge University Press, 2002), 5.

6. Hannah Arendt, *Between Past and Future* (New York: Penguin Books, 2006), 145.
7. Arendt, *Between Past and Future*, 155.
8. Arendt, *Between Past and Future*, 241.
9. Rabindranath Tagore, *Rabindra Rachanabali* (125th anniversary edition), 15 vols. (Kolkata: Visva-Bharati, 1986–1992 [1393–1398 Bengali Era]), (hereafter cited as *Rachanabali*), 5: 763. All citations are in translation from Bangla, and have been translated by myself, unless otherwise specified.
10. Arendt, *Between Past and Future*, 241–242.
11. Bernard Williams, *Truth and Truthfulness* (Princeton: Princeton University Press, 2002), 12.
12. *Rachanabali*, 12: 662.
13. *Rachanabali*, 5: 789.
14. *Rachanabali*, 12: 664.
15. *Rachanabali*, 12: 664.
16. Williams, *Truth and Truthfulness*, 207.
17. Williams, *Truth and Truthfulness*, 207.
18. *Rachanabali*, 5: 667.
19. *Rachanabali*, 5: 667–668. It may be interesting to compare the point of Tagore's argument with that of Glaucon regarding the virtue of justice in Plato's *Republic*, as interpreted in another context by Williams. Williams concludes reading the argument in, as he says, 'a very different, and differently democratic time': 'Perhaps the lesson of Glaucon's argument is just this, that precisely because we need justice as an instrument we need to admire it for its own sake; and what we need to do is to learn how to do this, while not forgetting why we are doing so.' Bernard Williams, *The Sense of the Past: Essays in the History of Philosophy*, ed. Michael Burnyeat (Princeton: Princeton University Press, 2008), 107.
20. *Rachanabali*, 5: 674.
21. Arendt, *Between Past and Future*, 259.
22. Tagore, *Selected Letters*, 283.
23. *Rachanabali* 5: 682.
24. *Rachanabali*, 9: 605.
25. Williams, *Truth and Truthfulness*, 206.
26. *Rachanabali*, 5: 668.
27. Rabindranath Tagore, 'Letter to C. F. Andrews', ed. Sabyasachi Bhattacharya, *The Mahatma and the Poet: Letters and Debates between Gandhi and Tagore 1915–1941* (Delhi: National Book Trust, 2005), 61.
28. *Rachanabali*, 9: 603.
29. Isaiah Berlin, *Russian Thinkers*, eds. Henry Hardy and Aileen Kelly (London: Penguin Books, 1994), 295.

104 ❖ Politics: truth and non-violence

30. Rabindranath Tagore, *The English Writings of Rabindranath Tagore*, 4 vols. (Delhi: Sahitya Akademi, 1994–2007 [hereafter cited as *Writings*]), 3: 88–89.

31. Isaiah Berlin, *The Crooked Timber of Humanity: Chapters in the History of Ideas*, ed. Henry Hardy (Princeton: Princeton University Press, 1990), 1–2.

32. Alex Aronson, *Rabindranath Through Western Eyes* (Calcutta: Riddhi-India, 1978), 62.

33. Tagore to Mussolini in a conversation on 13 June 1926. An account of the conversation was subsequently dictated by Tagore himself to his secretary on the same day. Cited in Aronson, *Rabindranath Through Western Eyes*, 63–64.

34. *Rachanabali*, 5: 790.

35. *Rachanabali*, 5: 666.

36. *Rachanabali*, 5: 674–675.

37. Malcolm X, *By Any Means Necessary* (New York: Pathfinder, 2008), 61–67.

38. Eugene Victor Wolfenstein, *The Victims of Democracy: Malcolm X and the Black Revolution* (New York: The Guilford Press, 1993), 370–371.

39. Frantz Fanon, *A Dying Colonialism*, trans. Haakon Chevalier (New York: Grove Press, 1965), 180.

40. Fanon, *Colonialism*, 27.

41. Fanon, *Colonialism*, 27–28.

42. Fanon, *Colonialism*, 23–24.

43. Fanon, *Colonialism*, 24.

44. Fanon, *Colonialism*, 25.

45. Wolfenstein, *The Victims of Democracy*, 344.

46. Berlin, *Russian Thinkers*, 207.

47. G. C. Pande, *Jaina Political Thought* (Jaipur: Prakrit Bharati Sansthan, Centre for Jain Studies, University of Rajasthan, 1984), 34.

48. Pande, *Jaina Political Thought*, 36.

49. Chinmohon Sehanobis holds one such view. See Chinmohon Sehanobis, *Rabindranath o Biplabi Samaj* (Calcutta: Visva Bharati, 1998), 15.

50. *Rachanabali*, 8: 185–186.

51. Williams, *The Sense of the Past*, 83. It might be interesting to likewise refer to Burckhardt's comment indicating the qualities of cogency and receptivity in thoughtful conversation on the dialogue form preferred by the Greek philosophers: 'For the Greeks the dialogue form was especially congenial, and as a practical teaching device it is perhaps as old as the *acroamatic* lecture, for the formal dialogue develops more sharply than any other kind of discussion and hence, as mentioned earlier, philosophy was primarily an oral discipline. Socrates, who wrote nothing himself, may well have stimulated his listeners to write down whatever they could remember of his conversation. This

may explain the next step philosophers took in composing well-wrought dialogues. That Plato and Socrates worked very hard on the form of their compositions is certain. To master the conversational tone, Plato is said to have studied Sophron's *mimes*, i.e., prose conversations taken from the life of the common people. A tradition reports that throughout his long life Plato kept polishing and filing at his dialogues. Even the impious parody of Lucian as seen in *The Carousal or the Lapiths* is above all lucid and dramatic.' Jacob Burckhardt, *History of Greek Culture*, trans. Palmer Hilty (New York: Dover Publications, Inc., 2002), 318–319.

52. For a concise and penetrating analysis of the themes of the two novels in comparison, see Ashis Nandy, *The Illegitimacy of Nationalism*, in *Return from Exile* (Delhi: Oxford University Press, 1998), 27–34.

53. Bhupendra Nath Datta, *Bharater Dvitiya Svadhinata Sangram* (Calcutta: Burman Publishing House, 1949), 82; cited in Sehanobis, *Rabindranath o Biplabi Samaj*, 96.

54. Tagore, *Writings*, 3: 718.

55. *Rachanabali*, 12: 553–568.

56. *Rachanabali*, 12: 563.

57. *Rachanabali*, 12: 563–564.

58. Sehanobis, *Rabindranath*, 68.

59. Sehanobis, *Rabindranath*, 69.

60. Sehanobis, *Rabindranath*, 69.

61. Tagore, *Four Chapters*, 22–24.

62. Rabindranath Tagore, *Four Chapters*, trans. Rimli Bhattacharya (Delhi: Shrishti, 2001), 21.

63. Arendt, *Between Past and Future*, 259.

64. Tagore, *Four Chapters*, 19.

65. Tagore, *Four Chapters*, 79.

66. Tagore, *Four Chapters*, 17.

67. Tagore, *Four Chapters*, 24.

68. Tagore, *Four Chapters*, 24.

69. *Rachanabali*, 12: 553–555.

70. *Rachanabali*, 5: 778.

71. Tagore, *Four Chapters*, 79.

72. Boris Pasternak, *Dr. Zhivago*, trans. Max Hayward and Manya Harari (London: Vintage Books, 2002), 228.

73. Bimanbehari Majumdar, *Heroines of Tagore: A Study in the Transformation of Indian Society 1875–1941* (Calcutta: Firma K. L. Mukhopadhyay, 1968), 282.

74. Tagore, *Four Chapters*, 63.

75. Tagore, *Four Chapters*, 77.

76. Tagore, *Four Chapters*, 80.

106 ❖ Politics: truth and non-violence

77. Adrian Moore in Williams, *The Sense of the Past*, ix–x.
78. M. K. Gandhi, *Non-Violence in Peace and War*, 2 vols. (Ahmedabad: Navjivan Publishing House, 1942), 1: 170.
79. Gandhi, *Non-Violence in Peace and War*, 1: 170–172.
80. Gandhi, *Non-Violence in Peace and War*, 1: 173.
81. *Selections from the Prison Notebooks of Antonio Gramsci*, trans. and ed. Quintin Hoare and Geoffrey Nowell Smith (Chennai: Orient Longman, 1996), 229–230.
82. Gandhi, *Non-Violence in Peace and War*, 1: 170–172.
83. Arvind Sharma, *Modern Hindu Thought: The Essential Texts*, Appendix II (Delhi: Oxford University Press, 2002), 290–301.
84. Sharma, *Modern Hindu Thought*, Appendix III, 302–310.
85. I owe this information to Daniel Raveh – grandson of Judah L. Magnes, personal communication.
86. Sharma, *Modern Hindu Thought*, 301.
87. Sharma, *Modern Hindu Thought*, 292.
88. Sharma, *Modern Hindu Thought*, 301.
89. Sharma, *Modern Hindu Thought*, 303.
90. Gandhi, *Non-Violence in Peace and War*, 1: 179.
91. Gandhi, *Non-Violence in Peace and War*, 1: 162.
92. It appears that Gandhi was perhaps not fully aware of historical instances of non-violent resistance by communities, such as by Jews against the Roman Empire; the Sakyas against King Vidudabha; and the Maoris against the British. But then, he may be implying that *nation* – with its implicit military organisation – and non-violence are mutually exclusive categories.
93. Gandhi, *Non-Violence in Peace and War*, 1: 163.
94. The religious traditions generally take a similar position, as in Jainism: 'Himsa and ahimsa relate to one's own soul and not to others. . . . Self-culture is the main problem of ahimsa'. T. G. Kalghatgi, *Study of Jainism* (Jaipur: Prakrit Bharati Academy, 1988), 202.
95. Michael Ignatieff, 'Introduction', in Primo Levi, *Moments of Reprieve*, trans. Ruth Feldman (London: Penguin Books, 2002), 6.
96. For the details of his inner conflicts as Chairman of the Warsaw Jewish Council (a unit of the Nazi administration), as well as the insensitivity and corruption of ghetto administration, see *The Warsaw Diary of Adam Czerniakow: Prelude to Doom*, eds. Raul Hillberg, Stanislaw Staron and Joseph Kermisz (Chicago: Ivan R. Dee Publishers, 1999). Rather than assisting in killing helpless ghetto children by handing them over for transportation to concentration camps as demanded by the SS, Czerniakow killed himself on 23 July 1942, writing in his suicide note to his wife: 'I am powerless, my heart trembles in sorrow and compassion. I can no longer bear all this. My act will show everyone the right thing to do.' Joseph Kermisz, 'Introduction', in Czerniakow, *Prelude to Doom*, 23.

Politics: truth and non-violence ❖ 107

97. Elie Wiesel, *A Beggar in Jerusalem*, trans. Lily Edelman and Elie Wiesel (New York: Shocken Books, 1985), 208. There is a likelihood of Wiesel's description drawing on the account of an extremely poignant incident read out at the Nuremberg courtroom by British prosecutor Hartley Shawcross from the sworn affidavit of Hermann Graebe, who was an engineer with a German firm posted in the Ukraine. The testimonial description of the 'comparatively minor mass execution' has been reproduced by the noted journalist, William Shirer. Shirer mentions that a 'hush of horror' had descended in the courtroom at the reading of this account of the execution of the 5,000 Jews residing in Dubno by the German *Einsatz* commandos in October 1942. This extract conveys both a sense of resignation and fortitude on the part of the victims immediately before the massacre: 'An old woman with snow-white hair was holding a one-year-old child in her arms and singing to it and tickling it. The child was cooing with delight. The parents were looking on with tears in their eyes. The father was holding the hand of a boy about 10 years old and speaking to him softly; the boy was fighting his tears. The father pointed to the sky, stroked his head and seemed to explain something to him. At that moment, the S.S. man at the pit shouted something to his comrade. The latter counted off about twenty persons and instructed them to go behind the earth mound . . . I well remember a girl, slim and with black hair, who, as she passed close to me, pointed to herself and said: "twenty-three years old".' William L. Shirer, *The Rise and Fall of the Third Reich: A History of Nazi Germany* [1950] (New York: Ballantine Books, 1983), 1252.

98. Primo Levi, *The Drowned and the Saved*, trans. Raymond Rosenthal (New York: Vintage International, 1989), 136.

99. Elie Wiesel, *Dawn*, trans. Frances Frenaye, in *The Night Trilogy* (New York: Hill and Wang, 2008), 195.

100. Dennis Dalton, *Nonviolence in Action: Gandhi's Power* (New Delhi: Oxford University Press, 2007), 137.

101. Dalton, *Nonviolence in Action*, 229–230nn177, 178.

102. Ronald J. Terchek, *Gandhi: Struggling for Autonomy* (Lanham: Rowman & Littlefield Publishers, Inc., 1998), 210–211. In this context, Terchek also cites Karl Jasper's comment: 'It was only under the British, and only under their attempt at liberal rule which is unique in the history of empires, that Gandhi could succeed.' Karl Jaspers, *The Future of Mankind* (Chicago: University of Chicago Press, 1961), 38.

103. Terchek, *Gandhi*, 212–213.

104. Hannah Arendt, *On Violence* (London: Allen Lane The Penguin Press, 1970), 53.

105. Arendt, *On Violence*, 56.

106. Arendt, *On Violence*, 80.

108 ❖ Politics: truth and non-violence

107. Arendt, *On Violence*, 83.
108. Rajmohan Gandhi, *Mohandas: A True Story of a Man, His People and an Empire* (Delhi: Penguin Books, 2006), 444.
109. Gandhi, *Non-Violence in Peace and War*, 1: 177.
110. Gandhi, *Non-Violence in Peace and War*, 1: 177.
111. *India's Foreign Policy: Selected Speeches of Jawaharlal Nehru, September 1946–April 1961* (New Delhi: The Publications Division, Government of India, 1983), 346.
112. Halifax, quoted in Earl of Avon, *The Eden Memoirs* (London: Cassel, 1962), 163; cited in Rajmohan Gandhi, *Mohandas*, 422.
113. *Hitler's Secret Conversations 1941–1944* (New York: Farrar, Strauss, 1953), 163; cited in Dalton, *Nonviolence in Action*, 229 n176.
114. *The Goebbels Diaries: 1942–1943*, ed. and trans. Louis P. Lochner (New York: Doubleday, 1948), 162; cited in Dalton, *Nonviolence in Action*, 229n176.
115. *The Collected Works of Mahatma Gandhi*, 100 vols. (Delhi: Publications Division, Government of India, 1958–1994,) [hereafter *Collected Works*], 72: 193.
116. In his Presidential Address to the Congress session of 1909 at Lahore, Madan Mohan Malaviya offered condolences to Lady Curzon Wyllie and the family of Dr. Lalkata who was killed by Dhingra while he was trying to save Wyllie, and deplored the rising creed of political assassins. But he felt compelled to express his frustration at the helplessness of the political leadership before this cult of violence. 'But we are grieved to find that these new political *ghazis* have now risen in our midst, and have become a source of shame and sorrow to the country. I am sure we are all of one mind in our desire to do all we can to eradicate this new evil from our land. But we do not know what steps should be taken to do so. We have repeatedly denounced these outrages, but those who commit them have obviously gone beyond the reach of our influence.' *Congress Presidential Addresses*, ed. A. M. Zaidi, 5 vols. (New Delhi: Indian Institute of Applied Political Research, 1986–1989), 2: 421.
117. Hannah Arendt, *Eichmann in Jerusalem: A Report on the Banality of Evil* (New York: Penguin Books, 2006), 59.
118. *Eichmann in Jerusalem*, 39.
119. Hayem Greenburg, 'We Are Treated As Subhumans – We Are Asked To Be Superhumans', in Gandhi, *Non-Violence in Peace and War*, 1: 464.
120. Gandhi, *Non-Violence in Peace and War*, 1: 219.
121. Like many of the accused, who subsequently feigned ignorance about its contents, Goering stated at his trial at Nuremberg, 'The first time I learned of these terrible exterminations was right here in Nuremberg.' Shirer, *Rise and Fall of the Third Reich*, 1256.

Politics: truth and non-violence   ❖   109

122. Hilberg reasons that it was hardly incredible that 'written directives would give way to oral ones'. 'Hitler himself may never have signed an order to kill Jews. On the other hand, there are records of his utterances in the form of comments, questions, or "wishes". What he actually meant, or whether he really meant it, might have been a matter of tone as well as of language. When he spoke "coldly" and in a "low voice" of "horrifying" decisions "also at the dinner table", then his audience knew that he was "serious". Oral orders were given at every level. Hoss was told to build his death camp at Auschwitz in a conversation with Himmler. Stangl received instructions about Sobibor from Globocnik on a park bench in Lublin. A railroad man in Krakow, responsible for scheduling death trains, recalls that he was told by his immediate superior to run the transports whenever they were requested by the S.S.' Raul Hilberg, *The Destruction of the European Jews* [Chicago: 1961] (Teaneck, NJ: Holmes & Meier Publishers Inc., 1985), 265.

123. For details, see Hilberg, *The Destruction of the European Jews*, 125–138.

124. Louis Fisher, *The Life of Mahatma Gandhi* (Mumbai: Bharatiya Vidya Bhavan, 1990), 447.

125. Dalton, *Nonviolence in Action*, 136–137.

126. It is perhaps also safe to assume that, given Gandhi's plausible familiarity with Jewish tradition through his close relationship with friends such as Kallenbach, with his statement that Jews should have thrown themselves into the sea as a means of resistance, he was referring to Kiddush ha-Shem or 'the sanctification of the divine name', embodying the steadfastness of faith, which involves prayer and willingness for martyrdom.

127. Gandhi, *Non-Violence in Peace and War*, 1: 192.

128. Greenburg, 'We Are Treated As Subhumans – We Are Asked To Be Superhumans', in Gandhi, *Non-Violence in Peace and War*, 1: 462.

129. Arendt mentions the bizarre nature of the case; on the one hand, the Nazi slander of the victim for homosexuality and 'illicit relations' with Jewish boys, and on the other making him 'a martyr and victim of world Jewry'. See Arendt, *Eichmann In Jerusalem*, 227–228.

130. Hilberg, *The Destruction of the European Jews*. However, it should be mentioned that Arendt was highly critical of some of Hilberg's subsequent observations on the Jewish psyche, such as the 'death wish of the Jews'; they never met and the relationship between Arendt and Hilberg was hardly congenial. For an interesting version of their attitude to each other, see Raul Hilberg, *The Politics of Memory: The Journey of a Holocaust Historian* (Chicago: Ivan R. Dee Inc., 1996), 147–157.

131. Arendt, *Eichmann in Jerusalem*, 61.

132. Arendt, *Eichmann in Jerusalem*, 61.

133. Gandhi, *Non-Violence in Peace and War*, 1: 191.

110   ✦   Politics: truth and non-violence

134. Joan Bondurant, *Conquest of Violence: The Gandhian Philosophy of Conflict* (Princeton: Princeton University Press, 1988), 227.

135. Robert Pendorf, *Morder und Ermordete. Eichmann und die Judenpolitic des Dritten Reiches* (Hamburg: 1961); cited in Arendt, *Eichmann in Jerusalem*, 117.

136. Elie Wiesel, *Night*, trans. Marion Wiesel, in *The Night Trilogy* (New York: Hill and Wang, 2008). 26.

137. Wiesel, *Night*, 26.

138. Hilberg, *The Destruction of the European Jews*, 24.

139. Hilberg mentions the post-war observation of a commander of two death camps and war criminal Franz Stangl on the victims: '[Stangl] said that only recently he had read a book about lemmings. It reminded him of Treblinka.' Hilberg, *The Destruction of the European Jews*, 299.

140. This description is representative of the life in the ghettos of Eastern Europe during the closing years of the war: 'Throughout Europe the Jewish communities strove for community. They treated the sick who would not have time to recover, they fed the unemployed who would not work again, they educated the children who would not be allowed to grow up. For a middle aged leadership there was no alternative. Younger people also were caught in the psychological web. The children, however, were least prone to fall into illusion. When in the Theresienstadt ghetto a transport of children was funneled to ordinary showers, they cried out: "No gas!".' Hilberg, *The Destruction of the European Jews*, 302–303.

141. Hilberg, *The Destruction of the European Jews*, 299.

142. Arendt, *Eichmann in Jerusalem*, 117. Hilberg had similarly deduced that the entire process of extermination depended largely on Jewish participation, both at the level of individuals as well as at the level of organised collective activity, as through councils.

143. Hilberg has noted in this regard: 'In writing about the Jewish councils I had emphasised the extent to which the German apparatus counted on their cooperation. The accommodation policy of the councils had ended in disaster. For me, however the problem was deeper. The councils were not only a German tool but also an instrument of the Jewish community. Their strategy was a continuation of the adjustments and adaptations practiced by Jews for centuries. I could not separate the Jewish leaders from the Jewish populace because I believed that these men represented the essence of a time-honoured Jewish reaction to danger.' Hilberg, *The Politics of Memory*, 150–151.

144. Arendt specifically refers Hilberg's *The Destruction of the European Jews* as conclusive evidence in this regard. Arendt, *Eichmann in Jerusalem*, 117.

145. Arendt, *Eichmann in Jerusalem*, 297.

146. Gandhi, *Collected Works*, 23: 118.

Politics: truth and non-violence ❖ 111

147. Among the most graphic and painful are those contained in Elie Wiesel's *Night* and in Primo Levy's *The Drowned and the Saved*.

148. Levy, *The Drowned and the Saved*, 20.

149. Arendt, *Eichmann in Jerusalem*, 295.

150. Peter Bamm, *Die Unsichtbare Flagge* (Munich: 1952); cited in Arendt, *Eichmann in Jerusalem*, 232.

151. For details of this psycho-social aspect of the Holocaust, see Hilberg, *The Destruction of the European Jews*, 274–293.

152. Gandhi, *Non-Violence in Peace and War*, 2: 8.

153. *Collected Works*, 19: 116.

154. *Collected Works*, 19: 89.

155. *Collected Works*, 19: 90.

156. *Collected Works*, 19: 90.

157. *Collected Works*, 19: 91.

158. *Collected Works*, 19: 118. It is interesting to recall in this context what Gandhi had said in a speech at Dacca in 15 December 1920: 'We do not possess so much strength that we can approach the cultivators and tell them not to pay taxes or ask a soldier to leave his service. We will use swords, when the time will come. He who does not draw the sword at the proper time is a fool and he who uses his sword at an improper time is also impudent.' *Collected Works*, 19: 122. However, given that he never once in later years discarded his public position regarding non-violence, the statement can be taken perhaps as a rhetorical reference to an adage, a momentary aside during a crucial public campaign.

159. *Collected Works*, 22: 421. The somewhat more difficult issue in this connection pertains to a report by Nirmal Kumar Bose of Gandhi's support to a group of young violently inclined Hindus who were resolved to use, if necessary, their usual weapons to save the lives of some Muslims endangered in the partition riots in Calcutta during September 1949. In spite of his managing to temporarily instill a semblance of sanity to a communally passionate Calcutta, poor and ailing Muslims, who were still living in Mianbagan, fearing for their lives by a renewed threat of communal violence in the city were about to start for a safer neighbourhood aboard a truck, when grenades thrown on the vehicle killed two of the passengers. The said group of Hindu young men approached Nirmal Kumar Bose with their offer of protecting the targeted minorities, but with a request to Gandhi to prevent the police from arresting them for possession of unlicensed arms. Bose reports that Gandhi agreed to help them in their resolve, saying that 'he was with them. If Prafulla Babu, the Chief Minister, could not protect the minority with his government forces, and the young men decided to do so, they deserved his support'. Gandhi's endorsing of violent intervention

112 ❖ Politics: truth and non-violence

in this case is apparently centred on the principle of preventive violence through the agency of the state in situations of group persecution. Additionally, it involves violence on the part of not the sufferers themselves but by the enabled against the vindictiveness of their own community. Only, it is as if Gandhi is substituting an ineffective state apparatus with the buttressing community of the state in the performance of its essential function, the protection of the life and liberty of its citizens. However, this instance needs to be distinguished from vigilante justice. According to Bose, a Jewish intellectual from Palestine University, Walter Zander, some years later professed to understand Gandhi's position, stating that 'Gandhiji was here not encouraging violence; he was trying to protect those who were against him from the hand of his own people. And if violence was condoned for this purpose, it was no more than cutting off one's own hand to prevent it from doing mischief.' Nirmal Kumar Bose, *My Days with Gandhi* (Delhi: Orient Longman, 1987), 236.

160. *Collected Works*, 77: 91.
161. *Collected Works*, 38: 69.
162. Arendt, *Eichmann in Jerusalem*, 232–233.
163. For a literary representation of the charges of inaction, or worse, concerning Pope Pius XII, see Rolf Hochhuth, *The Deputy*, trans. Richard and Clara Winston (New York: Grove Press, 1964). It is significant that Bernhard Lichtenberg, whose courageous protest against the Holocaust we have mentioned earlier, was a dedicatee of this play. It is interesting to recall Hannah Arendt's account of the response of Pope John XXIII when he had read the recently published play and was asked about the possible course of action against it. He had reportedly retorted, 'Do against it? What can you do against the truth?' Hannah Arendt, *Men in Dark Times* (San Diego: Harcourt Brace and Company, 1968), 63.
164. Pope Francis agrees: 'Where was man? – that is the biggest contradiction to human solidarity of that period.' Jorge Mario Bergoglio and Abraham Skorka. *On Heaven and Earth: Pope Francis on Faith, Family, and the Church in the 21st Century*, trans. Alejandro Bermudez and Howard Goodman (London: Bloomsbury Publishing, 2013), 176–177.
165. Bergoglio and Skorka, *On Heaven and Earth*, 185. We can recall an interesting formulation by Judith Shklar regarding class and a perception of injustice: 'Noblemen are dishonoured as members of a caste, but a democratic sense of injustice asserts itself when one has been denied one's dignity as a human being. There is a vast difference between an aristocratic and a democratic ethos. One could argue that no aristocrat could possibly acknowledge a sense of injustice in all its fullness. If wounded honour calls for satisfaction, the democratic sense of injustice cries out for more, for a public recognition that it is wrong and unfair to deny to anyone a

minimum of human dignity.' Judith N. Shklar, *The Faces of Injustice* (New Haven: Yale University Press, 1990), 85–86.

166. Bergoglio and Skorka, *On Heaven and Earth*, 183.
167. Gandhi, *Non-Violence in Peace and War*, 2: 116–117.
168. Sabyasachi Bhattacharya, ed., *The Mahatma And The Poet: Letters and Debates between Gandhi and Tagore 1915–1941* (New Delhi: National Book Trust, 2005), 49–50.

III ❁
Nationalism

Ethics and responsibility

The attempt to evaluate the relationship of Gandhi and Tagore with the phenomenon of nationalism is hardly uncomplicated and defeats easy categorisation, naturally drawing attention as it must, to the porosity of the concept of nationalism. Although it is the received wisdom in many quarters that Tagore unlike Gandhi was opposed to nationalism, a close analysis may reveal why Gandhi chose to call him 'an ardent nationalist'. Gandhi's obituary of Tagore might be recalled relevantly in this regard:

> In the death of Rabindranath Tagore, we have not only lost the greatest poet of the age, but an ardent nationalist who was also a humanitarian. There was hardly any public activity on which he has not left the impress of his powerful personality. In Santiniketan and Sriniketan, he has left a legacy to the whole nation, indeed to the whole world. May the noble soul rest in peace and may those in charge at Santiniketan prove worthy of the responsibility resting on their shoulders.[1]

Equating Tagore with nationalism and Santiniketan at the same time may sound intriguing. If anything, Santiniketan is located in the tradition of viewing humanity as transcending cartographical divisions. Tagore was ever vigilant against 'nationalistic prejudices' that were 'sedulously cultivated in our school-books, and also by the patriots who wish the boys to be proud of the exploits of their own country by running down other countries'.[2] Thus, for him, most schools distorted children's sympathy and made them 'incapable of understanding alien peoples with different languages and cultures'.

In India, as a response to the Macaulayan policy of acculturation, a genuine effort was initiated to create an alternative system of education which was not chauvinistic but was premised on the complementarities of cultures. It was believed that to privilege one single culture as supreme would in effect impede and asphyxiate the interchange of human values and cultures. While concluding his acceptance speech for the Nobel Prize in Stockholm, Tagore alluded to the global character of Santiniketan with an invitation to the world, in the 'name of the unity of men', in the 'name of love' and 'in the name of God' to 'join hands with us and not to leave this institution to us', to 'make it living and representative of the undivided humanity of the world'.[3]

The undoubted astuteness of Gandhi and his propinquity with Tagore even as they argued their way through some of the crucial periods of the nationalist movement indicate to the soundness of Gandhi's perception regarding Tagore. Was there a nationalist hidden in Tagore which appealed to Gandhi's nationalism? Was Gandhi not a nationalist in the conventional sense and so appreciated Tagore's similarly unconventional nationalism? Or is nationalism itself a complicated category and which is admitting of nuances?

Friedrich Waismann introduced the idea of open texture more generally used in the philosophy of language, which indicates that notwithstanding definition as applicable category, there still remain possibilities of a definition being inadequate, even though this entails that the definition in question will remain different from any kind of vagueness, insofar as the definition may be fairly accurate in actual situations.[4] It might be interesting to look at the definitions of nationalism.

Broadly defined nationalism is the assumption of an identity by a group of people primarily on the basis of territory, language, religion and culture. It is the political aspect of a categorisation of history in the industrial age.[5] Hans Kohn defined nationalism as initially a collective 'state of mind', which has been variously constituted across history. Different elements of this collective mind, such as language, territory and traditions, have mutated both in scale and intensity, and the idea of nationalism has motivated human beings towards different objectives and accomplishments, and these objectives have been considered to be possible and realisable mainly in a sovereign state. The building of an independent state has been the ultimate aim of the nationalities compelled to traverse the historical stages from political subjection to autonomy. 'Nationalism demands the nation-state; the creation of the nation-state strengthens nationalism. Here, as elsewhere in history, we find a continuous interdependence and interaction.'[6] One perilous development in the nineteenth century was investing a divine status to the nation. Seton-Watson connects the subsequent growth of this fledgling sentiment to the diminution of

116 ❦ Nationalism: ethics and responsibility

religious faith. 'Nationalism has become an ersatz religion. The nation, as understood by the nationalist, is a substitute god; nationalism of this sort might be called *ethnolatry*' (emphasis as in the original).[7] In the history of Indian nationalism, Gandhi and Tagore were opposed to this tendency to conflate the nation and godhead. Recently, some scholars have seriously debated the logical correctness of the claim of a national community to be regarded as a moral community, based in the concept that the ethnicities constitutive of nationality are inherently vested with ethical value. Margaret Moore points to the normative character of this argument: 'Nationalists see their arguments as arguments about what *should* be done, about what is *legitimate* state action. They often appeal to the good of the nation, as part of a claim about legitimate political action. They think that this sort of claim counts as a moral reason in favour of a particular policy' (emphasis as in the original).[8] Elie Kedourie regarded nationalism as a pretension contrived in Europe for rationalising autonomy of government for a component of a population in a specific geographical area. As a form of ideological politics, nationalism was contradistinct from constitutional politics, which supersedes sectional claims in the providence of a system of law and procedure to protect and promote common interests and aspirations of a society or state. Nationalism in the form of ideological politics is more oriented to establish an ethos, which will supposedly facilitate an ideal society repositing desired well-being and values. 'To do so, the ideologist will, to borrow Plato's analogy in the *Republic*, look upon state and society as a canvas which has to be wiped clean, so that his vision of justice, virtue and happiness can be painted on this *tabula rasa*.'[9] Some years into the twentieth century, a nation was defined by Stalin as 'a historically evolved, stable community of language, territory, economic life and psychological make-up, manifested in a community of culture'.[10] The universal applicability of this historical evolution has been contested in contrary formulations of the nation as a product of historical amnesia[11] or as an imagined community.[12] Marxist scholar James M. Blaut draws attention to the fact that whereas Stalin's definition later became immensely influential within Marxist circles, Lenin did not apply Stalin's nomenclature on the subject in his regular discussions of colonial nationalism through his speeches and writings from 1915 to the end of his life: 'In none of these did he refer to or use Stalin's definition of "the nation".'[13] Moreover, in the details of his formulation, Stalin was responding polemically particularly to the Jewish Bund and generally to the Bolshevik endorsement of the aspirations of nationalities within

Russia. Since the Jews did not have territorial rights or territorial possession, they were not entitled to the status and claims of a nation.[14] Blaut finds it difficult to accept the all too readily accepted linkage between nationalism and fascism in certain theoretical formulations. Nationalism is a composite of different ideologies in different historical contexts and it may become very simplistic to club them all under one common rubric from a particular theoretical point of vantage. 'Fascist movements can make use of the politics of national aggrandizement, and even the politics of secessionism. But nationalism has no direct and close connection to fascism, and the problem of fascism cannot be solved within the theory of nationalism.'[15] However, it is generally believed the exclusionary element is predominant in nationalism. On one plane, it 'connotes a tendency to place a particularly excessive, exaggerated and exclusive emphasis on values, which leads to a vain and importunate overestimation of one's own nation and thus to a detraction of others',[16] and on another, it denotes, as in Camille Julian's searching for spiritual France even while dealing with periods thousands of years preceding the existence of his country, an 'extreme case of the emotional and intellectual substitution of a nation for Mankind.'[17] Gellner is of the view that this exclusivity and imposition is practised by nationalisms not only in relation to other nationalisms across the borders of the nation states, but also, and more crucially, within the 'nation' by the 'high culture' which dominates the nationalistic consciousness. The apparatus of the national state assists in this imposition of a politically powerful high culture over the 'low culture' that was hitherto practised by the majority of almost the whole of the national population: 'It is the establishment of an autonomous, impersonal society, with mutually substitutable atomized individuals, held together above all by a shared culture of this kind, in place of a previous complex structure of local groups, sustained by folk cultures reproduced locally and idiosyncratically by the groups themselves.'[18] It is significant in this context to mention that P. Ananda Charlu, offering one of the earliest definitions of nationality in the history of Indian nationalism in his presiding address to Congress in 1891, relegated the commonality of language and religion, commensality and inter-marriage as at best only 'potent auxiliaries' of nationality. Favouring the Sanskrit word *prajah* as most aptly translating nationality, Charlu drew attention to the historical environing of diverse communities/races that for him constituted the basic element of a nationality. Charlu proceeded to adapt with approbation an illustration of the evolving Indian nation: 'In the next place [racial stem]

118 ❖ Nationalism: ethics and responsibility

gets added to, from time to time, by the accession of other peoples – like scions engrafted on the central stem, or like creepers attaching thereto – who settle in the country in a like manner, and come under the many unifying influences already referred to, though still exhibiting marks of separateness and distinctness.'[19] The metaphor of the trunk and the creeper is interesting.

Although the extent to which the category of nationalism can be stretched – without its becoming something of its opposite – is debatable, it does contain quite a variety in itself; for instance, Hobsbawm has likened *Mafias* to national movements inasmuch as they were also points of convergence for diverse social tendencies, divergent social and personal aspirations and focalised defence of social tradition against alien and disruptive tendencies: '[*Mafias*] are to some extent, like national movements, of which perhaps they are a sort of embryo fluid.'[20]

Tagore called nationalism 'a great menace', stating that he was 'not against one nation in particular, but against the general idea of all nations'.[21] However, his hostility to the nation is not monolithic and as intractable, in spite of similarities, as that of George Steiner, who has famously stated:

> Nationalism is the venom of modern history. Nothing is more bestially absurd than the readiness of human beings to incinerate or slaughter one another in the name of nationhood and under the infantile spell of a flag. Citizenship is a bilateral arrangement that is, that always ought to be, subject to critical examination and, if need be, abrogation. No city of man is worth a major injustice, a major falsehood. The death of Socrates outweighs the survival of Athens. Nothing dignifies French history more surely than the willingness of French men to go to the brink of communal collapse, to weaken the bonds of nationhood drastically (as they in fact did) over the Dreyfuss case. . . . Trees have roots, men have legs with which to leave after they have, in conscience, said no.[22]

There is, in this passage by Steiner, an interesting conflation of the nation and the state. There are also obvious echoes of Lincoln who had at one stage contemplated emigrating if America became more intolerant to minority groups.[23] But for the present purpose, I am drawn more to Socrates than to Steiner. Confronted by death, Socrates refused to leave Athens at the bidding of Crito. In spite of acknowledging that the state had 'injured' him and had given him 'an unjust sentence', Socrates nevertheless constructed a dialogue with the Laws before Crito for elaborating

Nationalism: ethics and responsibility   ❀   119

his reasons for not leaving the city state. Socrates states that the laws tell him that he had been 'the most constant resident' of Athens, renouncing the choice to 'go to a colony or any other city' and 'take his goods with him'. He had signed his covenant with the laws and leaving now would amount to an unworthy transgression. Socrates prefers to 'depart in innocence, a sufferer and not a doer of evil; a victim, not of the laws but of men'. The voice urging him in this is he says, 'murmuring in my ears, like the sound of a flute in the ears of a mystic; that voice, I say, is humming in my ears, and prevents me from hearing any other'.[24] Rather than individual secession from an unjust nation/state, the principle of bearing witness becomes overriding in this case, also perhaps indicating in the process the other, and the possible ethical foundations of the nation state.

Nationalism and cosmopolitanism

Similarly, for Tagore, as mentioned earlier, mere political freedom as understood in the modern West was of secondary importance, being mostly only inadequately realised and thereby catalysing in international disputes and tensions. It was publicly associated with contestable claims, and a sense of tensed alertness: 'Political freedom does not give us freedom when our mind is not free.'[25] In Tagore's perception, *dharma* transcended political liberty and was related to individual resilience rather than to external agency. Recurrently explored in his writings, his concept of *dharma* differed from common notions of religious code, and agreed with Gandhi's view of its living quality. For Tagore, the nation is apparently an amoral, rather immoral category, which 'will never heed the voice of truth and goodness'.[26] But more to the point is the fact that when he says that 'in the reign of the nation the governed are pursued by suspicions', his experience is primarily that of the repression practised by the colonial state; even though for him 'it is not a question of the British government, but of government by the nation', he nevertheless acknowledges that 'our only intimate experience of the nation is the British nation'.[27] But, '[this] government by the nation is neither British nor anything else; it is an applied science and therefore more or less similar in principles wherever it is used'.[28] However, thus far, the paradox of the nation and the no-nation remains unresolved. The paradox can perhaps be explicated and partially resolved by looking at what Amartya Sen has

120 ❧ Nationalism: ethics and responsibility

termed 'Tagore's dual attitude to Nationalism', and thereby recognising the open texture of nationalism as well.

> Tagore's 'dual' attitude to Nationalism – supporting its emphasis on self-respect but rejecting its patriotism – was not an easy one to get across, even in India. His criticism of Japan and of Britain were received with easy understanding in India, but when similar criticism were made of India and Indians, there were many attempts to see Rabindranath as a lukewarm Indian. But Tagore remained deeply committed to his Indianness, while rejecting both patriotism and the advocacy of cultural isolation.[29]

Tagore's combined stress – on studying the Indian classics and on the importance of Bengali as the medium of instruction on the one hand, and on courses studying the culture and traditions of the West as well as of the Far and the Middle East, evoke Sen's comment: 'Tagore attempted to reflect his dual emphasis, mentioned earlier, in the educational arrangements at Santiniketan.' Perhaps, this informed Gandhi's statement about Tagore, nationalism and Santiniketan.

However, it was of paramount concern for Tagore that the urge to unify into one nation should in no case destroy the natural diversity of culture and community in the nation. He had repeatedly observed the uniformalising tendencies that almost inevitably and naturally accompanied the rise of nationalistic sentiment. He was aware that innate divisions did not automatically indicate auspiciousness for any country. Early in 1909, he stated that the roots of India's impairment lay in the separateness of her people. 'Therefore it is our devotion to unify into one the many of our country. Who can make into one the many? It is Ethics. It is the discarding of ethics on the temptation of necessity that weakens the bonds of fidelity.'[30] He was aware that the catalysis of distinct identities and culture which had occurred on the dispersal of some of the empires in Europe had, on the one hand, caused the partition of countries as between Norway and Sweden, and, on the other hand, it had caused an equally powerful instinct on the part of certain empires to deny even a semblance of autonomy of culture and language to its constituent peoples. As with the seed growing into the flower, the genealogy of communities indicated no difference. However, the development of distinct communitarian identities commenced with the growth of national communities. The exacerbation of conflict had made very powerful the aspirations of separateness on the part of communities, and all around the world

Nationalism: ethics and responsibility ❖ 121

smaller communities and countries desired to survive on the basis of their distinct identities. The contrary aspiration to submerge differences into larger entities had lost its appeal. Tagore pointed out that nations are normally apprehensive that any kind of 'hesitancy' on the part of a constituent community with regard to 'national aspirations' results in the dissipation of national strength, and that it was this apprehension which lay at the heart of Russia's desire to homogenise Finland and England's imperialistic attitude with Ireland. He felt that the same spirit was now motivating the Hindus in their efforts to somehow achieve 'national unity' by convincing Muslims that their interests lay in a united India. He stated that the Muslims were rightly doubtful of this, and stable integration lay not in assimilation, but in the acceptance of the differences that lay between communities. 'Now the problem worldwide is not that of unity by dissolving differences – but how to meet while preserving differences. This task is difficult – because, therein no laxity is permissible, therein each other will have to leave each other's space.'[31] For Tagore, the actual ideal for modern India ought to constitute a cooperative of different communitarian aspirations, which would actualise the cosmopolitan consciousness that was necessary to the survival of a world being driven by the ambitions of dominance and exploitation. He wrote about this particularly during the non-cooperation movement of 1921, which he perceived to be encouraging of xenophobic emotions.

> The awakening of India is a part of the awakening of the world. The door of the New Age has been flung open at the trumpet blast of a great war. We have read in the Mahabharata how the day of self-revelation had to be preceded by a year of retirement. The same has happened in the world today. Nations had attained nearness to each other without being aware of it, that is to say, the outside fact was there, but it had not penetrated into the mind. At the shock of the war, the truth of it stood revealed to mankind. The foundation of modern, that is Western, civilization was shaken; and it has become evident that the convulsion is neither local nor temporary, but has traversed the whole earth and will last until the shocks between man and man, which have extended from continent to continent, can be brought to rest, and a harmony can be established. From now onward, any nation which takes an isolated view of itself will run counter to the spirit of the New Age, and know no peace. From now onward, the anxiety that each has for its own safety must embrace the welfare of the world. For some time, the working of the new spirit has occasionally shown itself even in the Government of India, which has had to make attempts

122 ❧ Nationalism: ethics and responsibility

to deal with its problems in the light of the world problem. The war has torn away a veil from before our minds. What is harmful to the world, is harmful to each one of us.[32]

In the West, notably in Europe, the rise of Latin scholasticism and a church administration constituted of representatives of varied communities as against the local visions of rural communities had symbolised the spirit of cosmopolitanism since the Middle Ages. William Chester Jordan has traced both the growth and the decline of cosmopolitanism in Europe. 'The system of papal legatees, nuncios, and judges-delegate, the pope's eyes and ears in even the most distant provinces of the church, knitted together the whole in an impressive, if fragile, pan-European administrative network. Over against this cosmopolitanism stands the relative self-sufficiency of the village economy, the extreme parochialism of rural priests and of the inmates of minor religious establishments, and the often restrictive impulses associated with concerns for family and lineage.'[33] The emphasis was thus clearly on urban, 'progressive' centres, including universities and on the larger markets as developing sites regarding cosmopolitan values.[34] According to many scholars, however, the growth of universities founded by rulers and governed on regional/national principles and requirements started the undermining of the cosmopolitan character of the European universities fairly early in the life of the universities, although the scholars continued with professions of and discussions on cosmopolitical concerns. Jordan notices the historical legacy of this tendency rather humorously: 'I am tempted to see a parallel in my home institution, Princeton. Scholars there talk often of their contributions and loyalty to the *world* of learning, but the university motto is "Princeton in the *nation's* service." '[35]

Tagore, in perhaps a unique logical turn, equated the growth of the chauvinistic national sentiment in India with the rising urban educated class – even associating a political insincerity in the profession of hollow solidarity on their part with the rural and exploited classes whilst they formed the educated leadership of the Congress and thus inverted the traditional view that identified cosmopolitanism with the urban professional classes. As mentioned earlier, Tagore was highly apprehensive of artificial concerns of wider identities undermining local mores that provided essential resilience to communities threatened with homogenising mobilisations that were generally the companions of nationalistic urges.

The theme is still relevant in mapping and gauging the growth and potential of many of our dominant ideas of culture and polity, both because Tagore was in a sense the autobiographer of the times in which these ideas generally acquired an outline and a substance, and because such issues as the identity and rights of immigrant/migrant/stateless communities and the changing perceptions of the home and the world seem fated to have a persistent and pervasive presence in the coming decades.

It can perhaps be said that the inter-relationship of the home and the world of late operates most illustratively within the philosophical category and the juridical norms of cosmopolitanism. As Seyla Benhabib has observed, 'The term "cosmopolitanism", along with "empire" and "globalization", has become one of the keywords of our times.'[36] The play within the term, however, contains themes that are of universal validity even when they are located within certain regional contexts, as they were in the times when Tagore was writing around these themes. This may be relatable to Jeremy Waldron's indication of the knitting of the different possibilities of the term as used by Benhabib. Waldron perceives the congealment of a variety of meanings around the idea of cosmopolitanism, beginning from a general inspiration towards the love of mankind and an attendant and accepted principle of indiscriminative human obligation and duty on the part of the individual towards every person on the planet regardless of her national or ethnic identity. The meanings of cosmopolitanism include, on the other hand, 'the fluidity and the evanescence of culture' and the extolment of a natural and gradual process of the historic mutation in the particularities of hitherto established and distinct cultures, and of the possibilities of a 'world of fractured and mingled identities'. For Waldron, the existence of still another aspect of the concept is considerably significant, and according to him, it is this aspect that is explored and prioritised by Benhabib that the sustenance of cosmopolitanism is crucially dependent upon the observance of standards and rule rather than the comparatively vague expressions of cultural similarity and honourable feelings. 'It [cosmopolitanism] envisages a world order, and (in some views) a world government or world polity. According to the cosmopolitan, there are already many norms in the world which operate at a cosmopolitan level, including (for example) the principles that define human rights and crimes against humanity, the laws that govern refuge, asylum, travel, and migration, and the dense thicket of rules that sustain our life together, a life shared by people and peoples, not just in any particular society but generally on the face of the earth.'[37]

124 ❧ Nationalism: ethics and responsibility

The genealogy of modern cosmopolitanism is by no means confined to the global west and includes the cosmopolitan consciousness of Chinese philosophers; the Arab and Muslim cultures; and also as seen embedded in, but not limited by, what is now described as 'colonial modernity'. Scholars such as Peter van der Veer have discerned, with particular reference to India and Vivekananda, the emergence of a 'nineteenth-century cosmopolitan consciousness based on universal spirituality', which was very different from the cosmopolitan ethos generated by the pronouncedly secular ethic of the Western European Enlightenment.[38] According to van der Veer, this prominence of *Vedanta* in the metaphysical foundations of a spiritual and variously non-modern and anti-colonial cosmopolitanism makes for a 'complex story connecting Immanuel Kant, Madame Blavatsky and Swami Vivekananda in a variety of ways, and which show global connections that are different from world capitalism or modernity as usually conceived'.[39] Conversely, with a rather obvious Western accent, Robert Fine and Robin Cohen trace certain cosmopolitan ideas which they find to be of current and particular relevance, through four contexts or moments; the word moment serving for them, not as a theoretical vessel but as 'a convenient device to anchor some key debates and antinomies'. Although we may not wish, for our present purpose, to examine the four moments which are enumerated as 'the ancient world (Zeno's moment), the enlightenment (Kant's moment), post-totalitarian thought (Arendt's moment) and the late North American thought (Nussbaum's moment)', it may be of our immediate interest to focus on Fine and Cohen's comment on Nussbaum. 'Nussbaum promotes a radically alternate vision, one that draws explicitly on the ancient cynics and stoics and, less convincingly, on the Indian novelist Rabindranath Tagore.'[40] There is no further elucidation of this comment. Although many of us will perhaps agree that Tagore's position regarding cosmopolitanism may not be very easily defined, it still comes quite close to some of the aspects of the term, as mentioned by Waldron earlier. So, does this comment refer to a deficit in Nussbaum's understanding of Tagore's cosmopolitanism? Or to a deficiency in Tagore's vision itself? Should one ignore this comment as being typically uninformed and thereby not needing any further explanation? Or, does it yield to further disputation and thus extends the scope of the concept?

In *Atmaparicahaya* (*Self-Introduction*), Tagore was defining the relationship between individual consciousness and group identity and thereby drawing the subtle distinction between nationalistic identity

Nationalism: ethics and responsibility ❖ 125

and the cosmopolitan tradition: 'If in human nature there were to be only that which is perpetual, if there were to be nothing that he can create himself, if in his own mind there were to be no space for exercising his own will, then he is but a lump of clay. Again, if there were to be no one perpetual current from his past, if all of it was to be unexpected or to be created of his own will, then it would be an insanity, a chimera.'[41] These questions may thereby follow: Is definitive identity indispensable and a vital necessity? And to what extent is it only an accretion inimical to changing times? Or, conversely, does it serve as affirmation in times of uprooting and exile? Elie Wiesel, the suffering writer of the Holocaust, has stated in the context of identity and displacement/effacement: 'I am seeking childhood; I will always be seeking it. I need it. It is necessary for me as a point of reference, as a refuge. It represents for me a world that no longer exists; a sunny and mysterious place where beggars were princes in disguise, and fools were wise men freed from their constraints.'[42] Such statements are significant and largely representative of the experience of alienation and exile cutting across space and time, and it might be appropriate to illustrate this from an extended quotation from Wiesel's description of his own dilemma of location and identity framed by his ethical concerns of suffering and social responsibility, and perhaps also by his view of social reality and social consciousness in India. This is as if a testament that in poignantly underlining what Jeremy Waldron calls the dense thicket of rules that sustain our life together and reinstates the issues of ethical choices confronting the apparent insensitivity and irresponsibility of societies/states during times of human crisis, as Wiesel attempts to recollect his negotiation with the choices of living after the death camps of Auschwitz. Repelled by the organised cruelty that he had witnessed in the war-trampled West, Wiesel was also attracted, during his many explorations of spiritual marginality in Europe, by Hindu mysticism and Sufism and considered relocating to India.

> If I had been able to settle in an ashram somewhere in India, I would have. But I couldn't. I had seen under the incandescent sky of India, an immeasurable, unnameable suffering. I couldn't bear it. In the face of this suffering, the problem of evil imposed itself on me with a destructive force. I could choose to steel myself against it or flee. I was not anxious to be an accomplice. Hindu friends would cross the street stopping over mutilated and sick bodies without even looking at them. I couldn't. I looked and I felt guilty.

126 ❖ Nationalism: ethics and responsibility

> Finally I understood: I am free to choose my suffering but not that of my fellow humans. Not to see the hungry before me was to accept their destiny in their place, in their name, for them and even against them. Not to mention their distress was to acquiesce to its logic, indeed to its justice. Not to cry out against their misery was to make it all the heavier. Because I felt myself too weak to cry out, to offer a hand to so many disfigured children, because I refused to understand that certain situations couldn't be changed, I preferred to go away. I returned to the west and its necessary ambiguities.[43]

It was Tagore's considered view that the Indian nation would essentially require a social conscience and an ethical arrangement among its diverse races and communities to exist as a viable nation, particularly with its diverse social hierarchies and its extended register of such historical difference, animosity even, between its social communities. He rejected the notion that the English had done service to the country by compelling the erstwhile differing groups to live together under a strong administrative centre, and that once the political movement had successfully invented the English as the enemy in public perception, the diverse groups would, in turn, perceive India as a common racial political home. He termed such an argument facile, which likened, and thereby avoiding, the chronic problem of divisive identities in India to a large family constituted of members having different natures but bound together by common feelings. In his opinion, such common feeling did not exist among the varied communities of India. The forming of a national union of various races in Switzerland evidenced that there was an effective element of unity among its peoples. In India, there was only diversity, and in the absence of any natural unity, the intrinsic particularities had prevailed, acquiring the shapes of language, caste/race, religion and custom, and kept this vast country divided into hundreds of units. He, therefore, personally did not feel any assurance in invoking metaphors and instances and thus in neglecting the reality of the country. He transferred this issue on to the plane of ethics in writing that even the principle of justice would not be served through the contention that a recently burgeoning national sentiment had accomplished unity, and that after somehow dislodging English rule from the political scene, communities like the Bengalis, Punjabis, Marathis, Madrasis, Hindus, Muslims, could possible live as free Indians with one mind and one interest. He said that actually whatever little unity that was apparent in India was mechanical and not organic. The unity among the diverse races of India

Nationalism: ethics and responsibility ❖ 127

had not been achieved naturally but by the outside bond exercised by the rule of a foreign power. Tagore raised uncomfortable issues, which confronted the staple political argument for linking political liberty and nationalism and which viewed the experience of the political movement itself as conducive to the creation of an abiding national sentiment. He argued against the theory of the binding of diversities of community by foreign rule and described the union of communities by invoking the example of the grafting of one variety of plant on to one belonging to a different group. The two different plants achieve, thereafter, an organic unity among themselves not by the force of the outside binding applied at the time of grafting – although the binding is essential till the unity is achieved – but by natural and intrinsic unification of the plants. The binding, therefore, howsoever painful, needed enduring till such time the inner unity was achieved and the process of uniting ought to commence immediately with the grafting together of the plants. Similarly, the diverse communities needed to accomplish a unity on the plane of relationship and of interests and values. English rule was endurable till the mechanistic unity of communities was succeeded by a real organic unity to be striven for by the people themselves, which could only occur without the passive dependence on the artificial binding provided by foreign rule. This unity of diversified India through one umbilical bond needed to be accomplished through service, love and by the removal of the artificial barriers to a true unity. This foundation of one's own country, out of a land perceived by many as a mere geographical unit and one native community out of a divided people would have to be performed through our own efforts towards a diversely creative process directed at the ultimate union of the people. He acknowledged that an impression was prevalent among some sections of the country that the archetypal hatred of the foreigner as being the inveterate enemy was an effective bond uniting the country. He cautioned in this regard that one day such unity, as was impressed by the hatred of the alien, would become defunct with the inevitable departure of the English rule from India. The simulated imagination of hatred nurtured by some people would then naturally be detached from popular consciousness, and in the absence of this binding from without the artificial thread of unity would be instantly snapped. In the absence of any alien enemy, the countrymen would then turn against each other with all the accumulated bloodthirstiness and hatred that had been long fostered in their minds.[44] Tagore, in this, reinforces the theory that it is its ethical basis that redeems nationalism and makes

128 ❈ Nationalism: ethics and responsibility

it a responsible means for the building of stable and just communities. In this sense, his description and his prayer in the *Jana Gana Mana* for an ideal India, which had attracted people of diverse identities and faiths to subsist and repose on its soil, represents only a part of his visualisation of India – it describes not so much the actual historical scene as it does the possibilities of the emerging of a caring nation in India enabled by the ideals of living. And this ideal is not the archetypal nation, which for him developed in the modern West, striving more towards empire than for internal peace and cohesion. Tagore was ever apprehensive of the threat of a similar militancy and exclusivism developing around the national movement in India. He argued in *The Cult of Charkha* in 1925 that individual ethics were indistinguishable from the ethics of the citizen, and therefore amoral nationalism was a travesty and a mistake, and that the true goal of nationalism was cooperation with the world.

> As is livelihood for the individual, so is politics for a particular people, a field for the exercise of their business instincts of patriotism. All this time, just as business has implied antagonism, so has politics been concerned with the self-interest of a pugnacious nationalism. The forging of arms and of false documents has been its main activity. The burden of competitive armaments has been increasing apace, with no end to it in sight, no peace for the world in prospect. When it becomes clear to man that in the cooperation of nations lies the true interest of each, – for man is established in mutuality – then only can politics become a field of endeavour. Then will the same means which the individual recognizes as moral and therefore true, be also be recognized as such by nations. They will know that cheating, robbery and the exclusive pursuit of self-aggrandizement are as harmful for the purposes of this world as they are deemed to be for those of the next. It may be that the League of Nations will prove to be the first step in the process of this realization.[45]

General critical opinion has agreed with the positing of Tagore in opposition to the majority and nationalistic view inhabiting the freedom movement. And it is completely valid to recognise that Tagore in his critique of nationalism was concerned more with the excessive chauvinism of national movements than with the cooperative potential of nationalism. Nepal Majumdar, a veteran Tagore scholar, has perceived the presidential address of C. R. Das at the Gaya session of the Congress in 1922, as also at one remove directed at Tagore's arguments against nationalism. But even such an instance might also and appropriately include the possibility that the definition of nationalism as outlined by Das is actually very close to the position of Gandhi and Tagore, especially since Tagore did not fully disagree with the cruciality of the idea of nationalism – whatever be its demerits – in the corporate life of nations. For purposes of further detail, the position of C. R. Das in his Gaya address approximates more closely to that of Gandhi. Das described the nationalism of the Indian movement in contradistinction to the nationalistic ideas prevalent in Europe. Nationalism was the natural expression of a nation's identity and spirit, and it existed not in opposition to that of other nations but as a step towards the larger unity of the world. The nationalism of Europe was a perversion of the nationalistic values, and it reflected itself primarily in commercial and imperialistic struggle between the major powers of the West. 'I desire to emphasise that there is no hostility between the ideal of nationality and that of world peace. Nationalism is the process through which alone will world peace come. A full and unfettered growth of nationalism is necessary for world peace just as a full and unfettered growth of individuals is necessary for nationality. It is the conception of aggressive nationality in Europe that stands in the way of world peace; but once this truth is grasped that it is not possible for a nation to inflict a loss on another nation without at the same time inflicting a loss on itself, the problem of Humanity is solved.'[46]

Gandhi's references to the 'nation' appear quite early in his writings. In the *Hind Swaraj* (1909), Gandhi's interlocutor offers the argument that it was the English, with their contributions such as the railways, who have created a spirit of nationalism in a disparate country like India. Gandhi's response argues against both the Western archetypes of modernity and nationalism. He not only refuses to concede that modern technology represents progress and unifies countries into nations but also rejects the customary Western notions of homogeneity of race and culture as the basic principle of nationalism. Gandhi posits unambiguously the idea that it was a composite identity of its people that represented the ideal and ultimately the resilience of the nation. Along the path of his argument, he also dismisses another archetypical notion regarding nationalism that historical and permanent enemies and allies were an essential political and psychological reality for the nation. Gandhi states that it was an English propaganda that India had never been a nation, and he invokes a distinctly non-Western idea of nationalism in presenting cultural symbols and not the European concept of cultural nationalism as a constitutive element of the nation. 'I do not wish to suggest that

130　❖　Nationalism: ethics and responsibility

because we were one nation we had no differences, but it is submitted that our leading men travelled throughout India either on foot or in bullock carts. They learned one another's languages, and there was no aloofness between them.'[47] He mentioned the cherished pilgrimage centres, such as Rameshwaram, Puri and Hardwar, as evidence of the early national imagination of the Indian thinkers who founded these centres not so much as merely religious locations, as statedly for them, worship could be performed within the consciousness of the devoted. 'But they saw that India was one undivided land so made by nature. They, therefore, argued that it must be one nation. Arguing thus, they established holy places in various parts of India, and fired the people with an idea of nationality unknown in other parts of the world. Any two Indians are one as no two Englishmen are. Only you and I and others who consider ourselves civilized and superior persons imagine that we are many nations.'[48] The 'reader' in the dialogue raises, considering originally modern Western notions of monochromic nationalism, the rather obvious question of the historical and cultural differences of the Hindus and the Muslims as an insurmountable obstacle for India's nation state: 'We thus meet with differences at every step. How can India become one nation?'[49] Gandhi offers a concise exposition of inclusive nationalism that is also of striking contemporary relevance:

> India cannot cease to be one nation because people belonging to different religions live in it. The introduction of foreigners does not necessarily destroy the nation, they merge in it. A country is one nation only when such a condition obtains in it. The country must have a faculty for assimilation. India has ever been such a country. In reality, there are as many religions as there are individuals, but those who are conscious of the spirit of nationality do not interfere with one another's religion. If they do, they are not fit to be considered a nation. If the Hindus believe that India should be peopled only by Hindus, they are living in dreamland. The Hindus, the Mahomedans, the Parsees and the Christians who have made India their country are fellow country-men, and they will have to live in unity if only for their own interest. In no part of the world are one nationality and one religion synonymous terms: nor has it ever been so in India.[50]

Allied to the issue of minority identity in nation states was the vexingly recurrent emphasis, in the majority opinion, on the allegedly natural relationship prevailing between minority institutions and communalism. One of the founders of the Hindu Mahasabha, B. S. Moonje, wrote to

Gandhi opposing the campaign to raise funds for Jamia Millia Islamia in the memory of Hakim Ajmal Khan, since Moonje felt that it was one of such sectarian institutions that had been 'emphasizing and exaggerating sectarian separateness, culminating eventually in such deplorable Hindu-Muslim tension'. He suggested that there be instead a fund for a common memorial dedicated to 'our revered and beloved late Hakim ji' and Swamiji (Shraddhanand). Gandhi, while agreeing to Moonje's general concern, asked, 'Can we enforce it only among Musalmans, or can we begin the reform with them? Have we not got in the country innumerable purely Hindu institutions . . . even a sectional institution may be called national if the outlook is national and is in reality utilized for national advancement.'[51] On numerous occasions, as in this observation, in 1924, on C. F. Andrews's positive comment on nationalism, Gandhi stated clearly his opposition to aggressive nationalism: 'Violent nationalism, otherwise known as imperialism, is the curse. Non-violent nationalism is a necessary condition of corporate or civilized life.'[52] Similarly, Gandhi wrote to an American correspondent in 1935 that 'Love has no boundary. My nationalism includes the love of all the nations of the earth irrespective of creed.'[53] Notably, Gandhi extended the possibility of a non-aggrandising, non-expansionist nation with regard to other countries as well, irrespective of even the colonising governments that headed some of these countries. His statement towards the end of the *Hind Swaraj* is especially significant: 'You English, who have come to India are not good specimens of the English nation, nor can we, almost half-Anglicised Indians, be considered good specimens of the real Indian nation. If the English nation were to know all you have done, it would oppose many of your actions.'[54] During the Congress boycott of the visit of Prince of Wales, Gandhi refuted any suggestion that the boycott could be translated as an insult to the people of England. He asked rhetorically whether the viceroy by this allegation implied that the British government in India could possibly be identified with the general British public: 'Does he wish India to infer that the British administrators here represent the British people and that the agitation directed against their methods is an agitation against the British people?'[55] Gandhi further declared that the Indian movement for self-rule could not be construed as xenophobic, also attempting to define thereby the essential code and resilience of nationalism conceived and practised on an ethical plane.[56] This conveyed a spirit which was not anti-thetical to that of Tagore who had, subsequent to his earlier stated opposition to the idea of the nation,

132 ❂ Nationalism: ethics and responsibility

nonetheless explained during his lecture on nationalism that 'Each nation must be conscious of its mission, and we in India must realise that we cut a poor figure when we try to be political, simply because we have not yet been finally able to accomplish what was set before us by our providence.'[57] The nation that Tagore is severely critical of is the colonising English nation. His comments on nationalism in India reflect more upon its impracticability – given the obnoxious caste system which occluded a common birthright and intermarriage and race amalgamation – than on its absolute undesirability in principle.[58] His statement that nationalism 'is the particular thing which for years has been at the bottom of India's troubles' was unmistakably a recoil from the recent emulation of the spirit of European chauvinism by Indians, rather than from the feeling of Indianness.

> India has never had a real sense of nationalism. Even though from childhood I had been taught that idolatry of the nation is almost better than reverence for God and humanity, I believe I have outgrown that teaching, and it is my conviction that my countrymen will truly gain their India by fighting against the education which teaches them that a country is greater than the ideals of humanity.[59]

Einstein, like Steiner, a Jew and categorised as a trenchant critic of nationalism, once famously calling it the 'measles of mankind', nevertheless believed that 'It is not enough for us to play a part as individuals in the cultural development of the human race, we must also tackle tasks which only nations as a whole can perform. Only so can the Jews regain social health.'[60] He despised national frontiers and armies, not national existence, the 'life of peaceful nations' was 'civilised and just'.[61] Palestine, thus, was 'not primarily a place of refuge for the Jews of Eastern Europe but the embodiment of the reawakening corporate spirit of the whole Jewish nation'.[62] Einstein wished that the state of Israel should aspire to embody three traditional ideals of Jewry: 'The pursuit of knowledge for its own sake, an almost fanatical love of justice, and the desire for personal independence.'[63] Likewise, Tagore may have aspired, as Einstein did for Israel, for creating India primarily as a social and spiritual centre, but nonetheless the centre did not negate the nation that was India. Gandhi and Tagore were both nationalists in this sense of the term, although their different understanding of the constituents of the nation – culture, language, history, idea of nationhood, memory, non-violence – led them

Nationalism: ethics and responsibility ❖ 133

to occasionally take stances that appeared to strike at the roots of the conventional notion of nation. For instance, in theories of nationalism, nationalistic consciousness is generally stapled with memories of racial injustice. It is rightly mentionable that colonised nations sought to preserve the scars of tortures perpetrated by the colonisers, in the collective psyche of the nation, as spurs to sentiments of resistance/nationalism. It is well known that Tagore had renounced his knighthood in protest against the massacre at Jallianwala Bagh. He, however, opposed the erection of a memorial for the victims, in a message sent to the first memorial meeting presided over by M.A. Jinnah on 13 April 1920. The message was read out by C.F. Andrews. This extract is relevant:

> Let those who try to burden the minds of the future with stones, carrying the black memory of wrongs and their anger, but let us bequeath to the generations to come memorials of that only which we can revere — let us be grateful to our fore-fathers, who have left us the image of our Buddha, who conquered self, preached forgiveness, and spread his love far and wide in time and space.[64]

Nationalism, violence and the state

The tragic massacre at Jallianwala Bagh constitutes the single-most brutal of such acts of repression that were executed by the British government during the national movement in India. It was followed by a reign of terror in Punjab. The historical reconstruction of the terrible incident, including the political dimensions, and the philosophical connotations that emerge from the process, all offer very significant pointers to a discussion of the responsibilities of nationalism. The outrageousness of the government action and the tragedy of Jallianwala Bagh generated intense political activity in the country and led to some irrevocable changes in the attitude regarding the general direction of the national movement. The response of Tagore to the massacre at Amritsar and the repression in all of Punjab has become memorialised, as being reflectional of his moral courage and of a kind of timeless statement of national self-respect, in contemporary discourse in Indian history. It is particularly significant in any analysis of Tagore's relationship with mainstream nationalism. According to Harish Trivedi, 'Tagore's response to the Jallianwala Bagh massacre constitutes perhaps the most decisive nationalist act of his whole life.'[65] For most

134 ❖ Nationalism: ethics and responsibility

of his biographers, it is seemingly evident that Tagore was considerably more forthright and courageous than Gandhi by the issuing of a public statement and therewith courting the danger of penal action provided in the Defence of India Act during a time of unfettered state repression. As a prominent Tagore scholar has written, men in those times had been subjected to very harsh sentences from the government for venturing to make far less blunt protest. Public positions taken by the Congress leadership on the Punjab repression are thought to be characterised by a general timidity, and it is indubitably implied as well that Gandhi can be unproblematically included in this category of diffidence and timidity that was in display during this period.[66] Biographers of Tagore have described his anguish at the silence of the leaders as the horrific details of martial law began to gradually seep through the censorship in Punjab. Travelling to Kolkata from Santiniketan, Tagore tried to get the political leadership to organise a public meeting to express formal protest against the persecution by the government in Punjab but received at best a dispirited response. P. C. Mahalanobis, a prominent intellectual, has alleged that he was told by Tagore that even C. R. Das was hesitant to involve himself with an open protest against the government.[67] Tagore wrote his famous letter to Viceroy Chelmsford, reportedly on the night of 29 May 1919, sending it and releasing it to the press within a couple of days. Prabhat Kumar Muhkopadhyaya mentions – somewhat contrary to Mahalanobis's claim of having been immediately privy to its contents – that Tagore did not disclose it even to his son Rathindranath, and it was only with C. F. Andrews that he chose to share the writing of his letter.[68] Written purportedly because of the listlessness of the political leadership, the letter was however hailed publicly and discussed widely in the press. Ramendra Sunder Trivedi, a respected scholar and outspoken nationalist of Kolkata was particularly moved on reading a Bangla version of the letter in the daily *Basumati*. Trivedi who was then on his death bed, sent a message to his elder friend Rabindranath that he wanted to pay his respects, in fact to do obeisance to him as in his own words: 'I want the dust of your [Tagore's] feet' (my translation). Tagore visited Trivedi and read out to him the original text at his bedside. After staying a while, Tagore left with Trivedi offering him the traditional *pranam*. According to Mukhopadhyaya, Trivedi then lapsed into drowsiness and shortly thereafter passed away in his sleep.[69] Justifiably moving as these accounts are, it is disappointing that almost all of them are characterised by analytical neglect of the cargo of ideas that Tagore's letter carried along with

Nationalism: ethics and responsibility ❄ **135**

its obviously symbolic value. In opting for an individual protest, Tagore was foregrounding the principle of individual responsibility, which was also for Gandhi absolutely inalienable from the concept of nationalism. However, in the absence of a contentual scrutiny, the letter risks the danger of being ultimately highlighted on the grounds of mere stylistic flourish and emotive value. Quite naturally, Tagore was aware of the perils of a merely eulogistic reception to his letter. Some years later, in 1925, he was to write in the *Modern Review* on the unabated discussion on the relinquishment of his knighthood, underlining that it was prompted solely by the atrocities in Punjab and that he intended not the slightest show of discourtesy and conceit in the returning of an honour that had been conferred on him for his literary attainments. He, perhaps, also cautioned against the tendency to privilege form over content: 'I greatly abhor to make any public gesture which may have the least suggestion of a theatrical character. But in this particular case, I was driven to it when I hopelessly failed to persuade our leaders to launch an adequate protest against what was happening at that time in the Punjab.'[70] Sadly, an uncomfortable suggestion which persistently emerges from the attitude of a prominent section of Tagore scholarship in this context is its regard simply for establishing the moral superiority of Tagore's response over that of Gandhi concerning the massacre at Jallianwala Bagh.

Although the text of the letter is well known in its detail, a delineative reference to its argument will be useful to the discussion. Marked by its tone of courtesy, the statement deplores the repressive measures which were 'without parallel in the history of civilised governments, barring some conspicuous exceptions, recent and remote'. But, rather than locating it only on abstract principles of hurt and redressal, Tagore makes it almost into an effective legal interrogation of the government on the basis of the principles of the civil state, confronting therein the arguments that would be advanced by the government regarding public lawlessness and its own obligation to restore peace and justice. The draconic acts of a militarily dominant power on a 'disarmed', disheartened and hapless population, which it was normatively enjoined to protect, could 'claim no political expediency, far less moral justification'. That the numerous insulting measures suffered by citizens was rooted in a racist bias of the authorities was coupled with and manifestly proven by the denial, through censorship, of the freedom of expression which could otherwise have provided a hope of justice, and the simultaneous and disproportionate indulgence towards 'most of the Anglo-Indian papers, which have in some cases gone to the

136 ☀ Nationalism: ethics and responsibility

brutal length of making fun of our sufferings', was another instance of depriving citizenry of their right of equality before law. Blinded by the 'passion of vengeance', the government was losing sight of its 'nobler vision of statesmanship' and debasing its obligation to 'magnanimity' that was appropriate to its 'physical strength and moral tradition'. As if putting the government to test on its observance of the rule of indiscriminative procedure of law with regard to all citizens, Tagore declared that he was perfectly prepared to endure the consequences of his protest against the submission of an entire people to silence and fear, and it was to open himself to such penalty by discarding any special status that he was with regret returning a title which he had in the past felt honoured to receive.[71]

Gandhi's response to the Punjab tragedy has so far been unfortunately under analysed for its content of ethical positions. It should be underlined at this point that almost not a single position, even though at times admitting of change and even then in very few instances, taken by Gandhi is ever improvisational. Also, as he was the major architect of the nationalist movement, his view of any political eventuality comprises more than one dimension and its evaluation naturally requires a wider scrutiny of the aggregate as well as contiguity of his views. A study of his role in the months leading to the Rowlatt agitation and in the subsequent Congress inquiry into the Punjab atrocities provide an enlightening indication of his assessment of the nature of protest and political liberty as well as that of the vitality of *Satyagraha* in even the most inclement political climates. By March 1919, Gandhi had been frankly puzzled as to the options of protest available to the country if the government ignored the agitation against the Rowlatt Bill and enacted it into law. He was in Madras on the invitation prominently of Kasturi Ranga Iyengar, and in what was his very initial series of meetings with Rajagopalachari at Iyengar's residence he discussed extensively with him the ethos and the ramifications of non-observance of laws promulgated by the state. 'I felt myself at a loss to discover how to offer civil disobedience against the Rowlatt Bill if it was finally passed into law. One could disobey it only if the Government gave one the opportunity for it. Failing that, could we civilly disobey other laws? And if so, where was the line to be drawn? These and a host of similar questions formed the theme of these discussions of ours.'[72] The idea of the *hartal* (general strike) which commenced the Rowlatt *Satyagraha* was to come to Gandhi in a dream, and he regarded the hartal as an act of self-purification wholly appropriate to a sacred fight. He later stated that he was unsure of the whole country and

Nationalism: ethics and responsibility ❖ 137

would have been reasonably satisfied if it had been correctly observed in the provinces of Bombay, Madras, Bihar and Sind. As it so happened, the hartal came to be a success in almost the whole of India. Gandhi was on a tour of northern and western India during the first week of April, by which time with the *Satyagraha* gripping the imagination of the country the government was already beginning to use force against civil resistance. The restive and then chafing gatherings began to turn violent, notably in Delhi, and Gandhi's presence was being sought in different parts of the country to variously enthuse – as by Dr Satyapal regarding Amritsar or to pacify the people – as by Swami Shraddhanand in Delhi. Gandhi planned a strictly private visit to Delhi on 9 April and invited Satyapal to come to Delhi for a meeting. Gandhi was immediately turned into a restrictee by the government, with a series of orders the issuance of which prohibited him from entering Delhi and Punjab, and confined him to Bombay. On non-compliance, he was arrested en route to Delhi and transported to Bombay. Gandhi had throughout stressed upon the leaders to take special care to prevent rowdyism and violence in public processions and meetings, but nevertheless violence erupted in Delhi and Ahmedabad with the news of his arrest. During 10–11 April in Ahmedabad, some Europeans were beaten up by mobs, which then began to destroy government property. More than fifty government buildings were burnt and a European army officer was killed. Viramgam and Nadiad were similarly wracked by violence and instances of looting of government property. These occurrences were, however, milder than the public violence followed by government repression which engulfed Amritsar beginning 10 April 1919.[73] Released in Bombay and horrified at the incidents of violence in Gujarat, Gandhi was severely critical of crowd behaviour and violence in his speech of 11 April at a mass meeting on the Chowpati beach. He pointedly praised the courtesy accorded to him during his detention and was unable to understand the mass resentment against it, terming the form of protest as 'worse than *duragraha*' (opposite of *Satyagraha*). Invoking the metaphor of *dharma*, he declared that he was opposed to any effort to obtain the release of persons connected with violent activity, as *Satyagraha* required deference to penal provisions consequent to the violation of law: '*It is breach of religion and duty to endeavour to secure the release of those who have committed deeds of violence*' (emphasis as in the original).[74] Almost prophetically, even as violence during mass protest started inflicting a kind of collateral damage, he outlined the duties of a *satyagrahi* and unequivocally declared that he would not hesitate to modify, oppose

138 ❖ Nationalism: ethics and responsibility

and ultimately stop any of his own political campaigns in the event of a single casualty involving any individual other than a civil resister – '*The time may come for me to offer satyagraha against ourselves*' (emphasis as in the original).[75] He had heard that Englishmen had been injured by mobs and apprehended and that some of them might have succumbed to their injuries. He clarified that although sorrowed at the death of a *satyagrahi*, he would at the same time regard it as a sacrifice in the struggle. But not one *satyagrahi* could be absolved from the responsibility of any injury done to a non-participant, even an opponent of the movement. He considered his own responsibility to be a 'million times heavier' in such an event and declared that he had commenced on his political journey with full awareness of 'such responsibility'. He was categorical that he would treat these incidents as sins that were 'simply unbearable'. And then Gandhi followed with a statement that needs detailed reference since it frames his position during crucial public moments throughout his life, evidenced as in the immediately subsequent events, and as equally through instances like Chauri Chaura to his martyrdom in 1948.

> But I know how to offer satyagraha against ourselves as against our rulers. *What kind of satygraha can I offer against ourselves on such occasions? What penance can I do for such sins? The satyagraha and the penance I can conceive can only be one and that is for me to fast and if need be by so doing to give up this body and thus to prove the truth of satyagraha* (emphasis as in the original).[76]

He declined to comment on the behaviour of the police as being irrelevant to the occasion, other than to laud them for withholding firing on the protestors so far. It is noteworthy that Gandhi applied a very significant phrase regarding the practise of non-violent resistance when he emphasised on the essentiality of the *satyagrahi*'s learning the way to '*undergo intelligent suffering*' (emphasis as in the original). The next day, he released instructions including the 'inviolable principles' concerning *Satyagraha* that were expected to be 'strictly obeyed'. Civil resistors were injuncted against processions, demonstrations, hartals and violence of any kind, as well as instructed to observe 'perfect stillness' at public meetings and not to clap hands or to shout slogans of any kind.[77]

Returning to Ahmedabad on 13 April, Gandhi issued a message to the citizens appealing for the resuming of their normal routine of work and for immediate suspension of all protest activity in order to facilitate

Nationalism: ethics and responsibility ❖ 139

the restoration of normalcy and to effectuate the redundancy of martial law in the city. The following day, he wrote to J. L. Maffey (private secretary to the viceroy) that he felt the 'deepest humiliation and regret' for the sheer lawlessness of the situation in which Englishmen and women in Ahmedabad had been compelled to abandon their homes for more secure dwellings. He conceded that he had erred in appraising the present reach of the ideals of *Satyagraha* on the public mind and that he had mistaken the 'power of hatred and ill will'. Although his personal faith in *Satyagraha* was entirely unaffected, he was temporarily retracing his steps on the offering of *Satyagraha* against the Rowlatt Act. He stated that he would not attempt to travel to Delhi and Punjab until he felt reassured in the capability of his colleagues in the movement to restrain and pacify the crowds of followers, and that his *Satyagraha* would at this juncture be 'directed against my own countrymen'. He was, however, convinced that his restraining order had been ill advised and had possibly contributed to the unrest, even though Amritsar might well have been an exception insofar as the incidents there were unconnected with *Satyagraha*. It must be mentioned here that Gandhi would be referring to incidents prior to the firing at Jallianwala Bagh. Gandhi expressed the hope that the withdrawal of the Rowlatt Act would indicate the goodwill of the government and would assist in the restoration of peace and order. It is not without meaning that at a time of racial antagonism, Gandhi felt it suitable to express his confidence in the continuance of his cherished friendship with Maffey and of the necessity of passing his thoughts to him, as well as expecting Maffey to 'do what you [Maffey] like with them'.[78] Thereafter, Gandhi addressed a mass meeting at Sabarmati Ashram announcing therein his decision to atone for the loss of life and property of Englishmen and women. Notwithstanding his continuously repeated assertions that violence and *Satyagraha* were fundamentally discordant, he said scathingly that the residents of the city had indulged in extortion, pillage, incendiarism and killing. 'If deeds such as these could save me from the prison-house or the scaffold, I should not like to be so saved.'[79] Gandhi announced, as atonement, a collection for the families of those Englishmen who had been killed by the acts of Indians, and 'each of us' was asked to contribute a minimum of eight annas to the fund. He hoped that none would evade contributing to the fund on the grounds that he was not one of the perpetrators, as non-resistance to wrongful action amounted to participation. The determining of responsibility of violence in Ahmedabad on to Indian protesters, it is needless to say, was

140 ❖ Nationalism: ethics and responsibility

an act of rare courage in the face of the most despicable massacre known to English India, and accounts of the incident of the previous day were already fast circulating in spite of censorship. Gandhi acknowledged that his own responsibility was a 'million times greater'. He acknowledged what was to him the rather limited validity of the allegation that he had hastily motivated huge numbers of people for *Satyagraha* and that this was largely responsible for the descent to mass violence. He had in response to this perception already performed penance by postponing his visit to Delhi for offering himself for arrest, and also by partially retracting *Satyagraha*. Although these two steps were 'more painful to [him] than a wound', he had in addition decided to fast for seventy-two hours. Any public empathy with his suffering, thereupon, would best be translated into complete abstinence from violence in the future. The country ought to take his word that it could not win freedom or serve itself through 'violence and terrorism'. 'I am of opinion that if we have to wade through violence to obtain swarajya and if a redress of grievances were to be only possible by means of ill will for and slaughter of Englishmen, I, for one, would do without that swarajya and without a redress of those grievances. For me life would not be worth living if Ahmedabad continues to countenance violence in the name of truth.'[80]

On 18 April, Gandhi announced through a letter to secretaries of the *Satyagraha Sabha*, which was released to the press that he was being compelled to temporarily suspend civil disobedience, not due to any of loss of faith on his part but following his undiluted faith and his understanding of the laws of *Satyagraha*. He believed that it was the pervasiveness of *Satyagraha* that had, if in very small measure, exercised restraint upon the aggressivity of the mob.[31] Tagore hailed Gandhi's position in a letter written to Andrews on 26 April from Santiniketan. Deploring the needless vehemence of the protest against government repression, Tagore reflected on the teaching of Gandhi regarding the transcendence of victimisation through a fearless endurance. Tagore felt that now – when Gandhi was being disowned equally by those who desired rapid success without being inclined to meet the value required in the adherence of ideals, and by those who were because of their timidity propendent towards sycophancy and endless supplication, 'Gandhi's personality shines before us with greater glory than when his light was blurred by the dust storm of popularity'.[82]

Amidst public addresses and a series of leaflets issued by Gandhi regarding the atonement for violence and the ethos of *Satyagraha*, the political community naturally became preoccupied with the details of the Amritsar tragedy and the subsequent public torture through martial law in Punjab. The accounts were initially indistinct and deficient due to censorship in the province, and it was only by early June that the full picture of the tragedy conveyed itself to Gandhi. Incredulous at first of the magnitude of the killing, he was incensed particularly over the enforcement of the crawling order in Amritsar: 'Before this outrage the Jallianwala Bagh tragedy pales into insignificance in my eyes, though it was this massacre principally that attracted the attention of the people of India and of the world.'[83] It is said that every year thereafter he fasted for twenty-four hours on the anniversary of the massacre.[84] Concerned by mid-May over the denial of the freedom in Punjab and at the punitive actions against eminent journalists B.G. Horniman and Kalinath Roy, Gandhi conveyed on 16 May his disquiet to Maffey, observing notedly that he had refrained from uttering a single word on the recent incidents in Punjab 'not because I have not thought or felt over them', but because in the absence of authentic information he had 'not known what to believe and what not to believe'. He said that he had been expecting an early and 'fullest investigation made as to the causes of disturbances and the measures adopted to quell them'.[85] As he was being both advised for and dissuaded from immediately travelling to Punjab, he called a discrete meeting – the related circular which was issued to select individuals on 21 May was not meant for publication in the press – of some prominent *satyagrahis* in Bombay on 28 May to consider the extension of Rowlatt *Satyagraha* to repression in Punjab.[86] The truncated meeting (not all invitees attended) found itself largely unable to agree, on the planes of technicality and practicality, with Gandhi's view of the appropriateness and feasibility of *Satyagraha* in the current situation. Gandhi himself was of the view that every individual *satyagrahi* needed to consider the extendability to Punjab of the *Satyagraha* Pledge regarding the Rowlatt Act. However, he was himself without doubt as to the practicability of *Satyagraha* in the present situation and had no apprehension of an inevitable accompaniment of violence with civil disobedience. He did not favour any kind of demonstration or strike as part of the civil disobedience, not even upon the arrest of a prominent leader during the movement. Very significantly, he sought the opinion of the committee on his proposal for him to approach the viceroy for setting an impartial committee of inquiry into the circumstances of the Punjab disturbances and martial law and for the revision of sentences from the Martial Law Tribunal. In the event of such demands remaining unachieved even after

142 ❖ Nationalism: ethics and responsibility

public agitation and representation to the secretary of state for India, Gandhi recommended the practise of *Satyagraha*. This idea was approved. The note on this meeting, dated 30 May and signed by Gandhi, was once again marked not for publication in the press.[87]

Accordingly, on 30 May, coinciding with the date of Tagore's letter to Chelmsford, Gandhi wrote to S. R. Hignell, the private secretary to the viceroy. He addressed his appeal to the viceroy, already made as he said in the press, for instituting an independent committee of inquiry regarding Punjab and which would also review the sentences passed on the alleged perpetrators of violence. The public mind, as his own, was disturbed at the unduly heavy sentences passed by the Martial Law Tribunal, the official response on public floggings and the numerous restrictions enforced on civilian activity. Censorship of the press had only contributed to the public anxiety about the reality of the situation. He reiterated that in the absence of 'reliable data' he had abstained from publicly speaking on the Punjab disturbances even 'at the risk of being misunderstood by my countrymen'. Importantly, he stated that he 'was not prepared to condemn martial law as such' and neither was he inclined to deduce that 'martial law measures would be unduly hard' from Michael O'Dwyer's record of severity of governance in Punjab. 'No one can dispute the right of the State to declare martial law under certain circumstances, but it will be conceded on behalf of the State that it should justify to the public the measures adopted under it, specially under circumstances described above.'[88]

Reading the official attitude as unchanged, Gandhi suggested to the *Satyagraha Sabha* within the fortnight that it consider his proposal to renew civil disobedience by July 1919. In his opinion, the earlier arguments advanced by members against its resumption were no longer operative, given the improvement in public awareness as to its norms and the preparedness of the government to control any violence that should as remote possibility occur during the same. He recommended a movement completely under his personal guidance, both regarding its area and scope and its participants. One argument that he offered in favour of its resumption can also be understood as a response to the apprehension that was to be repeatedly expressed by Tagore, beginning April 1919, of civil disobedience disintegrating into public violence. However, it should be mentioned that such assurance was invariably joined with his faith in Gandhi's moral power and his capacity to stand against public degeneration. Gandhi declined to be perpetually constrained by the ever

Nationalism: ethics and responsibility ❖ 143

present risk of a sabotage of a non-violent movement by provocateurs: 'A movement like Satyagraha, designed as it is to work a moral revolution in society so far as the method of attaining reforms are concerned, cannot be stopped for the vague fear of unscrupulous or ignorant persons misusing it. At the same time, every possible precaution must be taken by us against any such misuse.'[89] Gandhi was to reiterate his position on both issues – that mass reaction was, however difficult, avoidable in early April in Amritsar and that civil disobedience was unendingly contingent on the risk of fringe violence – in his letter of 8 August 1919 to Abdul Aziz. But he admitted that it would be mere calculus to apportion blame for Punjab violence without a full and proper inquiry of the circumstances around the incidents.[90] Gandhi, meanwhile, had taken over the editorship of two journals, *Navajivan* and *Young India*, and he focussed them on crucial contemporary concerns. He had been tirelessly petitioning for justice to Kalinath Roy along with the withdrawal of the Rowlatt Act, and on 18 June communicated to the viceroy through a letter to Hignell that he planned to resume *Satyagraha* in July unless these concerns were adequately addressed by the government. He was confident that *Satyagraha* did not have any destructive value, and far from vitiating Indian society with racial hatred for the English, it was actually 'designed to remove acerbity between two members of the Empire'. In the event of a renewal of civil disobedience, Gandhi assured the government that its practise would be limited to his own individual self.[91] This was followed by a telegraphed representation to the same effect to Secretary of State Edwin Montagu on 24 June. While Gandhi was engaged in preparing for civil disobedience involving circulars to potential civil resistors, the government communicated to him its intention to meet with a heavy hand any attempt at resuming civil disobedience, mentioning the moral responsibility that must lie with the leaders for the serious consequences that would inevitably accrue with the movement. However, it simultaneously conveyed that it would be setting up a committee of inquiry on Punjab and that the viceroy had commuted the two-year prison term of Kalinath Roy to three months. Gandhi must, of course, have deferred his decision on civil disobedience not at the threat of punitive action but at the meeting of two of his most important demands from the government. After the viceroy's announcement in the Legislative Council on 3 September, the committee was constituted under Lord Hunter on 24 October. The introduction in September of the Indemnity Bill effectively providing immunity to officials from penalty for their role in public repression had

144　❀　Nationalism: ethics and responsibility

resulted in a heated debate and opposition in the Council. Gandhi was, on the other hand, as ever realistic in his expectations from government per se and not overly enthusiastic about demanding systemic changes within the procedure of the system itself. His evaluation of the idea of state was singularly unromantic, and he was with foresight recognising the juridical norms of the independent Indian state. With characteristic honesty, he refused to expect such provisions – even from a government that he opposed – as he was sure a future Indian government as well would find itself unable to extend towards citizenry. Gandhi was clear that officials could not be immunised from departmental action, including dismissal from service for incompetence or misconduct. But for him, it was inadvisable to expect officials to be made liable to criminal charges, such as that of murder, for having discharged functions in a purely administrative capacity. It should in parenthesis be mentioned in this connection that an official acquiescingly assisting in pogroms or ethnic cleansing would automatically be excluded from this category as any deliberate action conceived against norms of humanity by itself contravenes, according to the general philosophy of government, the definition of constitutional obligation or administrative duty. Gandhi was pointing out that, as things stood in the present, even if such demands were to be made with force and conviction, there was no chance of their being met. In this, he was interrogating the concept of the modern state, and inviting serious introspection as to the enormity of the changes that would be necessary and the path that would have to be travelled for instituting alternative protocols of government and state, if the Indian political community was really sincere in aspiring for a reasonably equitable and representative political apparatus in the future Indian nation.

> Every state needs such protection. Even when we come to enjoy swaraj, the state will retain this power. The officers will then too commit grave mistakes and the public will get excited; even under swaraj the people will resort to violence; if the spirit of pure satyagraha has not come to prevail in India by then, there will be Martial Law and firing, followed by appointment of Commissions. Even under swaraj Indemnity acts will be passed to protect the authority of the state. But then, as now, the actual provisions will need to be looked into.[92]

The Punjab Sub-Committee nominated by the Congress in June 1919 was already in Punjab assembling evidence related to atrocities during martial law, and after deciding by November that it would not associate

Nationalism: ethics and responsibility ☀ **145**

itself with the Hunter Commission, it formed further a group of commissioners, including Gandhi, to collect evidence for a report by Congress on Punjab. Gandhi had written to Hignell on 30 September for rescission of restriction on his entry into Punjab and the orders were withdrawn on 15 October.[93] Gandhi reached Punjab by the end of October and remained in the province with the Sub-Committee for the next three months, touring affected areas, including remote villages, conducting hearings and preparing the Congress report. A series of Punjab letters written by him during this period constitute a valuable record, which in those days informed public opinion, and in the present serve to illustrate the principle of the extension through the openness of a leadership of the representative character of proceedings of such committees. Although compiled and signed jointly by Gandhi, C. R. Das, Abbas S. Tayabji and M. R. Jayakar, we have it on Jayakar's authority that the Congress report, entitled *Report of the Commissioners appointed by the Punjab Sub-Committee of the Indian National Congress*, in its conception and drafting reflects primarily the personal agency of Gandhi.[94] The report indicted the government for its violation of the basic principles of law, justice, governance and public morality. It censured O'Dwyer and a host of officials and suggested their dismissal from their position in the government and recommended the recall of Viceroy Chelmsford. Remarkably for an anti-colonial investigation into colonial excess, the report absolved, on the grounds of inexperience and their less brutal conduct, two junior officers from public action whom it otherwise found guilty of gross dereliction of their duty. As a document of record, it was appreciated for its probity, clarity and brevity in the legal community.[95]

The fact-finding tour of Punjab translates the nationalist response, crafted mainly by Gandhi, to an administrative calamity, from the petitionary to the juridical. This is distinctive of an alternative or shadow government and thus equates a public movement with the methodology of a state effectively establishing parity in matters of policy and structure. In this respect, Gandhi's utmost concern with fairness and restraint linked with his complete distrust of hyperbole and exaggeratory propaganda, and the permanent inhabitancy of this value in nationalist leadership during Gandhi's lifetime, becomes illustrative of the larger cosmopolitan concerns of Indian nationalism. Equally important, the raising by Gandhi of a fund for English victims of nationalist violence and his fasting for seventy-two hours as atonement strengthened the ethical presence in the public domain at a critical juncture of nationalist politics in India. This

146 ❖ Nationalism: ethics and responsibility

was in stark contrast to the frenzy among a section of English society and the Indian press for subscribing to the *Morning Post* fund for General Dyer, even after he had been subjected to disciplinary action by the government. As almost always in history, the general reaction on both the sides was not, however, entirely without nuance. In 1920, writing in the aftermath of the agitation, Gandhi warned the Indian public that the tendency to raise impulsive demands and use discourteous language in relation to individuals and offices even during inflamed situations would degrade public concerns and ill serve the national cause. In England, the debate on Dyer's conduct, and the criticism of the raising of the *Morning Post* fund, evidenced the democratic concerns and complexity of English politics.[96] The agitation against the Punjab repression culminated into Gandhi's 'real entrance into Congress politics', and he was frequently invited to informal meetings to envisage and draft crucial resolutions for the Subjects Committee. He was finally entrusted with drafting a constitution for the party. He also involved himself actively with the building of the Jallianwala Bagh memorial.[97]

It proceeds, perhaps inescapably, from the discussion that it is futile to try to establish any moral hierarchy in the responses of Tagore and Gandhi. Any such exercise will fail to avail of the opportunity to realise the essence of their respective, and perhaps broadly similar, positions concerned with the first principles of nationalism and freedom. We have earlier in the discussion mentioned Tagore's caution against memorialising hatred in the nationalist discourse. His refusal flowed also from his anguish that the Punjab tragedy did not embody courage on the part of the victims, and that neither the oppressors nor the oppressed reflected any trace of heroism in their conduct.[98] Gandhi, while taking a leading role in the construction of the memorial, as with him in all matters, meditated on the appropriate plane of memorialisation. He considered it as a potential site of nationalist secular pilgrimage drawing Indians of all faiths and denominations, as compared to religious sites which appealed only to a particular community. Writing in the *Navajivan* in April 1920, he opined that the contributors to the fund for the memorial wished only to honour the innocent dead and not to perpetuate ill will. Many of them believed that the site would inspire Hindu–Muslim unity. He, then, recalled the wisdom of Tagore's counsel: 'What Sir Rabindranath Tagore has said is perfectly true, that we shall certainly not advance by keeping alive the memory of General Dyer's cruelty. To perpetuate the memory of truth, firmness, courage and innocence, wherever these may be found – that is the people's real duty and in doing so lies the nation's regeneration.'[99]

Nationalism: ethics and responsibility   147

Scholars have traced Gandhi's almost absolute disillusionment with the democratic credentials of the British government to its attitude to the series of events that constituted the Punjab tragedy. Rabindranath also changed in course of time his early belief in the British traditions of fairness and decency in politics. By August 1920, in preparing the country for a sustained civil disobedience campaign, Gandhi returned his Kaiser-i-Hind medal to the government and advised all title holders to do likewise. In this, he perhaps pointedly evoked the phrase which Tagore had used in the same context, when he described government titles as 'badges of honour'. He might have been consciously suggesting the emulation of the step taken by Tagore, and Gandhi referred to erstwhile distinctions bestowed by the government as 'badges of dishonour and disgrace when we really believe that we cannot get justice from this government'.[100]

Before concluding this discussion, we would like to draw attention to another statement by Gandhi to hierarchical oppression made during his address to the Suppressed Classes Conference at Ahmedabad on the anniversary of Jallianwala Bagh in 1921, which for him was a day that was 'hallowed by the memory of innocents'. Speaking to the gathering Gandhi, however, invoked the act of massacre to point to its similarity to the terrible cruelty of untouchability that continued to be practised by Hindus over the disprivileged classes, and thereby reaffirmed that not sanctimony but moral responsibility represented the core value of nationalism. He prioritised for the nationalist agenda the difficult question as to whether it should be a test of the national conscience that the violation of its moral universe be found invariably to generate a righteous anger on the part of the nation.

> We are guilty of having suppressed our brethren; we make them crawl on their bellies; we have made them rub their noses on the ground; with eyes red with rage, we push them out of railway compartments – what more than this has British rule done? What charge that we bring against Dyer and O'Dwyer may not others, and even our own people, lay at our door? We ought to purge ourselves of this pollution. It is idle to talk of swaraj so long as we do not protect the weak and the helpless, or so long as it is possible for a single swarajist to injure the feelings of any individual.[101]

Responsible nationalism

Khilnani has mentioned the 'anti-statism' 'that had animated the thinking of both Tagore and Gandhi' and how the 'state was a dispensable

148 ❖ Nationalism: ethics and responsibility

nuisance' for them.[102] We have seen Gandhi's realistic assessment of the nature of the state. Tagore's attitude to law, and thus presumably the state was complex. His rejoinder in 1928, to a polemical claim regarding an academic institution and involving issues of social ethics and law, might be illustrative of his regard for the occasional necessity of arbitral law for preserving the social fabric of the nation. It is also noteworthy that the said incident held very disturbing connotations for the future Indian state. In early 1928, students residing in the Ram Mohun Roy Hostel of the Sadharan Brahmo Samaj-administered City College in Calcutta suddenly became zealous for performing the annual worship of the Goddess Saraswati inside the hostel premises. The Brahmo-managed institution, fully consonant with its established tenets of prayer and ritual, had no prior tradition of idol worship in its premises and was naturally opposed to the inauguration of any religious practice which was in contravention of its essential standards of religious ceremonies. It was reported that a rising but still junior political personality in Calcutta with grander ambitions was the soul of this unprecedented project of the students. The situation was doubly awkward as the hostel was named after Ram Mohun Roy, who was known for his lifelong opposition to idol worship. The authorities of the college attempted to forcibly prevent the performance of Saraswati Puja in the hostel. Certain politicians were industrious in creating a rift between the Hindu community and the Brahmo Samaj and exploited the latent anti-Brahmo feeling in orthodox Hindu circles. The already disputatious atmosphere was further aggravated with the Brahmo Samaj invoking the rights of minorities in this regard. Orthodox Hindu opinion began citing the Brahmo attitude in this case as an evidence of its illiberality.

Tagore made a public intervention in the debate through a detailed essay in May 1928. He described the claim of the students as reprehensible according to the principles of religion, public morality, social ethics, legal norms and on the encroachment on religious freedom. The obstreperous assertion by votaries to publicly worship their deity amidst an unwilling milieu in reality signalled the votaries' disregard for the deity. Tagore was disturbed at the quietude of the political class before an obviously pernicious sectarian mobilisation and stated that he would not avoid the risk of confronting discourteous behaviour in the fulfilling of his public obligation as a citizen. Transcending its own history of sectarian conflicts, modern Europe had been able to achieve both 'social order and political power' by successfully establishing protocols of diversity and unity. He defined swaraj as being characterised by individual and group self-restraint and in the recognising of the limits of liberty. As he had similarly said elsewhere, he cautioned that religious differences had historically been of a far serious degree in India and that this was the gravest challenge to the union of the country, and the cultivation of a maturity of view to preclude further antagonisms of this nature was crucial to the creation of 'national life'. 'Where a multitude of men live in the same country, social adjustment and freedom of self-determination become for them the greatest fulfilment. And every great people strives with disciplined effort and sacrifice to attain this fulfilment.'[103] He reminded the readers of the tenets of Hindu worship, which prohibited the worship of a deity in any place which was not appropriate to the ceremony and which might give annoyance to adherents of a different form of the divine. The believing Hindu thus would commit a grave transgression in doing otherwise, as was sought to be done by the Hindu students in this case. Along with the religious injunctions, Tagore focussed on the significance of the rules of social behaviour for internal polity and upheld state intervention in disputes involving religious sensibilities: 'If a particular religious community has charge of a certain college, then mere gentlemanliness dictates that the students of such a college should not wound the religious beliefs of that community. And if there be some amongst the former devoid of this quality, then it becomes a case for the external social force called law. It is the fear of this law that prevents any member of society from taking it on himself to forcibly discard the rights and privileges of any other members.'[104] Such demands were tantamount to Hindu students attempting to ritually worship the icon of Kali in the Aligarh College, which would be in addition to a social discourtesy an act 'against the law' which 'no civilised society' could allow, and along with suffering 'inward shame', the 'culprit' would 'be liable to the outward penalty prescribed by law'. And for deciding on questions of legality of the demands of the students as raised by them in this instance, reference must be made by the students in a 'constitutional way' to the overarching institution as the university in such cases or to a court of law, but 'never to their own boisterous wilfulness'.[105] Moreover, would Hindus be willing to accept the sacrifice of a cow by Muslims as part of their ritual in the City College? Obviously, the same arguments would be deployed by the latter in support of such an act as had been deployed by the Hindus. He compared the current Hindu orthodox intimidation of a marginal sect to the traditional domineeringness of the bridegroom's family over the bride's relatives in Indian society and drew attention to the danger of an identical attitudinal

150 ❋ Nationalism: ethics and responsibility

permeation in religion, politics or 'national work': 'Should it not rather be a source of the gravest anxiety to the national Leaders?'[106] It was a bad augury that a thoughtless attempt was being made to overwhelm through a ruckus an institution that had so far been regarded for its indiscriminative attitude towards students of all denominations. It was being unfortunately obscured that the entire campaign would ultimately end in the lasting embitterment of a minority group of compatriots: 'Would that be a hopeful outlook for our thousand-times divided people? Would it amount to a cultivation of the spirit of Swaraj which is to give legitimate freedom of self-expression to all natural differences in the communities that come under it?'[107]

As it subsequently happened, the students were provoked by some cliquish political leaders to picket, in the name of 'satyagraha', the house of a wealthy Hindu lady to whom the college authorities had pledged the building of the college against a loan from her to construct its present premises. The lady was compelled to ask the college for immediate repayment of the loan. The Visva-Bharati rescued the college from acute financial distress by advancing as investment the fund of one lac rupees, which had been donated to the Visva-Bharati by the Nizam of Hyderabad for pursuing Islamic Studies. Tagore wrote in a highly critical vein in a letter in May 1929 of the unholy alliance of orthodoxy and ambition, which had launched the campaign against the city college:

> Those who have accepted as the only aim of their efforts the national unification and liberty of India, when even they are encouraging by their partisanship this religious conflict, when even they are diffident of expressing even the slightest trace of opposition to the conduct of the students which is against the tenets of one's rule of one's self, then I clearly see that the technique of realising the spirit of politics in our country, due to its own cowardice and weakness, is standing on the road leading towards its own futility.[108] (my translation)

A mining of the stratum of his conceptual and literary writings may reveal that his ideas on the nation state are neither ahistorical, nor are they reducible to crude and absolutist assumptions. He was opposed to the modern commercial/capitalist/expansionist complex, which had donned the mantle of the nation, rather than the geographical/ethnic units which congeal together on the basis of shared characteristics that to an extent ensure the sustenance of a viable national entity. This conclusion seems logical if we look at his constant references to a particular genius that distinguishes every ethnic group in the world, and his sympathy for the emancipative struggles of people across continents. He had a great admiration for Asian nations like Japan and China, and he appealed to their intellectual communities to nurture the spirit of reconciliation, which could be manifested in their governments' general national and international policies. Some critics, however, would be doubtless led to infer that Tagore was generous in his criticism of Eurocentrism, but he refrained from a similar critique of Indian history and tradition because of his own orthodoxy and hegemonic inclinations. His pragmatism regarding the nation state is evident in his position on national armies, as in one of his lectures delivered in Japan: 'I do not for a moment suggest that Japan should be unmindful of acquiring modern weapons of self-protection. But this should never be allowed to go beyond her instinct of self-preservation.'[109] However, he went on to clarify that 'The living man has his true protection in his spiritual ideals which have their vital connection with his life, and grow with his growth'.[110] We should mention that he might appear to be somewhat in proximity to Immanuel Kant's conceptual universe regarding the community of nations. Kant can be said to, in some measure, combine the idealistic and the pragmatic in his study of the possible norms of fraternal association of states that would facilitate abiding peace in the world. War, in the employing of human beings by the state to destroy human life, entails the abrogation of the autonomy of the self as human beings surrender to the state their inalienable right over their own person. Inordinate accumulation of resources by a state was similarly considered undesirable by Kant, since states regarded monetary power as the most dependable weapon available to them, and therefore the financial resources were objects of plunder and appropriation. Kant had suggested that the practice of maintaining standing armies by states should be discontinued with time. Standing armies heightened the belligerence of states and provoked them into confrontation, and as this continuous process of acquiring parity in military capability became progressively more burdensome to the finances of the state, open war appeared preferable to them rather than the interminable struggle for superiority. However, he conceded that 'the periodic and voluntary military exercises of citizens who thereby secure themselves and their country against foreign aggression are entirely different'.[111]

Defining the ultimate goals of his nationalistic movement for *Swadeshi*, Gandhi was writing to a correspondent in January 1928 amid allegations in India and abroad that his movement was exacerbating elements of xenophobia within the country: 'Swadeshi does not mean drowning oneself in one's own little puddle but making it tributary to the ocean that is the nation. And it can claim to contribute to the ocean only if it is and keeps itself pure. It is therefore clear that only such local or provincial customs should have a nation-wide vogue as are not impure or immoral. And when once this truth is grasped, nationalism is transmuted into the enthusiasm of humanity.'[112]

There is an altruistic core to the nationalistic idea, insofar as it extends beyond the strictly individual, towards identifying itself with a wider group and occasionally, even frequently, it therefore involves some degree of selflessness on the part of the nationalist. But it becomes self-centred when rights for a group are demanded by individuals, primarily because of the realisation that the benefits would thereof automatically flow to them in their individual capacity. This constitutes chauvinistic, amoral nationalism. However, the kernel of altruism in the idea of nationalism retains its significance even when it is precariously placed between the 'two great powerful and attractive fallacies', as Isaiah Berlin called them, the imperialistic preaching of internationalism to the powerless; on the other hand, the compulsive desire of the weak to 'declare themselves bankrupt, and be struck off the roll, and lay down the burden of freedom and responsibility'.[113] In a climate of shallow internationalism paralleled with militarism, Tagore appreciated the basic fact of internationalism, which has been highlighted in a different context by Berlin when he writes: 'Internationalism is a noble ideal, but it can be achieved only when each link in the chain, that is, every nation, is strong enough to bear the required tension.'[114] In regarding the equation of the ideas of internationalism and nationalism, as obtained in the views of the leadership of the Indian national movement, it may be illustrative to refer to Gandhi's argument which he offered to Tagore in the explaining of the premises of his concept of non-cooperation. Gandhi argued that non-cooperation was on the part of Indians a refusal of any servility to colonial definitions imposed on them and not the rejection of cosmopolitan values. In fact, such servility as he refused to let be continued any longer was inimical to the formation of a principled and moral world order, where communities could only exist independently in the relationship of roles and ideas and not, as devised to happen in a colonial system, in a relationship of benefactor and beneficiary. 'We must refuse to be lifted off our feet. A drowning man cannot save others. In order to be fit to save others, we must try to save ourselves. Indian nationalism is not exclusive, nor aggressive, nor destructive. It is health giving, religious and therefore humanitarian. India must learn to live before she can aspire to die for humanity. The mice which helplessly find themselves between the cat's teeth acquire no merit from their enforced sacrifice.'[115] Within a nation, willed selflessness would ideally be the norm. In conceiving nationalism occasionally in familial terminology, Gandhi was at once using a reductionist turn to access the idea at more tangible levels of cognition and also opening the accessible terminology of family to a wider meaning involving much larger allegiances. 'After all, the truest test of nationalism consists in a person thinking not only of half a dozen men of his own family or of a hundred men of his own clan, but considering as his very own the interest of that group which he calls his nation.'[116] Of course, Tagore swayed neither towards sentimental traditionalism nor towards vague cosmopolitanism. Berlin, for one, affirmed this in his lecture at the centennial conference on Rabindranath Tagore in Delhi in 1961. But I am equally interested in Berlin's argument in the same city eleven years later, in the inaugural Humayun Kabir Lecture in 1972 rather intriguingly entitled *Kant as an Unfamiliar Source of Nationalism*. Illustrating the many connotations of the concept of nationalism, Berlin had argued that there was, howsoever paradoxical, a connection and a 'traceable line of influence' between Kant's ideas and the 'rise of nationalism'. Kant's expectable horror at such a connexion, if he were by any chance to traverse chronology and come to learn of such a linkage, did not rule out the fact that romantic nationalism was but 'two steps' away from 'Kant's impeccably enlightened rationalism'.[117] It is noteworthy that Berlin had also argued that the responsibility of the later extension of Kant's ethical and political ideas could not and should not be ascribed to Kant. 'Ideas do at times, develop lives and powers of their own and, like Frankenstein's monster, act in ways wholly unforeseen by their begetters, and, it may be, directed against their will, and turn on them to destroy them. Men, least of all thinkers, cannot be held responsible for the unintended and improbable consequences of their ideas.'[118]

Berlin's apology for Kant is similar to the presumption in Tagore's case, inasmuch as general opinion agrees that Tagore's relationship with the *Swadeshi* movement was complicated and apparently vexed, given his early support to the nationalist cause followed by his recoil at its developing an overtly violent and a dangerously communalist character. One of the prominent instances, recently advanced by critics in support of this theory of vexedness, is the supposed criticism of Tagore by some of his

154 ❀ Nationalism: ethics and responsibility

contemporaries – particularly in an essay written in 1908 in the *Prabasi* by Ramendra Sunder Trivedi – for incipiently extending unqualified support to *Swadeshi*, which had included composing songs for its propagation, before Tagore's withdrawal from the movement after noticing its increasing coerciveness: 'When the fire of swadeshi ignited, the pen of Rabindranath did not fail in spreading the fire.'[119] However, if Ramendra Sunder Trivedi's essay is read in entirety, it will be extremely difficult to support the contention that he was a critic of Tagore's early support to *Swadeshi*. It is well known that Trivedi was aggressively patriotic and very strongly in favour of *Swadeshi*, both politically and culturally. As an instructor in the University of Calcutta, he desired to give his lessons by reading from his treatise in Bangla, and on being refused permission to teach in the language, declined to give lectures till he was specially permitted by the vice chancellor to do so. Trivedi was one of the most gifted essayists in Bangla and his prose writings are distinguished by their range of themes, exceptional erudition and remarkable articulacy. This evaluation of Trivedi by Sukumar Sen, a highly respected scholar of Bengali culture, might be consequential for our discussion: 'As an intelligent prose writer and as a nationalist he was considered as second only to Tagore.'[120] This drawing of a nationalistic kinship between Tagore and Trivedi may not be entirely incidental. Trivedi had earlier written another and more famous essay entitled *Bangalakshmir Bratakatha* in protest against the partition of Bengal in 1905.[121] It was on his proposal that *arandhan* (a traditional Hindu festival in Bengal of abstaining from cooking every year on the last day of the month of *Bhadra*) was observed throughout Bengal in protest against Lord Curzon's partitioning of the state. But to return to Trivedi's essay in *Prabasi* written as rejoinder to Tagore's essay *Byadhi o Pratikar*, Trivedi could not agree with Tagore that there was no specific path to independence and that liberty could only be realised by liberating the mind which could be achieved only through difficult, constructive work and not political and cultural mobilisation. Trivedi, rather humorously, observed on the early enthusiasm and volubility of the *Swadeshi* movement and its subsequent waning at the strictness of the government, and said that Tagore, being pained at this dampening of public ardour and the general weakening of the movement, was now suggesting a more reserved attitude with the charting of more arduous paths to social uplift and political liberty. He recalled, it must be mentioned with the highest regard, Tagore's contribution in the awakening of public opposition to Lord Curzon's decree and how Trivedi shared wholly the nationalistic

Nationalism: ethics and responsibility ❖ **155**

passion, which was intensified with every song and poem that Tagore then was writing regularly for the *Swadeshi* movement. 'He has never advised for a futile and pointless movement; but in generating the violent excitement that had occurred at that time in Bengal, Rabindranth's achievement was not entirely inconsiderable' (my translation).[122]

But even in the midst of his partly acerbic criticism of Tagore's later refusal to support the political campaign for *Swadeshi*, Trivedi did not fail to hail Rabindranath for presenting by personal example an alternative attitude to nationalism through his initiatives in the realm of education and rural reconstruction: 'Robi Babu is not merely increasing the volume of the screaming by repeating, "work, work", but is also illustrating some appropriate ways of doing that work by taking them up in his own hands' (my translation).[123] Along with this appreciation of Tagore, Trivedi simultaneously underlined what appeared to him as a fallacy in Tagore's prescription of a 'constructive' operation of the present national emotion and his argument that the agency of the country's actual development ought not to be transferred into the hands of its rulers. Trivedi said that in the present circumstances of colonial rule that option was not practically available to the country, as the opportunity for initiative and space for constructive work could any time be denied to the people of the country by an indifferent and powerful government wielding untrammelled authority.

However, since we have alluded to Berlin on the issue of nationalism, and especially the apology for Kant's relationship with nationalism, it may be appropriate to our discussion to again refer to his essay titled 'The Bent Twig' on the positive aspects of nationalism. In this essay, Berlin has mentioned Schiller's description of nationalism as a 'bent twig' and has traced nationalism as occasionally an inevitable condition among subject peoples with memories of hurt and aspirations of assertion and very importantly not rejected the possibility of its non-belligerence. 'Nationalism is an inflamed condition of national consciousness which can be, and has on occasion been, tolerant and peaceful.'[124] This, for Berlin, does not entail the ruling out of the terrible excesses of violently nationalistic regimes around the world, and the undeniable fact that the hideous instances of ethnic cleansing in the twentieth century have proven the dangers of a heady combination of nationalism and atavism. The socialist revolutions have also failed to effectively substitute with 'progressive' thinking what appeared to them as mere 'reactionary, bourgeois' sentiment, and the pull of what constitutes national feeling continues to

156 ❖ Nationalism: ethics and responsibility

be strong. Nationalism may be construed as a variegated theme in collective psyche – nostalgia for imaginary pasts; desire for imagined moral orders; idyllic lives without the degrading conditions of post-industrial revolution, modern labour; and also to erstwhile suppressed ethnic groups it may represent 'the straightening of bent backs, the recovery of a freedom that they may never have had (it is all a matter of ideas in men's heads), revenge for their insulted humanity'.[125] It is paradoxical that in the West, to which is ascribed the genesis of the modern nationalistic emotion, the attraction of nationalism was thought to be the weakest in countries that had been able to maintain their political freedom for longer duration, and which have enjoyed the distinction of national accomplishments also in culture, science and knowledge. Political philosophies advancing theories of social restructuring in the West have not, according to their assessment of the phenomenon, considered nationalism either an effective ally in their cause or a significant obstruction in their plans, particularly given that nationalism was viewed by such philosophies as an instrument of class oppression. This rivetingly analytical and suggestive passage on nationalism's career by Berlin also indicates the variety of nationalism:

> In fact, nationalism does not necessarily and exclusively militate in favour of the ruling class. It animates revolts against it too, for it expresses the inflamed desire of the insufficiently regarded to count for something among the cultures of the world. The brutal and destructive side of modern nationalism needs no stressing in a world torn by its excesses. Yet it must be recognised for what it is – a world-wide response to a profound and natural need on the part of newly liberated slaves – 'the decolonised' – a phenomenon unpredicted in the Europe-centred society of the nineteenth century. How did the possibility of this development come to be ignored? To this question I volunteer no answer.[126]

Critics, Ramachandra Guha among them, have somewhat over-read Tagore's contrition over his own role in the *Swadeshi* movement. Guha particularly has seen some of Tagore's later essays on the theme as an autocritique.[127] But there is no consequential departure of ideas in his later and prominent writings such as *Raja Praja, Samuha, Swadesh* and so on. In fact, Tagore reiterates in these writings that Indian society has still continued to suffer at the hands of rulers the indignity accruing from the staple colonial attitudes of racial superiority, typically exemplified in the depictions of Indian life by writers like Kipling. That colonial rule

Nationalism: ethics and responsibility ❖ 157

was an artificial barrier and a hindrance to the normal development of the country, even if it was not the only one, was a fundamental idea in his writings, as it is in most such nationalist writings. Political liberty and autonomy of government may not in all such cases, and certainly not in the world view of Tagore, be an aspiration towards hegemony in the dominant native class; autonomy is rather perceived as a means of the general improvement of the socio-economic standard in the country. Even the portion of his letter to Aurobindo Mohan Bose that Guha cites as example is preceded by statements that reject the absolutist assumptions and *modus operandi* of the *Swadeshi* movement, not the idea of nationalism itself. Responding to the critique of his article entitled *Deshhit*, Tagore stated clearly that he had nowhere said that 'boycott should stop', only that 'unjust, untruthful and unrighteous methods' would ultimately not be beneficial for the country and its people. Equating patriotism with God and thereby making it the supreme ideal would result in patriotism becoming 'the blindest of superstitions, similar to the belief in omens about sneezing and lizards croaking, or the worship of goddesses to ward off cholera and skin diseases'.[128] The undue primacy of patriotism in the public imagination paradoxically disfigures the idea and deprives it of all redemptive value. Interestingly, an article by Tagore's renowned Santiniketan colleague Kshitimohon Sen, which instances the mutual regard of Rabindranath Tagore and the arch-nationalist Bal Gangadhar Tilak, compares Tagore's attitude towards his nation as a kind of praxis or devotion exclusive of all other goals, calling Tagore's nationalism *rashtriya sadhana*. It is likened to the ant-like approach of the ascetic towards true realisation: the *pipilikadrishti* of *munis*. This signifies the quality of meticulous dedication in Tagore's worshipful attitude towards his nation. Sen revealed that Tagore had recorded in his own hand his detailed advice and a kind of a plan of action regarding the fulfilment of the essential duties of citizens towards their local community as well as to the nation. This handwritten manuscript had been in the possession of his friends, who unfortunately came to regard it as an incriminating document and destroyed it through fire at their fear of its being discovered during the regular police search of houses during the *Swadeshi* move-ment.[129] This fact accomplishes two things: first, it dispels the notion of Tagore having at any point unconsciously subscribed to xenophobic nationalism; second, that the imagined shift in his attitude indicated the unintended consequences of his ideas with regard to the excesses of the

158 ❋ Nationalism: ethics and responsibility

Swadeshi movement. It both defines and defends his national sentiment and effectively emphasises his distancy from the pathology of nationalism.

The remoteness of Gandhi and Tagore from the pathology of nationalism is also marked in the civility of their political language and their unfailing social courtesy to the functionaries of the political regime to which they were implacably opposed. During crucial moments in the national movement, Gandhi consistently sought to purge any impression or element of intolerance and ethnic animosity, as in his stating on the occasion of the public boycott of the Prince of Wales during his visit to India in 1921 that it was intended on the matter of principle and not a show of disrespect: 'The boycott was purely a question of principle and directed against what we have held to be the unscrupulous methods of the bureaucracy.'[130] We have earlier seen Gandhi's scathing criticism of the uncivil language used for Lord Chelmsford by some delegates at the Amritsar Congress. He reacted strongly to reports of hooliganism and social coercion on the part of non-cooperators, in an article written in January 1922 entitled *Beware of Ourselves*. He said unsparingly that it was a contradiction in terms for the non-cooperators to claim country-wide support and then attempt ostracism of countrymen for non-participation. Any deviation from the ideals of non-cooperation, tolerance and respect of opponents being the most prominent among them, would accrue in ethical disaster.

> We have more to fear from ourselves than from the violence or mistakes of the Government. The latter if we use them aright, do us good, as they have already. Our own violence or untruth will be veritable death for us. If we are not able to set our own house in order, we shall certainly destroy ourselves. Non-co-operation will be a by word of execration and reproach.[131]

Non-violence and any kind of discourtesy were naturally incompatible for Gandhi as well as Tagore. Even theoretically, this indissoluble binding of the two values receives dissent and might thereupon admit the possibility of one's own fallacy. This was prominently reflected in Gandhi's impression of the violence of Chauri Chaura and his acceptance of almost sole responsibility for the incident: 'I am in the unhappy position of a surgeon proved skill-less to deal with an admittedly dangerous case.'[132] He acknowledged that it was the bitterest humiliation for him but recognised it as God's warning that the country had still not acquired the mental quality appropriate for practising non-violent mass protest.

Nationalism: ethics and responsibility ✤ 159

It was doubtful that even if in the event of the government granting self-rule consequent to the Bardoli *Satyagraha* – which he withdrew after the violent outbreak at Chauri Chaura – violent elements would have become uncontrollable in the absence of a morally committed political community. Even if at all politically erroneous, the withdrawal of the campaign was morally discerning and valuable, and the 'country will have gained by my [Gandhi's] humiliation and confession of error'.[133] For Gandhi personally, the current withdrawal of his political programme was not adequate penance, as more was required from an architect of a political edifice. 'I must undergo personal cleansing. I must become a fitter instrument able to register the slightest variation in the moral atmosphere around me. My prayers must have much deeper truth and humility about them than they evidence. And for me there is nothing so helpful and cleansing as a fast accompanied by the necessary mental co-operation.'[134] He expected that his penance might encourage his followers and co-workers to aspire for self-restraint and non-violence in 'thought, word, and deed or the spread of that spirit'.[135]

There was an occasion in the case of Tagore when he had to confront non-cooperation from some of his own valued colleagues at Santiniketan for extending hospitality to the Governor of Bengal Lord Lytton, who was particularly unpopular for his severity and imperiousness. On being communicated that Lytton wished to visit Santiniketan, he was formally invited by the poet in 1922 when general feelings were still running high in the aftermath of the non-cooperation movement. Tagore respected the wishes of senior colleagues, such as the highly respected Bidhushekhar Shastri, to abstain from the ceremonials but nevertheless received the governor ritually and with perfect courtesy in the famous mango grove in observance of the traditional welcoming rites of Santiniketan. Similarly, in 1925, Lytton came to Santiniketan on a personal visit while returning to Calcutta from an official tour, and just after a bitter correspondence between Tagore and himself over his support of police brutality on nationalist protestors in Dacca, but Tagore was as ever the perfect host. He was assailed in some newspapers for having shared a meal with the governor. Tagore's public courtesy was put to further nationalist test during Viceroy Irwin's visit to Santiniketan in December 1925. For the first time in the history of the institution, police entered the premises with Tagore's approval. The employees had to wear ochre-coloured robes for easy identification by the police. Tagore accepted these conditions as necessary for reasons of feasibility and propriety.[136]

160 ❖ Nationalism: ethics and responsibility

Returning to the issue of the genesis and extension of the idea of nationalism in unlikely epistemic climates, Tagore unlike Kant was still living during the nationalistic apotheosis in his nation and could thus respond to its positions and ideology. To mention yet another difference in the case of Tagore, the idea of 'the autonomy of the will of a nation or a society' had been already launched on the political plane, and he was in effect also refining these ideas. Berlin's essay on Kant and Nationalism foregrounds the possibility of an inclusive, liberal and democratic nationalism, as in Mazzini and Michelet. Berlin has stated that the nationalist consciousness was rooted in 'the uniqueness of particular traditions, languages, customs – of occupation, over a long period, of a particular piece of soil on which intense collective feeling is concentrated'.[137]

It is undeniable that Indianness, embodying some unique qualities, was precious to Tagore, whether it is called love of homeland or local attachment. He ascribed at times very noble features to the subcontinent, which it should be remembered became three nations. For instance, he wrote in the *Swadeshi Samaj* in 1904 that the 'realisation of the one in many, attaining unity in diversity – this is the inherent quality of Bharatvarsha'. For him, this India never equated difference with animosity and did not deem aliens to be enemies. Because of this, it aspires to accommodate everybody within a wide system, mindful of the importance of each in its assigned place: 'Since India possesses this quality, we will never imagine any society to be our enemy and be fearful. With ever new conflicts we will aspire for the expansion of ourselves. Hindus, Buddhists, Muslims, Christians will not die fighting each other in the case of India – here they will discover a harmony. This harmony will not be non-Hindu; in fact, it will be Hindu in its essential sense. The limbs and organs of this harmony may come also from alien countries; however, its life and soul shall be Indian.'[138] This love for a homeland is considered by scholars of nationalism, such as Boehm, to be 'an ethical concept fundamental to all nationalism'.[139] It is significant that this love acquires a universal character in Tagore. It is, of course, evident that it does not allow any scope for chauvinism; overzealous patriots by trying to cite it for their benefit will inevitably cause the vandalism of the entire idea. But it still remains that Tagore cherished a regional-national sentiment, which has elsewhere been defined as being 'conducive to nationalism of a defensive and intensive rather than of an aggressive and extensive nature', and an idea which 'in regions of mixed nationality . . . may serve as a unifying

Nationalism: ethics and responsibility ❖ **161**

element for rival nationalities and also as a check on the development of a conscious and too ardent nationalism'.[140]

Gandhi was likewise a consistent defender of composite nationalism. Although he personally continued with his reservations regarding the salutariness of religious conversion, he was absolutely clear that conversion, even if to other faiths than the faith of the numerical majority, was never inimical to national loyalties, indicating thereby his other prominent concern with the nation as a secular state and indeed a secular nationalism. In a public speech in 1927 at Tinnevelly, he referred to a communiqué from the Indian Christian Association which stated their identification with the national movement. Gandhi affirmed his position on religion as a personal virtue, without even the least of nationalist overtones. 'There is no doubt in my mind that it is as it should be. Acceptance of Christianity or any other faith should never mean denationalization. Nationalism need never be narrow or inconsistent with internationalism. That nationalism, which is based upon pure selfishness and the exploitation of other nations, is indeed an evil. But I cannot conceive of internationalism without a healthy and desirable national spirit.'[141] It may be in this connection relevant to add that Gandhi in stating some years after that the earthquake in Bihar was a 'divine chastisement' for the sin of untouchability, may have invoked the category of moral nationalism inasmuch as the universal Godhead chooses not to extend benediction on military adventures, but to rebuke a people for its violation of human norms.[142] This indicates at a societal conscience and introduces the principle of the morality of the nation/state. The origins of Gandhi's concept of the ethical state can perhaps be traced also to the Jain *niti* tradition, particularly the tenets pertaining to the moral duties and obligations of a ruler in *Laghavarhnniti* composed for King Kumarpala in twelfth-century Gujarat, by his minister Hemchandra who like Gandhi belonged to the Modh Bania community of the Kathiawar region.[143] In 1944, Gandhi's interview to Stuart Gelder of the *News Chronicle* was published in the *Times of India*. His position in the interview on the issue of a possible national government in India assisting in the war effort became controversial and it was alleged in some quarters that Gandhi had shifted his position from the August Resolution of the Congress. Gandhi, during a subsequent press conference in July at Panchgani, mentioned his detractors' allegation that he had 'betrayed' the Congress at the behest of the affluent lobby. It is extremely significant that Gandhi said that he now welcomed the premature publication of the interview which he had till then criticised as ill timed. He was now pleased that it provided him an opportunity to state his position on his political affiliations:

> I do not want to sail under false colours. The country as well as the Government should know me exactly as I am. I have never concealed the fact that I am a friend of everybody – moderates, moneyed men, English-men, Americans or any other, irrespective of caste or colour or persuasion . . . I may say that the favourable war situation had nothing to do with my proposal, if only for the simple reason that, in the flush of approaching victory, my proposal was not likely even to receive a fair hearing. But as a lover of peace, not merely in India but peace among all mankind, I could not but make a proposal for what it is worth. After all, there is such a thing as world opinion, apart from the opinion of authorities.[144]

This ethical position is more crucially evident in Gandhi's fast against the decision of his country's independent government to freeze Pakistan's share of the common assets during the Kashmir war, culminating in the government's revocation of its earlier decision and the release of the funds. The fast probably precipitated the insane passion that his fundamentalist opponents had nurtured against his moral authority, into plans for his assassination. We should perhaps profitably, for our discussion, recall the remark on Gandhi that Romain Rolland had made in his diary in 1922, which reflects on the moral stature of Gandhi in the history of nationalism: 'I see in Gandhi something quite different from an internationalist of my type: he is a nationalist, but of the greatest, the loftiest kind, a kind which should be a model for all the petty, base, base, or even criminal nationalisms of Europe. An idealistic nationalist who wants his nation to be the greatest in spirit – or nothing'[145].

The convergence of Tagore and Gandhi, on the morality of the state and the ethics of nationalism, attests as much the category of their nationalism as it perhaps does the open texture of nationalism itself.

Notes

1. Sabyasachi Bhattacharya, ed., *The Mahatma and the Poet* (Delhi: National Book Trust, 2005), 216.
2. Rabindranath Tagore, *Letters from Russia*, trans. Sasadhar Sinha (Calcutta: Visva-Bharati, 1984), 203.

Nationalism: ethics and responsibility   **163**

3. Rabindranath Tagore, *The English Writings of Rabindranath Tagore*, 4 vols. (Delhi: Sahitya Akademi, 1994–2007 [hereafter *Writings*]), 3: 966.

4. A common example is the open texture of the term mother in the case of *in vitro fertilization*, where the producer of the ovum is different from the bearer of the foetus and in cases even from the one who rears the baby. The question of the 'real mother' thus becomes inapplicable, since the term is inadequate under the changed circumstances. I am aware of the dimensions introduced into this issue by custody suits as in the celebrated custody case of Melissa Stern, or Baby M. However, it only reinforces the appropriateness of the example rather than dispute it.

5. Toynbee states: 'The spirit of nationality is a sour ferment of the new wine of democracy in the old bottles of tribalism.' According to Toynbee, Western democracy tries to reconcile the contradictory principles of fraternity and militant tribalism. See Arnold Toynbee, *A Study of History* (London: Thames and Hudson, 1995), 34.

6. Hans Kohn, *The Idea of Nationalism: A Study in Its Origins and Background* (New Brunswick, NJ: Transaction Publishers, 2005), 19.

7. Hugh Seton-Watson, *Nations and States: An Enquiry into the Origins of Nations and the Politics of Nationalism* (London: Methuen & Co., 1977), 465.

8. Margaret Moore, *The Ethics of Nationalism* (New York: Oxford University Press, 2001), 33.

9. Elie Kedourie, *Nationalism* (Malden, MA: Blackwell Publishing, 1993), xiii–xiv.

10. Joseph Stalin, *Marxism and the National and Colonial Question* (London: Lawrence & Wishart, 1936), 8.

11. See Earnest Renan, 'What Is A Nation', in ed. Geof Ely and Ronald Grigor Suny, *Becoming National: A Reader* (New York: Oxford University Press, 1996), 42–55.

12. See Benedict Anderson, *Imagined Communities: Reflections on the Origin and Spread of Nationalism* (London: Verso, 2001).

13. James M. Blaut, *The National Question: Decolonizing the Theory of Nationalism* (London: Zed Books Ltd., 1987), 153.

14. Blaut, *The National Question*, 148–149.

15. Blaut, *The National Question*, 88.

16. Max Hildebert Boehm, 'Nationalism: Theoretical Aspects', in ed. Edwin R. A. Seligman *et al.*, *Encyclopaedia of the Social Sciences*, 15 vols. (New York: The Macmillan Company, 1963), 11: 231.

17. Julian imagined a France that is at once spiritual and material, to the extent that he would probably not have felt spiritually depleted even if, hypothetically, the whole world perished with the exception of France. He collapsed entire periods into recent memory, so that 'in the twinkling of an eye, the scientific Western historian of the Neolithic age has been transfigured into the French patriot in AD 1918'. See Toynbee, *A Study of History*, 36.

164 ❖ Nationalism: ethics and responsibility

18. Ernest Gellner, *Nations and Nationalism* (Ithaca, NY: Cornell University Press, 2008), 56.
19. *Congress Presidential Addresses*, ed. A. M. Zaidi, 5 vols. (New Delhi: Indian Institute of Applied Political Research, 1986–1989), 2: 114–115.
20. E. J. Hobsbawm, *Primitive Rebels: Studies in Archaic Forms of Social Movement in the 19th and 20th Centuries* (New York: W. W. Norton & Company, 1965), 30.
21. Tagore, *Nationalism*, ed. Ramachandra Guha (Delhi: Penguin Books, 2009), 73.
22. George Steiner, 'The Cleric of Treason', in George Steiner, *A Reader* (Harmondsworth: Penguin Books, 1984), 195–196.
23. Lincoln wrote to Speed: 'Our progress in democracy appears to me to be pretty rapid. As a nation we began by declaring "all men are created equal". We now practically read it "all men are created equal except negroes". When the know nothings get control, it will read "all men are created equal except negroes, and foreigners and Catholics". When it comes to this I should prefer emigrating to some country where they make no pretence of loving liberty – to Russia, for instance, where despotism can be taken pure, and without the base alloy of hypocrisy'. Carl Sandburg, *Abraham Lincoln: The Prairie Years* (New York: Dell Publishing House Co. Inc., 1960), 205.
24. Plato, *Crito*, reproduced in Jewett's translation, in ed. Doris A. Hunter and Krishna Mallick, *Nonviolence: A Reader in the Ethics of Action* (Delhi: The Gandhi Peace Foundation, 1990), 35–36.
25. Tagore, *Nationalism*, 80. Goethe had somewhat similarly asked Luden during the German uprising: 'But is the people really awake? Does it know what it wants and what it can achieve? And is every movement an uprising? Does he arise who is forcibly stirred up? . . . You say Freedom. Perhaps it would be better if you were to call it liberation . . . '. Rudolph Rocker, *Nationalism and Culture*, trans. Ray E. Chase (California: Rocker Publications Committee, 1937), 204.
26. Tagore, *Nationalism*, 59.
27. Tagore, *Nationalism*, 41.
28. Tagore, *Nationalism*, 43.
29. Amartya Sen, 'Foreword', in ed. Krishna Dutta and Andrew Robinson, *Selected Letters of Rabindranath Tagore* (Cambridge: Cambridge University Press, 1997), xx.
30. Rabindranath Tagore, *Rabindra Rachanabali* (125th anniversary edition), 15 vols. (Kolkata: Visva-Bharati, 1986–1992 [1393–1398 Bengali Era]), [hereafter cited as *Rachanabali*], 5: 790. All citations are in translation from Bangla, and have been translated by myself, unless otherwise specified.
31. *Rachanabali*, 9: 606.
32. *Writings*. 3: 423–424.

Nationalism: ethics and responsibility · **165**

33. William Chester Jordan, '"Europe' in the Middle Ages', in ed. Anthony Pagden, *The Idea of Europe: From Antiquity to the European Union* (New York: Cambridge University Press, 2002), 73.

34. For a very thoughtful and informative study of early cosmopolitanism in Europe, see Margaret C. Jacob, *Strangers Nowhere in the World: The Rise of Cosmopolitanism in Early Modern Europe* (Philadelphia: University of Pennsylvania Press, 2006).

35. Jordan, '"Europe" in the Middle Ages', 83.

36. Seyla Benhabib, 'The Philosophical Foundations of Cosmopolitan Norms', in ed. Robert Post, *Another Cosmopolitanism* (New York: Oxford University Press, 2006), 17.

37. Jeremy Waldron, 'Cosmopolitan Norms' in *Another Cosmopolitanism*, 83.

38. Steven Vertovec and Robin Cohen, 'Introduction: Conceiving Cosmopolitanism', in ed. Vertovec and Cohen, *Conceiving Cosmopolitanism: Theory, Context, and Practice* (New York: Oxford University Press, 2002), 15.

39. Peter Van der Veer, 'Colonial Cosmopolitanism', in *Conceiving Cosmopolitanism*, 174.

40. Robert Fine and Robin Cohen, 'Four Cosmopolitan Moments', in *Conceiving Cosmopolitanism*, 155.

41. *Rachanabali*, 9: 592.

42. Elie Wiesel, *From the Kingdom of Memory* (New York: Shocken Books, 1995), 135. In his famous study on aggregate memory, Halbawchs has offered a reason for nostalgia for the early years of one's life, in the fact that the past has noticeably less obtrusiveness on one's life, and does not in the same measure as the present does, represent the pressures of society in our everyday living. This 'retrospective mirage', as Halbwachs calls it, is more evident in one's recollections of childhood and youth while one convinces oneself that the better portion of one's life is already behind oneself. This may be the case even in the lives of those who have suffered considerably during their early years. According to Halbwachs: 'That faraway world where we remember that we suffered nevertheless exercises an incomprehensible attraction on the person who has survived it and who seems to think he has left there the best part of himself, which he tries to recapture. This is why, given a few exceptions, it is the case that the great majority of people more or less frequently are given to what one might call nostalgia for the past.' Maurice Halbwachs, *On Collective Memory*, trans and ed. Lewis A. Coser (Chicago: The University of Chicago Press, 1992), 49.

43. Wiesel, *From the Kingdom of Memory*, 140–145.

44. *Rachanabali*, 5: 675–676.

45. *Writings*, 3: 544.

46. *Congress Presidential Addresses*, ed. A. M. Zaidi, 5 vols. (New Delhi: Indian Institute of Applied Political Research, 1986–1989), 2: 57.

166 ❖ Nationalism: ethics and responsibility

47. M. K. Gandhi, *Hind Swaraj and other Writings*, ed. Anthony J. Parel (Delhi: Cambridge University Press, 1997), 48.
48. Gandhi, *Hind Swaraj and other Writings*, 49.
49. Gandhi, *Hind Swaraj and other Writings*, 50.
50. Gandhi, *Hind Swaraj and other Writings*, 52–53.
51. M. K. Gandhi, *Collected Works of Mahatma Gandhi*, 100 vols. (Delhi: Publications Division, Government of India, 1958–1994) [hereafter *Collected Works*]), 35: 497–498.
52. *Collected Works*, 25: 359.
53. *Collected Works*, 61: 27.
54. Gandhi, *Hind Swaraj and other Writings*, 115.
55. *Collected Works*, 22: 88–89.
56. Gandhi said: 'I repeat for the thousandth time that it is not hostile to any nation or any body of men, but it is deliberately aimed at a system under which the Government of India is being today conducted and I promise that no threats and no enforcement of threats by the Viceroy or any body of men will strangle that agitation or send to rest that awakening.' *Collected Works*, 22: 88–89.
57. Tagore, *Nationalism*, 64.
58. Tagore, *Nationalism*, 83. It may be pertinent in this connection to refer to Ambedkar's speech of 25 November 1949 to the Constituent Assembly: 'There was so little solidarity in the U.S.A. at the time when this incident occurred that the people of America did not think that they were a nation. If the people of the United States could not feel that they were a nation, how difficult it is for Indians to think that they are a nation. I remember the days when politically-minded Indians, resented the expression "the people of India". They preferred the expression "the Indian nation". I am of opinion that in believing that we are a nation, we are cherishing a great delusion. How can people divided into several thousands of castes be a nation? The sooner we realize that we are not as yet a nation in the social and psychological sense of the world, the better for us. For then only we shall realize the necessity of becoming a nation and seriously think of ways and means of realizing the goal. The realization of this goal is going to be very difficult – far more difficult than it has been in the United States. The United States has no caste problem. In India there are castes. The castes are anti-national. In the first place because they bring about separation in social life. They are anti-national also because they generate jealousy and antipathy between caste and caste. But we must overcome all these difficulties if we wish to become a nation in reality. For fraternity can be a fact only when there is a nation. Without fraternity equality and liberty will be no deeper than coats of paint.' *Constituent Assembly Debates: Official Report*, 5 Books. (New Delhi: Lok Sabha Secretariat, 1950; rpt. 1999), 5: 980.

Nationalism: ethics and responsibility ❖ **167**

59. Tagore, *Nationalism*, 70–71.
60. Albert Einstein, *Ideas and Opinions*, ed. and trans. Sonja Bargmann (London and New York: Crown Publishers Inc., 1954), 181.
61. For an analysis of Einstein's nationalistic views, see Isaiah Berlin, 'Einstein and Israel', in ed. Henry Hardy, *Personal Impressions* (Princeton: Princeton University Press, 2001), 66–77.
62. Einstein, *Ideas and Opinions*, 181.
63. Einstein, *Ideas and Opinions*, 183.
64. *Writings*, 3: 753.
65. Harish Trivedi, 'Tagore on England and the West', in ed. G.R. Taneja and Vinod Sena, *Literature East and West: Essays Presented to R K DasGupta* (New Delhi: Allied Publishers, 1995), 169.
66. This argument is common in Tagore scholarship. Two of the prominent instances which may be of helpful reference are Prabhat Kumar Mukhopadhyaya, *Rabindrajibani*, 4 vols. (Kolkata: Vishvabharati Granthanbibhag, 2008 [1415 Bengali Era]), 3: 16–24; and Nepal Majumdar, *Bharate Jatiyota o Antarjatikata ebong Rabindranath*, 6 vols. (Kolkata: Dey's Publishing, 1988 [1395 Bengali Era]), 2: 34–48.
67. Majumdar, *Bharate Jatiyota o Antarjatikata ebong Rabindranath*, 2: 35.
68. Mukhopadhyaya, *Rabindrajibani*, 3: 20–21.
69. Mukhopadhyaya, *Rabindrajibani*, 3: 23.
70. Majumdar, *Bharate Jatiyota o Antarjatikata ebong Rabindranath*, 2: 48.
71. For the full text of the letter, see Tagore, *Selected Letters*, 223–224.
72. M. K. Gandhi, *An Autobiography or The Story of my Experiments with Truth* (Ahmedabad: Navjivan Publishing House, 1988), 533.
73. For a concise account of public violence and government reprisal in the states of Bombay, Punjab, Bengal and Delhi during the Rowlatt *Satyagraha*, see Sushila Nayar, *Mahatma Gandhi: India Awakened* (Ahmedabad: Navjivan Publishing House, 1994), 266–287. For a detailed and useful, if very slightly pro-government, narration of the events leading to the firing at Jallianwala Bagh and martial law in Amritsar, including the debate in the English House of Commons, see Alfred Draper, *Amritsar: The Massacre that Ended the Raj* (London: Cassel Ltd., 1981).
74. *Collected Works*, 15: 211.
75. *Collected Works*, 15: 211.
76. *Collected Works*, 15: 212.
77. For details, see *Collected Works*, 15: 213–214.
78. *Collected Works*, 15: 218–220.
79. *Collected Works*, 15: 221.
80. *Collected Works*, 15: 223.
81. *Collected Works*, 15: 243–245.
82. Tagore, *Selected Letters*, 221.

168 ❖ Nationalism: ethics and responsibility

83. Gandhi, *An Autobiography*, 548.
84. Robert Payne, *The Life and Death of Mahatma Gandhi* (New Delhi: Rupa, 1997), 342.
85. *Collected Works*, 15: 311. Gandhi recounted that he faced a dilemma on offering *Satyagraha* in this regard, as his requests for rescission of the preventive order against his entry in Punjab were being rejected, and in this situation any attempt to enter that province would at the most be limited to a symbolic act. 'I therefore decided not to proceed to the Punjab in spite of the suggestion of friends. It was a bitter pill for me to swallow. Tales of rank injustice and oppression came pouring in daily from the Punjab but all I could do was to sit helplessly by and gnash my teeth.' Gandhi, *An Autobiography*, 548–549.
86. *Collected Works*, 15: 314–315.
87. *Collected Works*, 15: 332–333.
88. For the text of the letter, see *Collected Works*, 15: 334–335.
89. *Collected Works*, 15: 364–365. Tagore had written on 12 April 1919 in answer to Gandhi's solicitation of his opinion on the ensuing civil disobedience against the Rowlatt Bill: 'Power in all its forms is irrational, it is like the horse that drags the carriage blind-folded. The moral element in it is only represented in the man who drives the horse. Passive resistance is a force which is not necessarily moral in itself; it can be used against truth as well as for it. The danger inherent in all force grows stronger when it is likely to gain success, for then it becomes temptation. I know your teaching is to fight against evil by the help of the good. But such a fight is for heroes and not for men led by the impulses of the moment.' *The Mahatma and the Poet*, 49.
90. Gandhi wrote to Aziz: 'I miscalculated the capacity of the people to stand *any* amount of suffering and *provocation*. It *was possible* for the Punjab people to remain quiet in spite of the provocation offered by the arrests I have mentioned. But what happened was beyond endurance. The people of Amritsar could not restrain themselves and brook the deportation of their leaders. Neither you nor I can apportion blame for what followed. Satyagraha apart, the question will have to be solved whether the people were provoked into madness by the firing or whether the military were provoked to action by the mob.' *Collected Works*, 16: 15.
91. *Collected Works*, 15: 377–378.
92. *Collected Works*, 16: 141.
93. For details of the relevant order, as well as short extracts from confidential government reports on the subject, see *Collected Works*, 16: 239–241.
94. For the full text of the report, see *Collected Works*, 17: 114–292. Gandhi later acknowledged that he was entrusted with the drafting of the report. He recommended the report as a historical document which accurately records the atrocities in Punjab without any kind of exaggeration and unsubstantiated statement. 'Not a single statement, regarding the validity of which there was the slightest room for doubt, was permitted to appear in the report . . . So

far as I am aware, not a single statement made in this report has ever been disapproved.' Gandhi, *An Autobiography*, 554.

95. Jayakar recounts what Inverarity, one of the luminaries of the Bombay High Court, commented after reading the report: 'It is a damaging document, and you know its effect is largely due to the very careful way in which you have presented your facts and the restraint with which you have drawn your conclusions . . . And you can take it from me that, when this report is read in England, it will produce a far greater effect than in India, where people delight in hyperboles.' M. R. Jayakar, *The Story of My Life*, 324–326.; cited in Nayar, *Mahatma Gandhi*, 296.

96. Gandhi was particularly severe in his comment on the tone of some of the delegates in the Congress session at Amritsar, saying that the speeches for the recall of Lord Chelmsford were 'shameful and deserve condemnation': 'To regard Lord Chelmsford unfit for his post is one thing; but it is quite another to insult him and to use discourteous and unmannerly language about the Emperor's representative. We shall lower ourselves in the estimation of others thereby and such language, if it became common among the people, would be a blot on the virtues of humility, courtesy and magnanimity which still remain ours. I just do not believe that the nation can gain anything through exaggeration. Exaggeration is a particularly bad species of falsehood; even if the nation can advance through untruthfulness, it would be better for us to refuse to advance in such a manner because, ultimately, such advance will bring about our fall.' *Collected Works*, 16: 467. Speaking in the English House of Commons, Montagu faced a generally hostile audience as he ripped into Dyer's conduct as having been essentially against the norms of democracy and the code of government, but also as ultimately inimical to the relations between India and England: 'I invite this house to choose, and I believe that the choice they make is fundamental to the continuance of the British Empire and vital to the continuation, permanent, I believe it can be, of the connection between this country and India.' Montagu's viewpoint was shared only partially by Winston Churchill. The general bitterness against Montagu was noticeable and was commented on by some in the British press. A Jew by denomination, Montagu probably also received a share of racial animosity in the bargain. It was even alleged that he had exercised undue influence in the Indian government against Dyer. On Chelmsford's reported offer to divulge their private correspondence in order to demolish this allegation, Montagu significantly replied: 'Public life becomes impossible if, because a minority chooses to believe in the bad faith of a Viceroy or a Secretary of State, correspondence not intended for publication has to be produced. If we are not to be believed we should be dismissed.' For details, see Draper, *Amritsar: The Massacre that Ended the Raj*, 227–235. For references to hostility in the House linked to Montagu's Jewish origins, see Arthur Herman, *Gandhi & Churchill: The Epic Rivalry that Destroyed an Empire and Forged our Age* (London: Hutchinson, 2008), 254–255.

170 ❋ Nationalism: ethics and responsibility

97. Gandhi, *An Autobiography*, 564–566.
98. Majumdar, *Bharate Jatiyota o Antarjatikata ebong Rabindranath*, 2: 46–47.
99. *Collected Works*, 17: 322.
100. *Collected Works*, 18: 151.
101. *Collected Works*, 19: 572.
102. See Sunil Khilnani, *The Idea of India* (London: Penguin Books, 1997), 167–181.
103. *Writings*, 4: 392.
104. *Writings*, 4: 393.
105. *Writings*, 4: 393.
106. *Writings*, 4: 395.
107. *Writings*, 4: 395.
108. Cited in Mukhopadhyaya, *Rabindrajibani*, 3: 345.
109. Tagore, *Nationalism*, 20.
110. Tagore, *Nationalism*, 20.
111. Immanuel Kant, *Perpetual Peace* [1795] (Minneapolis: Filiquarian Publishing, LLC, 2007), 9.
112. *Collected Works*, 35: 505.
113. Isaiah Berlin, 'Rabindranath Tagore and the Consciousness of Nationality', in Isaiah Berlin, *The Sense of Reality: Studies in Ideas and their History*, ed. Henry Hardy, (New York: Farrar, Strauss and Giroux, 1999), 265.
114. Berlin, *The Sense of Reality*, 264. Gertrude Himmelfarb takes a more conservative even if not entirely anti-cosmopolitan position on the balancing of modern democracy with nationalism. According to her, identities are not options but inheritances of a kind, and a crossing over in this area of living can cause critical deficiencies in ones consideration of public situations. 'The "protean self", which aspires to create an identity de novo, is an individual without identity, just as the person who repudiates his nationality is a person without a nation.' Gertrude Himmelfarb, 'The Illusion of Cosmopolitanism', in Martha C. Nussbaum, *Love of Country*, ed. Joshua Cohen (Boston: Beacon Press, 1996), 77.
115. *Collected Works*, 21: 291. It might be relevant to refer to Seton-Watson's criticism of the superciliousness and the 'unconscious nationalist prejudice' against the nationalist aspirations of 'newer nations' on the part of many of the powerful nations, who have enjoyed political independence and economic prosperity for many generations: 'The unconscious, though obvious and unmistakable, arrogance with which they view those nations which they regard as tiresome upstarts, leaves an unpleasant Pecksniffian taste.' Seton-Watson, *Nations and States*, 466.
116. *Collected Works*, 35: 321.
117. Isaiah Berlin, 'Kant as an Unfamiliar Source of Nationalism', in *The Sense of Reality* ed. Henry Hardy, 242.

Nationalism: ethics and responsibility ❖ 171

118. Berlin, *The Sense of Reality*, 234.
119. For this reference and a gist of Trivedi's critique of Tagore, see *Rachanabali*, 5: 819. For a slightly more detailed summary, also see Mukhopadhyaya, *Rabindrajibani*, 2: 212.
120. Sukumar Sen, *History of Bengali Literature* (Delhi: Sahitya Akademi, 1992), 293.
121. A *Bratakatha* is a narrative concerning a deity and includes the vow of devotion, the method of austerities and worship of the deity, along with the description of the fruits which are bestowed on the devotee for the practice of the recommended austerities. *Bangalakshmir Bratakatha* described Bengal as a deity to be worshipped and recommended the method of nationalistic devotion and the fruits of selfless nationalism.
122. Mukhopadhyaya, *Rabindrajibani*, 2: 212.
123. Mukhopadhyaya, *Rabindrajibani*, 2: 213.
124. Isaiah Berlin, 'The Bent Twig: On the Rise of Nationalism', in Isaiah Berlin, *The Crooked Timber of Humanity: Chapters in the History of Ideas*, ed. Henry Hardy (Princeton: Princeton University Press, 1990), 245.
125. Berlin, *The Crooked Timber of Humanity*, 261.
126. Berlin, *The Crooked Timber of Humanity*, 261.
127. See Ramachandra Guha, 'Introduction', in Tagore, *Nationalism*, vii–xviii.
128. Tagore, *Selected Letters*, 71–72.
129. Kshitimohon Sen, 'Rabindranath o Tilak', in ed. Pronoti Mukhopadhyaya, *Rabindranath o Santiniketan* (Kolkata: Punascha, 2009), 218.
130. *Collected Works*, 22: 88.
131. *Collected Works*, 22: 258.
132. *Collected Works*, 22: 419.
133. *Collected Works*, 22: 417.
134. *Collected Works*, 22: 419.
135. *Collected Works*, 22: 420.
136. Mukhopadhyaya, *Rabindrajibani*, 3: 186, 249, 366.
137. Berlin, *The Sense of Reality*, 232.
138. *Rachanabali*, 2: 640.
139. Boehm, 'Nationalism', 234–235.
140. Boehm, 'Nationalism', 234–235.
141. *Collected Works*, 35: 92. It appears that Gandhi was addressing a prevalent concern in political circles and allaying apprehensions in this regard. Nehru was to comment on the pro-British attitude of the Church of England in India around 1936: 'A recent instance of how the Church of England indirectly influences politics in India has come to my notice. At a provincial conference of the U.P. Indian Christians held at Cawnpore on the 7th November, 1934, the Chairman of the Reception Committee, Mr. E. V. David, said: "As Christians we are bound by our religion to loyalty to the

172 ❦ Nationalism: ethics and responsibility

King, who is the Defender of Our Faith." Inevitably that meant support of British Imperialism in India. Mr. David further expressed his sympathies with some of the views of the "diehard" Conservative elements in England in regard to the I. C. S., the police, and the whole proposed constitution, which, according to them, might endanger Christian missions in India.' Jawaharlal Nehru, *Jawaharlal Nehru: An Autobiography* (London: The Bodley Head, 1942), 376n1. Gandhi in 1922 mentioned a contrary example that of the All India Christian Conference passing a *Swadeshi* resolution, which included the condemnation of government repression, the urging of amnesty to political prisoners, the suspension of non-cooperation for a possibility of a round table conference and prohibition. The resolution was prefaced by a declaration of national faith: 'We must demonstrate by words and deeds that Christianity has made us neither un-Indian nor un-national. Can it be for a moment conceived that we as a community shall dissociate ourselves from our brethren, Hindus and Mussulmans, whatever differences there may be in our religious convictions?' *Collected Works*, 22: 169.

142. In Jewish history, Amos had reminded Jews that being the chosen people meant in reality that they qualified for greater punishment for transgressions rather than for being privileged for especial rewards. More recently, Maxine Hong Kingston, linking imperial havoc with natural havoc, somewhat conflated a natural disaster as the fire in California with the regular exploitative military actions of the United States around the world. For details, see Maxine Hong Kingston, *The Fifth Book of Peace* (New York: Alfred A. Knopf, 2003).

143. Jain canon is generally very critical of the hard state and compares its enforcers, such as policemen and executioners, to robbers and murderers, and describes war as a form of organised and large-scale brigandage. For details, see G. C. Pande, *Jain Political Thought* (Jaipur: Prakrit Bharati Sansthan, 1984).

144. D. G. Tendulkar, *Mahatma: Life of Mohandas Karamchand Gandhi*, 8 vols. [1951–1954] (Delhi: The Publications Division, Government of India, 1963), 6: 260–261.

145. 'Extract from Romain Rolland's Diary', in *Romain Rolland and Gandhi Correspondence* (Delhi: Publications Division, Government of India, 1976), 5.

IV ✲

In argument

Considerance of the political

The debate between Gandhi and Tagore frames their larger and common concerns regarding the political community. The usual observation regarding the apparency of a fundamental divergence between their viewpoints might actually be more of a speculation rather than a decisive conclusion. Occasionally, even separate intellectual categories may seem appropriate to the two personalities – that of the moral activist and the moral philosopher – which are suited to two distinct activities. The two activities have been distinguished philosophically as 'the activity of the moralist, who sets out to elaborate a moral code, or to encourage its observance, and that of a moral philosopher, whose concern is not primarily to make moral judgements but to analyse their nature'.[1] One may, in haste, be inclined to understand Gandhi as primarily a moralist and Tagore as a moral philosopher. It is, perhaps, more worthwhile a position to study both of them as a combination of the moral philosopher and the activist, inasmuch as they are engaged simultaneously in reasoning a moral vocabulary and using it to ethical purpose. The debate between them can perhaps be meaningfully understood on the plane of a conversation shared by two individuals with similar ethical imperatives and accomplishments that involve the determining of proper means of thought and action in pursuit of their ethical purpose. The conversation is thus relevant to the study of ideas with having not merely archival or exegetical value but as also being illustrative of the conception and operation of political thought. An early evaluative comment in 1925 by Romain Rolland in his diary, who had been receiving impressions of Gandhi's movement from various sources, reflects the opinion that the attitudinal difference between Gandhi and Tagore was irreconcilable. Rolland's comment on Elmhirst's support for Tagore's criticism of Gandhi's politics is at once interesting and also anticipative and a rebutment of some points of the later criticism of Gandhi:

174 ❀ In argument: considerance of the political

But the whole of Gandhi's policies meet with Tagore's disapproval. L. Elmhirst, who reflects him in this, speaks of them (following his master) with obvious hostility and little understanding. The thinker who does not act finds it easy to point out discrepancies, at least apparent discrepancies, between the doctrine and the actions of a man who has the responsibility for 300,000,000 men. He even goes so far as accuse him of betraying the cause of the untouchable because, in order not to complicate the present entente between the Indian parties over immediate action, Gandhi did not speak about the untouchables at the last Congress. One senses at the bottom of this the invincible antipathy between the free mind in love with all forms of life (and with a fair dose of dilettantism) and the puritan who imposes rules of mortification, asceticism and harsh disciplines on his disciples – so as to build them into a militia ready for any sacrifice. Gandhi's indifference to suffering – to his own as to that of others – when it is offered as a sacrifice to a noble cause, revolts Tagore to the point of injustice. It seems that he refuses to recognize its moral grandeur. Elmhirst presents Gandhi's unmoved reaction to the strikes that he decreed and the resultant ruins as the sign of a cold politician. He could hardly misunderstand more the soul of this heroic believer. Tagore, Gandhi: two worlds, moving further and further apart.[2]

There are, however, insistent and perceptible indications of a convergence relating to the genealogy and the influence of their aspirations and concerns. Tapan Raychaudhuri has traced their intellectual and ethical kinship to the 'shared concerns of the nineteenth-century Indian intelligentsia trying to work out world-views and agenda in the context of their colonial experience'.[3] Raychaudhuri has outlined the similarities of their thought on the plane of rural uplift and social reconstruction, as well as in the contiguity of their attitude to Western civilisation. 'Gandhi had described Indian infatuation with the West as *moha*, the high road to cultural suicide. The poet compared the western impact with disease.'[4] Even Tagore's opposition to any rejection of a culture was not directed against Gandhian principles but was actually the articulation of his misgivings regarding the imminence of cultural chauvinism. It is therefore necessary to carefully consider the content of their criticism of the cultural enslavement that was an inalienable component of the intellectual dominance of Western models.

The argument between Gandhi and Tagore – especially significant in the context of the conflicting interpretations being advanced of the quintessence of 'Indian civilization' in support of political claims – was centred on the vital issues of the day, and wherein the 'higher human

In argument: considerance of the political   ❉   **175**

ideals are confronted' and which almost seems to be, in Rolland's words, 'a controversy between a St. Paul and a Plato' that 'embraces the whole earth'.[5] Perhaps, they were able to hone their views, by the 'debate their differences compelled them to enter'.[6] On one plane, the debate appears to be located on the political plane in its criticism of Gandhi's political programme, and apparently posits Tagore as an opponent of Gandhi's nationalism. However, even while speaking of Tagore's opposition to nationalism, his universalism ought not to be confused with mere cosmopolitanism. His was more a faith in the harmony of influences and traditions and spoke of the 'web of unity' in Indian culture, 'which binds all of us' without our 'knowing or not knowing it', and the 'truth of which was not contingent on our knowledge and acknowledgement of it'. In 1915, drawing an outline of his own identity, he emphasised on the retaining of the distinctiveness of traditions in building bridges between culture. Gandhi's position was identical. And even if their differences were, as some have contended, fundamental, why should thus there be an overriding aspiration to reconcile their respective positions? The cordiality of their relationship, which remained undiminished by Tagore's criticism of some of Gandhi's essential positions, indicates the nuances of the nationalist idea, besides being instructive in a world of acrimonious political difference.

I do not propose to describe the details of the very substantial content and extent of the debate but only hope to look at the outline and delineate some basic issues. It should also be mentioned at this point that the separately published compilations of the debate so far are yet not fully inclusive of all the nuances of the arguments that were stated, both because in certain cases some of the letters have been rather inexplicably shortened, excluding crucial portions, and because a study of the debate needs to examine parallel correspondences that explain concerns and positions. It is also necessary to mention that the debate was on occasions mediated through letters to counterparts, such as C. F. Andrews, and regarding which detours into related correspondences become necessary. The arguments similarly impinge on significant public expressions by leading personalities, most notably the Congress Presidential Addresses, such as in the presidential speech by C. R. Das in the Gaya Session of 1922, defining the Congress's ideal of nationalism, which was as mentioned earlier also probably in part aimed at Tagore's apparently implacable opposition to the principle of nationalism.

In a sense, Tagore along with Gandhi, is the embodiment of the spirit of his own country or *home*, representing almost the essence of its culture – starting

176 ❖ In argument: considerance of the political

from the *Upanishads* and the first principles of the thought of Buddha and continuing through the medieval Bhakti tradition, particularly Kabir, the other Indian languages, and the aspirations born of the cultural and ideological contact with Europe in the nineteenth century. Tagore welcomed secular knowledge along with an interlocution of traditions, and it was anathema to him that Western science should be rejected because it 'belongs to the West'. His debate with Gandhi delineates his differences and his underlying affinity with him over the nature of the 'home' of a community.

The study of the debate between Tagore and Gandhi can be gainfully prefaced, relevant to our discussion, by Tagore's comment made early in 1909 on the nature of political difference in contemporary times. Tagore stated that the debate on the respective merits of diverging ideas of the politically beneficial and the best means of achieving that end has never been concluded in any country. He said that in human history, this debate has resulted in bloodshed and its subsidence on one plane had been paralleled by a continual regeneration in other guises and directions. In the generally controlled atmosphere of political activity in the closing years of the nineteenth century, before the commencing of the *Swadeshi* agitation, the articulacy of differences regarding the welfare of the country had till now been largely confined to discussions in meetings and in the papers of the press and was comparatively tame and merely smouldered, without as he said igniting with the 'flame' of conviction. However, as in the present, viewpoints were generally perceived to be imminently linked with the welfare of the country and not as merely the echoing of poetic metaphors; he could not be unhappy if there was occasionally certain rudeness in the protest against his own views by those with whom he had had disagreements. He felt that it was an auspicious sign of the times that nobody was let off easily on expressing a view on the affairs of the country, and with politics becoming more intense and active, there was he said in matters of political difference an auspicious element of acrimonious articulation in political discourse. Very significantly for his own and occasionally fundamental later differences with Gandhi, Tagore stated for his critics in 1909 (years before the debate) that howsoever intense be the excitement of the argument with those whom he had occasion to differ – as there was no reason to doubt their genuine dedication to attaining the welfare of the country – it was necessary to clearly understand each other's statements and volition. To be either annoyed at the outset or to become suspicious of the sanity of the other's mind would perhaps deceive one's own mind. Tagore felt that as the disagreements arose from an intensified concern with the affairs of society, there was no cause to doubt the basic commitment and the soundness of reasoning that underlay the differing point of view.[7] It is worth mentioning that the only notable exception that he made in his life to this belief was arguably with regard to the path of violent political method, and this attitudinal exception was perhaps essentially due to the fact that political violence on behalf of an ideology never accepts the possibility of its ideological fallibility. It was Tagore's expressed belief that 'it can never be true that to respect the difference in opinion was to disrespect one's own discernment'.[8]

Issues in the debate: the programme of the national movement

The debate between Gandhi and Tagore is located squarely on the political plane – the way of developing the character of the people of India and with reference to some aspects of the national movement, particularly boycott and charkha. Most critics have seen the initial period of their disagreements as 'the one time in their lives when there surfaced real tension between them. It was during this period [1920–22] that the differences became manifest and if they were to disagree thereafter this would be the norm for their mutually respectful dissent'.[9] The debate also can be described almost wholly as arising from Tagore's criticism of some of Gandhi's positions and Gandhi's explanation of his ideas while replying to Tagore's criticism. Some of Tagore's criticisms, beginning 1921, were almost foundational in some respects and quite severe, expressing reservations about Gandhi's policies, who always responded with grace and sincerity to the critical positions taken by Tagore.

Tagore's first major and publicly critical statement on Gandhi's programme of action related with the idea of non-cooperation and boycott, particularly of government schools, was conveyed in 1921 in his letters to C. F. Andrews, which were subsequently published in May 1921 in the *Modern Review*. Gandhi's response to Tagore's position, through a couple of articles in June 1921 in *Young India*, drew a rejoinder from Tagore in the *Modern Review*, and which were further responded to by Gandhi in three articles in the *Young India*, all within the same year. Bhattacharya views the differences as arising from Tagore's 'abhorrence [of] an instrumentalist view of *satyagraha*', and his unhappiness at the

178 ❖ In argument: considerance of the political

Mahatma being used by the political class as merely 'a stratagem in politics'.[10] It may be appropriate to indicate at the outset that Tagore's criticism of the instrumental view of *Satyagraha* was also addressed to Gandhi himself, and hence it may be necessary to clarify that as regards the instrumentality of *Satyagraha*, Gandhi had ever since the earliest phase of his political programme in South Africa attempted to explain, particularly in comparison to the Western idea of civil disobedience, the programmatic inclusivity of *Satyagraha*. A recent study has referred to the epistemic gap in this respect between India and the West, inasmuch as *Satyagraha* was persistently seen in a limiting way as a political technique which was akin to Thoreau's concept of civil disobedience.

> Gandhi himself was familiar with Thoreau's work. He reproduced the American's essay in his own publications, and used the concept of 'civil disobedience' routinely, and with great care. For Gandhi, Thoreau's term referred to 'deliberate opposition to law'. This was a particular version of non-violent protest, and it represented but a fraction of the Mahatma's practice. Indeed Gandhi repeatedly stressed that the concept of 'civil disobedience' did not convey 'the full meaning' of the Indian struggle. As he put it most bluntly: 'Satyagraha does not mean civil disobedience only and nothing else.'[11]

Even in India, perhaps mainly because of its primarily political manifestation, *Satyagraha* was generally perceived almost exclusively as a mobilisation of mass protest. For Tagore, *Satyagraha* with its emphasis on boycott of English education became representative of the agitational politics and the militant spirit of the West. Even as he eulogised Gandhi, for rousing the 'immense power of the meek' reposed in the 'destitute and insulted humanity of India', he pointed out his hopes for the essential destiny of India: 'To raise the history of man, from the muddy level of physical conflict to the higher moral altitude. What is *swaraj*! It is *maya*, it is like mist, that will vanish leaving no stain on the radiance of the Eternal. However, we may delude ourselves with phrases learnt from the West, *Swaraj* is not our objective.'[12] Tagore protested that the non-cooperation movement's natural spirit was in places manifesting itself in social boy-cott: 'We have no word for Nation in our language. When we borrow this word from other people, it never fits us.'[13] He thought that Western science should not be rejected just because it 'belongs to the West'. The boycott of schools and colleges constituted 'arrogant nationalism'. Tagore continued in bitter vein, likening the current movement to a midnight

In argument: considerance of the political   179

orgy of potential violence. 'The idea of non-cooperation is political asceticism. Our students are bringing their offering of sacrifices to what? Not to a fuller education but to non-education. It has at its back a fierce joy of annihilation which in its best form is asceticism and in its worst form is that orgy of frightfulness in which human nature, losing faith in basic reality of human life finds a disinterested delight in unmeaning devastation, as has been shown in the late war and on other occasions which came nearer home to us. *No* in its passive moral form is asceticism and in its active moral form is violence. The desert is as much a form of *himsa* as is the raging sea in a storm, they both are against life.'[14] He thought it would be impossible to recompense the injury that was being inflicted upon the careers of the boys, who were for him real persons and not 'phantoms', by calling them out of schools for an abstraction. It was for him, and statedly, an unhappy destiny that in opposing the non-cooperation movement he was compelled to go against his natural instinct as a poet to identify himself fully with his surroundings and instead 'ply my boat where the current is against me'. But believing as he did in the convergence of the East and the West, the idea of rejection of culture stirred him deeply to protest. 'Love is the ultimate truth of soul. We should do all we can, not to outrage that truth, to carry its banner against all opposition. The idea of non-cooperation unnecessarily hurts that truth. It is not our heart fire but the fire that burns out our hearth and home.'[15] There was also, however, an ethical question, which was for Tagore involved in a hypothetical situation wherein he could contemplate supporting the non-cooperation movement, and this was that of individual responsibility. This ethical principle is consistently reflected in Tagore's political thinking. It may be recalled that as has been discussed earlier, all throughout beginning with his initial writings on the country's political movement, he had been severely critical of the leadership class for their remoteness, in actual living, from the people of the country and their consequent disconnect from the real issues in the public domain. He was especially critical of the political elites of the country for having, since the very beginning of 'modern politics', indulged in a 'non-attributive discussion of patriotism that excluded the people of the country' and the monetary resources for which were provided by either the landlords or the industrialists; the language for this was supplied by the lawyers.[16] In the quote in question, he referred to the insistent ethics against advising others on a sacrificatory course of action without being prepared to offer one's own self for the same end. His endorsing of the politics of

180　❖　In argument: considerance of the political

non-cooperation would require his own readiness to forsake their position of rent collectors, without which any appeal to others to sacrifice their profession or property would be immoral. Tagore conveyed this clearly in his letter of 5 March 1921 to Andrews. The entire paragraph stating his ethical dilemma needs to be quoted in full, particularly since the edited version of the letter subsequently carried in May 1921 in *Modern Review* inexplicably omitted this crucial portion, and subsequent compilations have generally reproduced the version in *Modern Review*, presumably to protect Tagore against any aspersion of pusillanimity. In fact, this introspective statement actualises Tagore's commitment to ethical politics and demonstrates the normative relevance of the debate between Gandhi and Tagore. The statement is as follows:

> While I have been considering the noncooperation idea one thought has come to me over and over again which I must tell you. *Bara Dada* and myself are zamindars, which means collectors of revenue under British Government. Until the time comes when we give up paying revenue and allow are lands to be sold we have not the right to ask students or anybody else to make any sacrifice which may be all they have. My father was about to give up all his property for the sake of truth and honesty. And likewise we may come to the point when we have to give up our means of livelihood. If we do not feel that the point has been reached by us then at least we should at once make ample provision out of our competency for others who ready to risk their all. When I put to myself this problem the answer which I find is that by temperament and training all the good I am capable of doing presupposes [a] certain amount of wealth. If I am to begin earning my living, possibly I shall be able to support myself but nothing better that that. Which will mean not merely sacrificing my money but my mind. I know that my God may even claim that, and by that very claiming repay me. Utter privation and death may have to be my ultimate sacrifice for the sake of some ideals which represent immortality. But so long as I do not feel the call or respond to it myself how can I urge others to follow the path which may prove to be the path of utter renunciation? Let the individuals choose their own responsibility of sacrifice, but are we ready to accept that responsibility for them? Do we fully realise what it may mean in suffering or in evil? Or is it a mere abstraction for us which leaves us untouched [by] all the concrete possibilities of misery [for] individuals? Let us first try to think [of] them as the nearest and dearest to us and then ask them to choose danger and poverty for their share [in] life.[17]

In addition to these concerns that motivated his opposition to non-cooperation, Tagore stated further objections to the assumptive

In argument: considerance of the political   ❧   181

principles of non-cooperation, saying that contrary to being swamped by foreign influence, India, having been so long insulated practically from the essential principles of her own culture, had lost the energy necessary for cultural transaction and her view of Western culture was extensively biased. On the plane of culture, he implied, the constitutive vision of non-cooperation was skewed. 'When we have the intellectual capital of our own, the commerce of thought with the outer world becomes natural and fully profitable. But to say that such commerce is inherently wrong, is to encourage the worst forms of provincialism, productive of nothing but intellectual indigence.'[18]

However, Gandhi was equally unrelenting on his position on non-cooperation and on the discriminatory potential in the over-use of the English language. He pointed out that the principle of non-cooperation principally or even practically, with a few disapproved exceptions, did not entail disrespect and boycott of other cultures. He referred to Tagore's misperception on this score and cautioned him against 'mistaking its excrescences' for the movement itself: 'How much better it would have been, if he had refused to allow the demon doubt to possess him for one moment, as to the real and religious character of the present movement, and had believed that the movement was altering the meaning of old terms, nationalism and patriotism, and extending their scope.' He stated that the English language had been reduced to a commodity for social advancement and that boys learnt English only insofar as they understood its employment possibilities. Gandhi outlined the contemporary situation for girls that even today is so apparent to many teachers of English in small towns and rural colleges in India: 'Girls are taught English as a passport to marriage. I know several instances of women wanting to learn English so that they may be able to talk to Englishmen in English. I know husbands who are sorry that their wives cannot talk to them and their friends in English. I know families in which English is *made* the mother tongue. . . . All these are for me signs of slavery and degradation. It is unbearable to me that the vernaculars should be crushed and starved as they have been. . . . [*Tagore had been saying exactly the same in many of his writings.*] I hope I am as great a believer in free air as the great Poet. I do not want my house to be walled in all sides and my windows to be stuffed. I want the cultures of all the lands to be blown about my house as freely as possible. But I refuse to be blown off my feet by any. I refuse to live in other people's houses as an interloper, a beggar or a slave. I refuse to put the unnecessary strain of learning English upon my sisters for the sake of false pride or questionable social advantage. I would

182 ❖ In argument: considerance of the political

have our young men and women with literary tastes to learn as much English and other world-languages as they like, and then expect them to give the benefits of their learning to India and to the world, like a [J C] Bose, a Roy, or the Poet himself.'[19] The mastery of Gandhi's language is unqualifiedly impressive, and it is almost as if he is solemnly bearing witness and with cadences reminiscent of an Edmund Burke.

Gandhi in his second article on the topic welcomed, as he said, the Poet's misgivings regarding any blemish to India's reputation on the count of xenophobic rejection of Western culture during non-cooperation, which Tagore had understood as 'a doctrine of separation, exclusiveness, narrowness and negation', and stated that 'No Indian can feel anything but pride in the Poet's exquisite jealousy of India's honour.' However, he categorically rejected all apprehensions regarding the possibility of cultural atavism in non-cooperation.

> Nor need the Poet fear that non-co-operation is intended to erect a Chinese Wall between India and the West. On the contrary, non-co-operation is intended to pave the way for real, honourable and voluntary co-operation based on mutual respect and trust. The present struggle is being waged against compulsory co-operation, against one-sided combination, against the armed imposition of modern methods of exploitation masquerading under the name of civilization. Non-co-operation is a protest against an unwitting and unwilling participation in evil.[20]

Gandhi was adamant on the boycott of state-run schools. The education provided by the government had only assisted the reinforcement of colonial systems and cultivated the psychology of imitating Western mores and systems, contributing to the first principle of colonialism, the willingness of the colonised to associate with their own colonising. State schooling, in obstructing character building and increasing discontent and despondency, had 'unmanned us, rendered us helpless and godless'. 'I hold that as soon as we discovered that the system of government was wholly, or mainly, evil, it became sinful for us to associate our children with it.'[21] Gandhi, in this regard, expressed his understanding of the Poet's instinctive objection to anything that was negative in character and said that Tagore's main opposition to boycott of schools was that it, like non-cooperation, was a negative act, and as such was devoid of redemptive value. He referred to Tagore's statement that he could not accept even negative doctrines such as the Buddhist concept of *nirvana* as it evoked allusions to denial and extinction, and that whereas terms such as *mukti* indicated to positive attitudes, *nirvana* directed attention to the 'negative side of truth'. Gandhi reiterated that rejection had equal value as an ideal along with acceptance. He differed with Tagore on the question of nirvana, saying that all religions postulate that 'the human endeavour consists in a series of acceptances and rejections', and suggested that 'the Poet has done an unconscious injustice to Buddhism in describing *Nirvana* as merely a negative state . . . *mukti*, emancipation, is as much a negative state as *Nirvana* . . . *Neti* was the best description the authors of the *Upanishads* were able to find for *Brahma*'.[22] He concluded his argument by emphasising the constructive possibilities of non-cooperation, inasmuch as it was a harbinger of a different era, with equality instead of hierarchy becoming the determinant in international relations. And only in this would India be able to realise the swaraj of 'the Poets dream'. 'Non-co-operation is intended to give the very meaning to patriotism that the Poet is yearning after. An India prostrate at the feet of Europe can give no hope to humanity. An India awakened and free has a message of peace and goodwill to a groaning world. Non-co-operation is designed to supply her with a platform from which she will preach the message.'[23]

However, Tagore's experience of the *Swadeshi* movement in Bengal only strengthened his unease, and he had a tangible premonition that Gandhi's non-cooperation movement could also lead towards the growth of atavistic passions in the country. By August 1921, he was reading in Bangla his critique of Gandhi's movement, *Satyer Ahovan*, in a public meeting in Calcutta. Gandhi visited Tagore's Jorasanko residence in September to 'persuade Tagore to give open and active support to his political programme'. Only C. F. Andrews was privy to their unrecorded conversation. Even while it was in progress, there were intemperate displays of xenophobia by non-cooperation enthusiasts, who burnt foreign clothes in Tagore's courtyard. Seeing this, Tagore reportedly wondered at Gandhi's confidence that his movement would be non-violent. However, in spite of their vital differences on this issue, they 'parted as friends, agreeing to disagree'.[24]

Tagore's idea of India, detailed in the English version of his above mentioned lecture, *Satyer Ahovan*, written again apropos Gandhi in 1921 entitled *The Call of Truth*, subverted the prevalent idea of nation and identity and relatedly the defining premises of movements of liberation. Tagore questioned the impulse of non-cooperation as being necessarily marked by a reaction and not a creative aspiration. This interrogation of the credentials of an idea was also related essentially with his central concern regarding the freedom of conscience, and he perceived an unreasoning acquiescence in the participants of the movement. This deferment of one's own discernment on the part of his countrymen defeated his own ideals of *Swaraj*, which Gandhi had claimed non-cooperation was a means of achieving, and in a way he directly addressed himself to Gandhi's position on this: 'They have not achieved Swaraj in their own nature, and so are deprived of Swaraj in the outside world as well.'[25] He preferred an emphasis on the evolution of the personality and not on sudden, passionate mobilisation which comes far easier. Peoples' movements were easily appropriated if they were founded on 'hatred of the foreigner, not love of country'. For him, the nation was not centred round flags and emblems; it was an experience subtly varying from individual to individual, yet binding them together. India was and it was not. Its spirit had to be realised by people aware of the true quality of freedom, through service and renunciation: 'The Creator gains Himself in His universe. To gain one's own country means to realize one's soul more fully expanded within it. This can only be done when we are engaged in building it up with our service, our ideas and our activities.'[26] Tagore recalled that enunciation of such ideas in *Swadeshi Samaj* in 1905, made not only 'the hooligans of journalism' but also 'men of credit and courtesy . . . unable to speak of [him] in restrained language'. But eventually, those who had practised terror in those times 'realized at length that the way of bloody revolution is not the true way; that where there is no politics a political revolution is like taking a short cut to nothing . . .' He, however, paid tribute to them for offering themselves as the 'first sacrifice to the fire which they had lighted': 'Their physical failure shines forth as the effulgence of spiritual glory.' Perhaps it was their first step towards self-realisation.[27] Tagore presented here the virtue of reasoning, which he traced as a characteristic value of Western thinking. This premise cannot, however, be seamlessly incorporated into Tagore's overall position on Western education and on Eurocentric values. But this was not the only occasion when he had criticised the implicit conformity of Indian social thought, and this absolute criticism compared to his acknowledgement of the progressivity of Western traditions is fundamentally opposed to Gandhi's rejection of any claim of a civilisational modernity on the part of the West. Tagore linked the urge of non-cooperation to an unthinking compliance to a doctrine, which he said would aggravate a tendency 'under which our country has all along been languishing'. 'So far, we have been content with surrendering our greatest right – the right to reason and judge for ourselves – to the blind forces of shastric injunctions and social conventions. We have refused to cross the seas, because Manu has told us not to do so. We refuse to eat with the Muslaman, because prescribed usage is against it. In other words, we have systematically pursued a course of blind routine and habit, in which the mind of man has no place.'[28]

This essay acclaims the countrywide awakening brought about by Gandhi – non-cooperation was more extensive than the *Swadeshi* campaign. But Tagore was disappointed that Gandhi, endowed with a vision largely unknown to political leaders, did not initiate a movement which would be more edifying. The earlier political leadership was obsessed with English parliamentary mores and practices unconnected with the reality of their country, which was only 'the bookish aspect' of the British history of India: 'Such a country was merely a mirage born of vapourings in the English language, in which flitted about thin shades of Burke and Gladstone, Mazzini and Garibaldi. Nothing resembling self-sacrifice was visible.'[29] Nehru's well-known description of Gandhi's political arrival appears to echo Tagore who wrote that Gandhi 'was the truth at last not a mere quotation out of a book': 'Who else has felt so many men of India to be of his own flesh and blood? As soon as true love stood at India's door, it flew open: all hesitation and holding back vanished. Truth awakened truth.'[30] But the true import of Gandhi's message was drowned in the chorus of obedience set up by leaders desiring immediate results, stifling dissent: 'When I wanted to enquire, to discuss, my well wishers clapped their hands over my lips saying; Not now, not now.'[31] This apprehension arose from the ambition for achieving results within a time frame. Tagore reminded his readers that the poor had suffered economic hardship because of a similar ambition on the part of the *Swadeshi* leadership in Bengal, when they were compelled to make sacrifices 'not always out of the inwardness of love, but often by outward pressure'.

The experiential metaphysics of Tagore, perhaps, inspired a particular language and style which involved a constant tussle with words to express the essentially inexpressible. The essay on non-cooperation contains the idea of preparing the people for real freedom, arguably akin in principle to the idea of revolution; Lenin remonstrated with Italian communist leaders that they wanted to 'reap a revolution [that they had] not sown'. Gandhian revolution too needed great sacrifice. It included, but did not stop at, political freedom. These aspirations were thwarted by boycott. Burning cloth, where thousands suffered the indignity of nakedness, betrayed insensitivity.

186 ❀ In argument: considerance of the political

> Even today, our worldly wise men cannot get rid of the idea of utilizing the Mahatma as a secret and more ingenious move in their political gamble. With their minds corroded by untruth, they cannot understand what an important thing it is that the Mahatma's supreme love should have drawn forth the country's love. The thing that has happened is nothing less than the birth of freedom. It is gain by the country of itself. In it there is no room for any thought, as to where the Englishman is, or is not. This love is self-expression.[32]

It was as if a novice musician of the *vina* (Tagore), who is on a search for a master player rather than skilled craftsmen and on ultimately meeting one such master (Gandhi) whose very first notes melt away the 'oppression within', is offered a cheap substitute for the exacting art of making a perfect *vina*. Tagore found this unacceptable. The master ought to teach the art instead of offering palliatives. The cult of *charkha* and boycott were easy substitutes for the arduous task of realising *Swaraj*, in which 'the economist must think, the mechanic must labour, the educationist and statesman must teach and contrive': 'Above all, the spirit of inquiry throughout the whole country must be kept intact and untrammelled, its mind not made timid or inactive by compulsion, open or secret.'[33] Gandhi was endowed with 'the voice that can call, for in him there is the Truth'. But his call, 'spin and weave', was simplistic.[34] For Tagore, this represented the substitution of a dictum for an argument. He returned here to his concern for freedom, and his statement is highly significant for realising the meaning of intellectual freedom and for the working of modern democracy. It is worth indicating at this point that his apprehension was perhaps not so much motivated from an innate disquiet with mass politics as is generally understood but with the overriding concern for the working principles of politics itself.

> If nothing but oracles will serve to move us, oracles will have to be manufactured, morning, noon and night, for the sake of urgent needs, and all other voices will be defeated. Those for whom authority is needed in place of reason, will invariably accept despotism in place of freedom. This is like cutting at the root of the tree while pouring water at the top. This is not a new thing I know. We have enough magic in the country, magical revelation, magical healing, and all kinds of divine intervention in mundane affairs. That is exactly why I am so anxious to re-instate reason on its throne. As I have said before, God himself has given the mind sovereignty in the material world. And I say today, that only those will

In argument: considerance of the political 187

be able to get and keep Swaraj in the material world who have realised the dignity of self-reliance and self-mastery in the spiritual world, those whom no temptation, no delusion, can induce to surrender the dignity of intellect into the keeping of others.[35]

Tagore reasoned that the burning of foreign clothes symbolised similarly the predominance of injunction over reason. The overloading of, what was and should have been treated as, a primarily economic question with emotive principle was indicative of a fatal tendency in his countrymen, and the remedying of which should be uppermost in the country's agenda as untruth was not merely materially debilitative but ethically incapacitating. Tagore found himself unable to obey the 'command to burn our foreign clothes', both because it was obligatory on his part to resist what essentially subverted his freedom of reasoning, and he could not burn clothing that did not belong to him but to those who were in critical need of them, and among the needy were included women who were confined in their homes because they did not have sufficient clothes in which to go out of their homes. However, he reiterated that he was a willing follower of the Mahatma in his campaign against the pressing and worldwide domination of the machine over human life. But Tagore cautioned against any action that denoted the acceptance of unreason and illusion, which had in fact been generative of the greatest misfortunes of the country. 'Here is the enemy itself, on whose defeat alone Swaraj within and without can come to us.'[36] He hoped that India would not turn parochial at the hour of its awakening.

Gandhi, in his reply through the *Young India* in October, welcomed from the 'Bard of Shantiniketan' the 'brilliant essay on the present movement' and gave a reasoned argument in support of his own position, fully appreciating at the outset the unquestioned significance of Tagore's warnings of the dangers of slavish followings.

I am quite conscious of the fact that blind surrender to love is more often mischievous than a forced surrender to the lash of a tyrant. There is hope for the slave of the brute, none for that of love. Love is needed to strengthen the weak, love becomes tyrannical when it exacts obedience from an unbeliever. To mutter a *mantra* without knowing its value is unmanly. It is good, therefore, that the Poet has invited all who are slavishly *mimicking* the call of the charkha boldly to declare their revolt. His essay serves as a warning to us all who in our impatience are betrayed into intolerance or even violence against those who differ from us.[37]

188 ❖ In argument: considerance of the political

Gandhi, however, refused to concede that non-cooperation was despotic and affirmed that he had in his political mobilisation appealed consistently to reason and not to emotional loyalty, and that it was his considered belief that the *charkha* had come to be accepted by the country after deliberation and not merely in momentary enthusiasm. Maybe even somewhat provocatively, he exhorted Tagore to take up spinning as it was the need of the times, indicating possibly at what he considered the superfluity of engaging in overfine distinctions on a course of action regarding which he himself had no ethical doubts whatever. Firmly locating the village as the central consideration in any political programme for India, Gandhi traced the recurrent crises in villages to systemic failures of modern government that neglected to understand that famines were generated in villages because there was no employment for the villagers. He was confident that non-cooperation and the spinning wheel represented a remedy on the economic as well as on the cultural plane, and that ensuring of the means of livelihood, which would feed the hungry, was the noblest vocation in a land of the poor such as India. Addressing Tagore's arguments for progressivism, innovation and absolute intellectual freedom, Gandhi responded: 'I do want growth, I do want self-determination, I do want freedom, but I want all this for the soul. I doubt if the steel age is an advance upon the flint age. I am indifferent. It is the evolution of the soul of to which the intellect and all our faculties have to be devoted.'[38] He acknowledged that he did not distinguish between ethics and economics, and considered economics harmful, which were deleterious to either the individual or the nation, and that he felt morally bound to advocate and restore such relegated economic practices as weaving and spinning, as they, were beneficial to the nation. He was obviously emphasising that his own position on individual responsibility was as equally insistent as that of Tagore. To Tagore's crucial objection on burning of clothing that was not one's own and that too in a land severely afflicted by scarcity of clothing, Gandhi's response was unqualifiedly direct:

> I venture to suggest to the Poet, that the clothes I ask him to burn must be and are his. If they had to his knowledge belonged to the poor or the ill-clad, he would long ago have restored to the poor what was theirs. In burning *my* foreign clothes I burn my shame. I must refuse to insult the naked by giving them clothes they do not need, instead of giving them work which they sorely need. I will not commit the sin of becoming their patron, but on learning that I had assisted in impoverishing them, I would

In argument: considerance of the political ❁ **189**

give them neither crumbs nor cast-off clothing, but the best of my food and clothes and associate myself with them in work.[39]

This was similar to his statement of a few months ago in July, wherein he had replied to his critics' 'rebuke regarding the burning of foreign cloth'. Even though the Provincial Congress Committee had made it optional for burning foreign cloth or despatching it to places like Smyrna, Gandhi had felt constrained to unequivocally declare that 'destruction is the best method of dealing with foreign cloth', and that the 'propriety of destruction depends upon the intensity of one's belief in the necessity of discarding foreign cloth'.[40] Gandhi's position here on the value of causal suffering towards superior aims was somewhat affinitive to revolutionary ideologies, and he said that it would be derogatory towards the deprived to think of them as being unsuitable for sacrifice because of their deprivation, and to thereby construe that they were any the less disposed to abnegation as they were otherwise compelled to perpetual situational denial. He had maintained that foreign clothing could not be gifted to the poor, and the objection was so much more potent when the clothing was being discarded as a mark of slavery.

> Should not India's poor have a sense of patriotism? Should they not have feelings about dignity and self-respect in the same manner as we have? I would not have the meanest of us remain without a spirit of true patriotism. Just as we would or at least ought to recoil with horror from giving them rotten food or food we will not eat, so should we feel about giving them foreign cloth. A moment's thought would also show that much of the finery we are throwing away is perfectly useless for the poor . . . But I do not base my argument for destruction upon the uselessness of the clothing discarded. My argument goes much deeper if only it is based upon a sentiment on which alone the noblest in us is and can be reared . . . What harm is there in gaining a million by concealing my faith for a moment? But I am not for the kingdom of the world. For exactly the same reasons we may not use foreign cloth for the poor in India.[41]

In his reply to Tagore's critique on the count of the exclusionary character latent in non-cooperation, Gandhi claimed that far from being an exclusive doctrine, non-cooperation was India's message to the world community and to be so acknowledged must appropriately be accepted and practised first in India. Such a message would also contribute to changing the usual image of India, which in the present was only known as the

190 ❀ In argument: considerance of the political

land of deprivation and disease. The ancient Indian philosophical texts, available in print and in many editions for readership, were neglected by the world as India itself did not practise the principles of living detailed in its own texts. He stated that the present India was different than the vital images presented by the Poet. It was a famished land without the energy to soar on the wings of imagination, and required material nourishment to survive, and not in the shape of charity or benefice but the scope and the means to earn its nourishment. 'For millions it is an eternal vigil or an eternal trance. It is an indescribably painful state which has to be experienced to be realized. I have found it impossible to soothe suffering patients with a song from Kabir. The hungry millions ask for one poem – invigorating food. They cannot be given it. They must earn it. And they can earn only by the sweat of their brow.'[42] In a note a few days later, Gandhi clarified that Tagore himself was not against the principle of spinning but objected to expectation that every Indian must spin as patriotic duty and economic remedy. Gandhi, however, added that given the general enthusiasm for the idea, he was certain that the whole country including Bengal would come to accept the *charkha* as an effective instrument for the elimination of poverty in India.

Tagore's position in the debate was given further and nuanced expression in his play *Muktadhara*,[43] which he wrote in 1922 within a year of *The Call of Truth*, and which centres in a major way on the theme of leadership, with renunciation as the keynote of the play. Kripalani found it 'in a sense a noble tribute to the personality of Gandhi and his campaign of non-violence'.[44] The dialogue of the play offers valuable insights into Tagore's views on leadership; the relationship of Gandhi and his followers; and more importantly, into Gandhi's viewing of his relationship to his followers and of his own duties. Tagore, in his insightful way perhaps, presented a true picture of Gandhi and his mind. Towards the close of the play, the denizens of Uttarkut, unable to find their prince, Abhijit, who has sacrificed himself to the machine so as to break the machine designed by the royal engineer, Bibhuti, which was installed by Abhijit's father, fall on Dhananjaya, binding him with ropes, while saying that he was neither saintly nor their leader. Dhananjaya retorts with a line that is highly suggestive: 'You are fortunate. I know some miserable wretches, who have lost their teacher by following him.'[45] It may be worthwhile to recall that within a few days of the publication of the *Muktadhara*, Tagore, explicating its underlying psychological themes in a letter written to Kalidas Nag, stated that criticism of the 'machine', in this implying perhaps also device, constituted a portion of the play. 'It is a terrible plight to those who hurt people with machine – because the humanness that they kill is also within them – it is their machine that is killing their own inner human being.'[46] Tagore stated that Abhijit could break the machine which hurts life only by giving up his own life, and that in the play the character of Abhijit depicted the tortured inner human being of the torturer, and that he gave up his life to free himself from his own tool. 'And Dhananjaya is the inner human being of him that is being hurt by the machine. He is saying, "I am above damage; hurt does not reach me – I will overcome injury by not being affected, I will ward off the blow by not striking in return." '[47] Tagore wrote that he who was being struck could through that strike upon him pass beyond injury, but the tragedy of the soul was visited on the person who was inflicting hurt, as it was he who would have to undertake the praxis of freedom, it was his responsibility to break with his life the machine. The wielder of the machine, or machinator, desired to be victorious by inflicting injury. The counsellor exhorts the mind to achieve victory by moving beyond the instinct of retaliation, and the human being that was captive to its own machine aspired to freedom from its machine by giving up its own life and to give freedom. 'Bibhuti is the machinator, Dhananjaya is the counsellor, and the human being is Abhijit.'[48] Ira Zepp has described the play as 'Tagore's mature objection to political tyranny in the name of the humanizing energy unleashed by the Buddha'.[49] Zepp's interesting comment on Tagore's reading of the political psychology of non-cooperation and concluding speculation regarding a historical hypothetical is equally relevant for the later discussions between Tagore and Gandhi.

> We are not certain that Gandhi read *Mukta-Dhara*. However, Gandhi already knew of Tagore's sympathetic treatment of *Ahimsa*, including non-cooperation. But it might have been to the Mahatma's advantage to have studied carefully the character of Dhananjaya. In the latter, Tagore's more calculating, detached analysis, especially about leadership of the Indian masses, could have helped Gandhi see the deficiencies in his symbolic leadership and take more seriously what kind of political legacy his *Satyagraha* was bequeathing to India. It is problematical, however, whether the power and communicating skills of the dramatist would have been any more convincing than the conventional prose of the Calcutta verandah.[50]

However intensely sensitive to the issue of idolatrous public followings, Gandhi had throughout the national movement, and particularly

192 ❂ In argument: considerance of the political

during the mobilisations for the non-cooperation and civil disobedience movements, shared with the readers of his journals and his interlocutors across the country his apprehensions regarding the perils of unquestioned acceptance of his proposals. Almost coincidentally with the writing of *Muktadhara*, Gandhi stated in March 1922 in the *Navajivan* that even though he was essentially an optimist, he was cruelly disappointed at the automatic acceptance of his proposals in the Working Committee in its recently concluded meeting in February at Bardoli. This scepticism is striking and wholly uncharacteristic of a masterful leader, who would have been reasonably satisfied at the ideological and programmatic deference that was offered to him by the apex body of the pre-eminent political organisation of the country. He suspected that the committee had accepted his constructive programme without commensurate faith, and he felt 'crushed under the weight of majority opinion'. He conveyed his dislike of shouts of salutation and that he had had to literally block his ears. He reminded his readers that it was with such slogans that mobs had engaged in murder and pillage in Ahmedabad, Viramgam, Amritsar, Chauri Chaura. The members had supported his proposal without inward approval, and this degeneracy of will was portentive for the future maturity of public opinion. The form and circumstances of his individual victory, he felt, had relegated truth and principle:

> How far will the wagon go, having thus to be pushed all the time? My soul testifies that, even if we do not accept non-violence in thought, word and deed, that is, even if we regard non-violence only as a matter of expediency, we should see, as clearly as we do the full moon, that after Chauri Chaura, there can be nothing but the Bardoli resolutions. And yet if the Bardoli resolution has been confirmed [by the A. I. C. C.], it was not on its merits but for my sake. The sailors, who without knowing the directions continue to pilot their ship relying solely on their pilot, will see their ship sink if the latter happens to die or they lose faith in him. It would be dangerous to sail in a ship piloted by such men. Similarly, those who pass Congress resolutions without understanding them will see the ship of the Congress go down.[51] (parenthesis as in the original)

To revert to the issue of individual discretion regarding *charkha*, the Congress passed, two years after *Muktadhara* was written, a resolution instructing members to wear *Khadi* and to submit a stipulated length of cloth woven personally on their *charkha* to the Congress office every month. Gandhi envisaged that this would extend the reach of the *charkha*

In argument: considerance of the political ❖ 193

and, in a sense, transform the Congress leadership. Predictably, Tagore did not agree with such a move. Purportedly, he was among those who were prominently indicted in an article by the venerable Acharya P. C. Ray.[52] Tagore called it 'censure in printer's ink', and responded with *The Cult of Charkha* in *The Modern Review* explaining his position, while recording his agony at having to differ from the Mahatma on a matter of conscience. Tagore commented that the injunction of the Congress on *charkha* and the unqualified enthusiasm for it around the country reflected the habitual and absolute deference by Indians to dictums emanating from morally irreproachable personalities, and such dictums were especially attractive if they held out shortcuts substituting arduous efforts to serious goals. He observed that this was contradicting the natural, since the natural variety of temperament and choice should be sought, as in the advocacy of *charkha* spinning, due to ambition for certain goals kneaded variety 'into a lump of uniformity'. The absence of rebellion to such enforced uniformity caused concern, as it represented the loss of the possibility of alternatives. In this, he was reiterating his concern with the freedom of conscience. 'If in any country we find no such symptom of such rebellion, if we find its people submissively or contentedly prone on the dust, in dumb terror of some master's bludgeon, or blind acceptance of some *guru's* injunction, then indeed should we know that for such a country, *in extremis*, it is high time to mourn.'[53] The caste system, based on the theory of *Karma*, had been one such instrument and reflection of the subservience of the individual conscience by Indians in general to the astute and the holy. 'From age to age they have been assaulted by the strong, defrauded by the cunning, and deluded by the *gurus* to whom their conscience was surrendered.'[54] Acutely conscious as he was of the extremity of his political isolation, he nevertheless asserted his moral right to abide by his conscience and follow his own dissenting path, instinctively feeling that, as with any other ideal, it was among the most vociferous adherents of *charkha*, that there could be counted those who were among the grossest cynics and unbelievers to the principles of austerity and dedication. It were the constitutive defects of the Indian psyche that were the cause of deprivation and poverty, and here he uncharacteristically referred to the depredations of foreign rule, 'Moghul and Pathan', and the capitulation of 'jerry-built edifices of Hindu sovereignty' before the foreign invaders during an age when there had been no dearth of 'thread', only perhaps the communitarian will enliven our life with renewed effort and replenishing ideas. He indicated at our 'lack of vitality, our

194 ❖ In argument: considerance of the political

lack of union'. Tagore, at this point, apparently rejected the notion that modern colonialism had destroyed the self-sufficiency of the pre-colonial economy, and that even during Muslim rule when Indians did not have sovereign power, the villages were at least provided with the bare necessity. It needs to be pointed out that his position on this issue around ten years later, in his writings on traditional political structures, had been directly opposed to this. At the present, however, his line of argument virtually dismissed the virtues of indigenous political systems in India, saying that any apparent qualities of traditional adequacy could only be functional during times that had been lived in insular fashion and were markedly unsustainable when confronted with the infusion of ideas and organisations. The luxury of seclusion was appropriately no longer feasible in the modern world; 'No longer will it be possible to hide ourselves away from commerce with the outside world; moreover such isolation itself would be the greatest of deprivations for us.'[55] He, thus, reinforced his argument against insulating the country from modern science and technology. The predominance of a mechanical device smothered creativity and introduced simplistic ideas of national regeneration. Also, the unilateral imposition of a principle implied silencing dissent; this held an added danger in the case of judgmental error on the part of the leader. The primary aim of introducing the *Charkha*, of enabling the poor to fulfill one basic necessity of life – clothing – was belied as spinning became a mere ritual. It was also artistically disagreeable insofar as the ritual involved the muscles and not the mind: 'That is why in every country, man has looked down on work which involves this kind of mechanical repetition.'[56] It may be mentioned that spinning was not an organic craft like weaving, where patterns reflected the artistry of the weaver. Ruskin had stated that the work done by the head was superior to the work done by the hand. Tagore, however, referred to Carlyle: 'Carlyle may have proclaimed the dignity of labour in his stentorian accents, but still a louder cry has gone up from humanity, age after age, testifying to its indignity.'[57] Regarding the argument that *Charkha* was but one component of regeneration, Tagore argued that the reticence about other means indicated otherwise. He questioned the capacity of the *Charkha* to absorb the multifarious talents of the Indian community.[58] Tagore emphasised that religion was an improbable platform for achieving unity in India, and the fruition of the recent attempts at political unity though practicable would be long in coming. The earliest effective unity in the country could only be possible in the domain of economics, and economic cooperation provided scope for the eradication of the instinct of competition and struggle. Cooperative ventures, in leading to the realisation of the indivisibility of existence, helped to instill values essential for a non-violent world order. 'Co-operation is an ideal, not a mere system, and therefore it can give rise to innumerable methods of its application.'[59] He admitted that recommending as he was a solution, which would involve unflagging devotion and arduous labour on an unimaginably large scale over the years and the inevitable setbacks before nearing accomplishment, he anticipated scepticism. But he was certain that superior aims could never be accomplished through easy methods. Tagore was not against the concept of *Charkha* as a means of fulfilling a basic need; however, it was 'doing harm because of the undue prominence which it has thus usurped'.[60] He frankly confessed the poignancy of his engaging in a debate with Gandhi over fundamental positions:

> It is extremely distasteful to me to have to differ from Mahatma Gandhi in regard to any principle or method. Not that, from a higher standpoint, there is anything wrong in so doing: but my heart shrinks from it. For what could be a greater joy than to join hands in the field of work with one for whom one has such love and reverence? Nothing is more wonderful to me than Mahatmaji's great moral personality. In him divine providence has given us a burning thunderbolt of *shakti*. May this *shakti* give power to India, – not overwhelm her, – that is my prayer! The difference in our standpoints and temperaments has made the Mahatma look upon Rammohan Roy as a pygmy, while I revere him as a giant. The same difference makes the Mahatma's field of work one which my conscience cannot accept as its own. That is a regret which will abide with me always. It is, however, God's will that man's paths of endeavour shall be various, else why these differences of mentality?[61]

Tagore concluded by renewing his stand that howsoever frequently and powerfully his esteem for Gandhi had moved him for enlisting himself as a votary of *charkha*, his conscience had motivated him to desist in ascribing to *charkha* a disproportionate value, and thereby from extending the deflection of the attention of his countrymen from issues that were greater than spinning cloth. He was, however, confident that Gandhi would understand his position and retain his affection as always for him.

Gandhi replied to this critique in *The Poet and the Charkha* in November 1925, acknowledging the unease that Tagore's criticism had generated in some quarters and the desire on their part that he should

196 ❖ In argument: considerance of the political

respond at the earliest possible opportunity. Gandhi, however, took quite a long time to respond, not the least because he desired an intervening break in the dialogue to ensure a dispassionate readership for understanding the two differing points of view. He mentioned that as Tagore had informed him that he might not be pleased at his writing on *charkha*, he had been expecting a critical statement from him. Gandhi pointed out that the variety of views were an essential condition of life and disagreements need not indicate displeasure. 'On the contrary, the frank criticism pleases me. Friends to be friends are not called upon to agree even on most points. Only disagreements must have no sharpness, much less bitterness, about them. And I gratefully admit that there is none about the Poet's criticism.'[62] His reply was brief, and he responded on the counts of uniformity and superficiality, prefacing his argument with a caution that the poet in Tagore had indulged in poetic license and his arguments had involved magnification of the dangers of the advocacy of *charkha*. 'Those therefore who take the Poet's denunciation of the *charkha* literally will be doing an injustice to the Poet and an injury to themselves.'[63] Mildly ironical, he clarified that the excesses of the *charkha* were largely imagined on the part of Tagore, based as his knowledge of the movement was largely on table talk due to a perhaps perfectly understandable unawareness on his part of Gandhi's arguments through the *Young India*. He clarified that he had never, as alleged, advocated the *charkha* to the exclusion of all else: 'So far is this from truth that I have asked no one to abandon his calling, but on the contrary to adorn it by giving every day thirty minutes to spinning as sacrifice for the whole nation . . . If the Poet spun half an hour daily his poetry would gain in richness. For it would then represent the poor man's wants and woes in a more forcible manner than now.'[64] He dismissed the misgiving that *charkha* would impose a barren uniformity upon the country as misplaced and asserted that the *charkha* being adopted as a general mode would no more displace the variety of talents and dispositions than the universally acknowledged essence of human life displacing the multifarious activities of humanity. He asserted that an exploitative Europe may fail to realise the significance and vital action of personal labour as it was presently able to live off other peoples, implying thereupon that it was because of Europe's neglect of the virtue of bodily labour that modernity could be portrayed as inimical to supposedly primitive forms of economic activity. He was relocating the question of labour in a climate that was fast becoming machinist. 'Machinery has its place; it has come to stay. But it must not be allowed to displace the necessary human labour.'[65] The *charkha* could induce people towards cooperation by opening them to the value of physical labour, and cooperative initiatives could be imagined, as had indeed in cases occurred, in rural areas regarding eradication of malaria, sanitation, communitarian adjudication and other economic and civic activities. Gandhi specified that he did not intend to respond extensively to Tagore's critique as their positions were not diametrically opposite, and as regards their positional similarity 'there is nothing in the Poet's argument that I cannot endorse and still maintain my position regarding the *charkha*. The many things about the *charkha* which he has ridiculed I have never said'.[66] Gandhi, however, entered a note of wounded sentiment regarding Tagore's riposte on his oft-mentioned comment on Rammohan Roy, to which we will return presently in slightly more detail. At this point, a reference to Gandhi's response becomes necessary. Gandhi stated: 'One thing, and one thing only, has hurt me, the Poet's belief, again picked up from table talk, that I look upon Ram Mohun Roy as a "pygmy". Well, I have never anywhere described that great reformer as a pygmy much less regarded him as such. He is to me as much a giant as he is to the Poet.' Gandhi mentioned that he had only once made public reference to Rammohun, and in the context of Western education wherein he referred to the easy possibility of high cultural accomplishment without the advantage of Western education, and mentioned Roy as a pygmy before the authors of the *Upanishads*. He maintained that such comparison as he had made between great personalities was not a disparagement but an appreciation. 'If I adore the Poet as he knows, I do in spite of differences between us. I am not likely to disparage the greatness of the man who made the great reform movement of Bengal possible and of which the Poet is one of the finest fruits.'[67]

Before studying his position on Rammohun, it might be appropriate to revisit the outline of Gandhi's stated views on *charkha* since, in what tells us both the importance of the charkha and the layers of his relationship with and consideration for Tagore. He continued on occasions to explain, even after Tagore's passing away, the nuances of the similarity of Tagore's and his position on *charkha*. Before the above mentioned statement of November, Gandhi had shared in January with his readers the approbation for *charkha* by the elder brother of Rabindranath, Dwijendranath, whom Gandhi in deep regard called *Boro Dada* (elder brother). As is evident in Gandhi's note, Dwijendranath was among his staunchest allies. 'Baro Dada Dwijendranath Tagore as the reader knows has a weakness for me.

198 ❖ In argument: considerance of the political

Almost everything I say or do appeals to him with an irresistible force. The reader is therefore entitled to discount his approval of my ideas and schemes. But he cannot but admire Baro Dada's zeal and devotion for his country which make him keep in touch with the current thought in our politics.'[68] Dwijendranath had referred to the *charkha* as a visionary scheme and had said that even though it might appear improbable to less insightful people, the *charkha* could be the single most important means of advancing the cause of India's economic freedom. On 9 January, Gandhi, to college students in Bhavnagar, likened the *charkha* to any initially bitter savoured remedy that as enjoined in the *Gita* provides immortality and offered it as the greatest *yajna* (sacrifice) in contemporary times for bringing peace and spiritual value to a student's life.[69] Some months earlier, he had responded in detail to M.N. Roy's criticism of spinning as a waste of energy, and his argument that the leisure of the peasantry that was sought to be otherwise occupied by their spinning was sorely needed for their rest and recuperation. Gandhi's tone had been implicitly different from that in his responses to Tagore: 'It appears to me that the critic has little if any experience of the peasantry in India. Nor has he been able to picture to himself the way charkha would work, and indeed is working today.'[70] Peasantry throughout the world depended on a subsidiary income from leisure time to make their ends meet, and in India particularly, women traditionally spun cotton to earn and occupy themselves. The experiment of *charkha* could not be evaluated merely from the failure of the contemporary workers, and experiences from certain parts of the country even now demonstrated the resilience of the idea, and such instances held concrete hopes for a chronically famine-afflicted country such as India, especially in parts like Orissa where hunger and unemployment had resulted in beggary as practice among the peasantry. Regarding Roy's suggestion for improved agriculture, Gandhi explained that *charkha* was not exclusive of agricultural innovation and would in all possibility be the harbinger of progress in a sphere of economy which was hampered by government neglect and peasant apathy. He enumerated eleven points of merit for the charkha in this respect. 'If there is one activity in which all is gain and no loss, it is hand-spinning.'[71] Gandhi, in a subsequent writing a few months later, shared a formative experience he underwent in Puri in witnessing, on the one hand, a group of children from famine-stricken families in an orphanage who were now energised and well and happily engaged in crafts like spinning, weaving, basket making; and on the other, hundreds of emaciated and torpid adults who appeared without hope and life and somehow just managed to eat the food that was charitably distributed among them. They did not want to work and apparently prepared to die in that state. 'There is on the face of earth no other country that has the problem India has, of chronic starvation and slow death – a process of dehumanization. The solution must therefore be original.'[72] Institutional and behavioural solutions would require years to activate and only the spinning wheel represented something of an immediate answer to the problem, wherein educated and well-provided sections will have to in practice demonstrate the value of spinning. This would, in turn, require a transcending of class inhibitions and identification with deprived and demoralised compatriots: 'An ocular and sincere demonstration by thousands who need not spin for themselves cannot fail to move these starving men and women to do likewise.'[73] Four years later, Gandhi advanced into exploring possibilities of principled partnership with domestic industry in extending the scope of *charkha* and boycott, notwithstanding apprehensions by many of his colleagues in the spinning movement that he was 'coquetting' with mill owners. Characteristically, he was prepared to go alone, demonstrating his principled pragmatism. Gandhi's explanation for this move both answer old questions of profiting mill owners through boycott and indicate issues of programmatic partnership between entrepreneurial ability and social conscience. The mills could augment the production of *khadi* for those who were not self-spinners, while the rural demand could be met by self-production. It could hopefully extend into effecting sartorial preferences in favour of *khadi*, provided the *khadi* workers were prepared to dedicate themselves completely to this aim. 'I have "coquetted" with mill-owners and discussed the possibility of immediate boycott of foreign cloth in association with them, in order to show that if they mean it they can give themselves the privilege of serving the nation at the same time that they serve themselves.'[74] He saw the weaving of *khadi* as an 'empirical science' which crucially had an ethical imperative. Similar to the textile mills, which depended and had developed a sophisticated science of manufacturing cloth, *khadi* would need an exact science of production extending from the gathering of cotton to the weaving of cloth, and in this *khadi* workers would need more attention to even those details which were usually not included in the science of mill production, such as the ecological sensitivity to the maximal utilisation of the entire process from gathering to ginning. He pointed out that unlike the mills which felt no need to utilise the remains of the ginned seeds, *khadi* workers would

200 ❋ In argument: considerance of the political

need to exercise utmost caution in even these and similar aspects, such as ensuring the retention of organic residue in the cotton seeds, which would be used for oil extraction and then for cattle fodder. It was of the utmost significance for *khadi* workers to be ever mindful that *khadi* was a national service and maintain a strict work ethic even in the environment of the *khadi* units from which all structures of punitive discipline were entirely absent. The ideal *khadi* worker should aspire to cherish his calling similar to the dedication and passion that a J. C. Bose brought to his scientific pursuit which was without any kind of desire for external reward, save that for acquiring of knowledge and the satisfaction of performing a duty, and the *khadi* worker with knowledge of the science of *khadi* and with devotion would, too, derive a cognate happiness that was of a divine origin. However, Gandhi insisted that sheer knowledge would not be enough to accomplish the mission of *khadi*:

> Mere knowledge would be useful in mills only. We need character in addition to this knowledge. You have come here not for earning your livelihood but with a desire to serve, to dedicate your life to the cause of khadi, and for this character will be very essential. How will you go among the people without character? Who will accept your service? Nobody bothers about the character of people working in the mills but everybody will enquire about your character. You have to go to the people as servants, not as tyrants. If possible, you have to be labourers living in their midst. For doing this a disciplined life is needed.[75]

Over the years, the national movement developed through events and situations, and Gandhi increasingly located social initiatives in the centre of his political programme. Expectedly, this was not received uncomplicatedly by congressmen, and Gandhi publicly shared his introspection on the role of his social agenda in the movement for *Swaraj*. By the close of 1939, amidst intimations of a decisive convergence of circumstances regarding the future direction of the freedom movement, he stated: 'I swear by the old constructive programme of communal unity, removal of untouchability and the charkha.'[76] For Gandhi, non-violence could not sustain without communal amity and the eradication of untouchability, and the *charkha* and its allied programmes involving the village crafts were of central importance in the upliftment of the villages. The indifference of the congressmen to *charkha* signified either that they totally lacked any inclination for non-violence or that Gandhi himself was entirely

In argument: considerance of the political ❧ 201

ignorant of the working of non-violence. It is an indication of his core identification with these themes and that this unsure attitude of the Congress towards his social initiatives was causing a deep unease in him that Gandhi felt it necessary at this stage to unequivocally declare: 'If my love of the charkha is a weakness in me, it is radical as to make me unfit as a general. The wheel is bound up with my scheme of swaraj, indeed with life itself. All India should know my credentials on the eve of what can become the last and decisive battle for swaraj.'[77] Soon after, he conveyed to Barin Ghosh (the younger brother of the former revolutionary and now recluse Aurobindo) that leadership entailed not merely the accomplishment of certain political ends but also the convincement of people as to the integrity of the political cause: 'The difference about the charkha is not immaterial. My whole life is bound up with it. If you cannot support it, you cannot whole-heartedly support non-violence. And of what use am I without non-violence?'[78] About a year later, it was with his growing doubts about the *charkha*'s acceptance within the Congress that Gandhi continued with explaining that the humble spinning wheel was for him not a whimsical obsession but the central link with a human instinct for equanimity as well as the epitome of non-violence:

> The spinning wheel is a symbol of non-violence for me. The wheel as such is lifeless, but when I invest it with symbolism it becomes a living thing for me. Its sound, if it is musical, is in tune with non-violence. If it is unmusical, it is not in tune with it, for it indicates carelessness on my part. The steel spindle one can use as a deadly weapon, but we have put it there for the best possible use. So we have to be meticulously careful about every part of the wheel. Then and only then will it produce fine music and spinning will be a true sacrificial act.[79]

In 1944, Gandhi, during a meeting of the *Charkha Sangh* held after two years of governmental persecution of the *Sangh*, traced the inception and development of the *charkha* to outline its indispensability for the country and to therefore impress upon the significance of the *Charkha Sangh* to its members. He had contemplated on the correctives required for the programme that had become necessary, insofar as he had until now allowed the mechanics of spinning to disproportionately dominate the outlook of the *Sangh* over the vision and the spirit of the movement. He admitted that his reflection on the many dimensions of the programme of *charkha* had been inadequate. But with his experience over the years,

202 ❧ In argument: considerance of the political

and since his recent stay in jail when he had thought intensively on the subject, he was now better placed for making a realistic assessment and conceptualise the future of the *Sangh*. 'The fault is not yours but mine and when I say this, it is not so much to blame you, but to whip up your intelligence and my own. We plied the charkha but mechanically, not intelligently. Had you yourselves appreciated the full significance of the charkha, you would have given it the same importance as I do. It also has political significance. It has however no place in the dishonest game of politics. More than any other thing it is the charkha that stands for clean, noble politics.'[80] The real import of the *charkha* had eluded the *khadi* workers, as also the larger nation, because in spite of their sacrifices offered in the course of the national movement Indians in general had failed to become non-violent, and thus failed to grasp the true meaning of spinning. They were, therewith, unable to realise the full scope of the movement for *khadi*. This situation was especially disappointing at a point when the achieving of political freedom was assured, was possible 'perhaps sooner than we believe'. Gandhi urged the members to consider his proposal to disband the *Sangh* and distribute its properties, so that it could continue not as a resourced organisation but as an ideal in the houses across the villages of India and also become a source of employment and discourage migration to the cities. 'The problems of Hindu–Muslim differences, untouchability, conflicts, misunderstandings and rivalries will melt away. This is the real function of the Sangh. We have to live and die for it.'[81] This aim was based in the universal dignity of labour and the idea of such a dissemination of physical labour as manifested in the *charkha* underlay the philosophy of new education or *Nai Talim*. A complete faith in *charkha* was required for this, and this faith along with the innate vastness of the idea would endure the disbanding of the *Sangh*, and with it dissipate the most appalling fears of possible persecution from the government. 'If they want to liquidate us we shall submit to it cheerfully. And what does it matter if a few million of us are done away with? An ocean does not dry up if a few drops evaporate.'[82] Within a couple of days, there was a marked intensification in Gandhi's arguments for the *charkha*. He proceeded to a decisive position regarding the future of the *Charkha Sangh*, asking its members to evidence principled adherence to the *charkha*. He emphasised that the *charkha* had only been accepted by the Congress for its deference to him, and that with the prevalent attitude towards it he had no answer to the socialist critique of the idea. The *charkha*, producing in the past muslin for the rich, so far a tool of oppression and slave labour in the history of India and reduced to a symbol of 'poverty, helplessness, injustice and forced labour', had been sought to be transformed by him as the symbol of 'mighty non-violent strength, of the new social order and of the new economy'. 'We want to change history. And I want to do it through you.'[83] He emphasised that believing in the *charkha* as a realiser of non-violence would require a different kind of perception on the part of his followers wherein they would 'approach it with a heart like [him]'. In this, he demonstrates a complete awareness of Tagore's point regarding the facilitating of attitudinal change as being the aim of leadership and was himself introducing once again the issue of the psychology of politics, not, it should be mentioned, to be used as a stratagem but as a possibility of changing the character of politics itself. He served an ultimatum to the *Sangh* to reconstitute both their perception and priorities, and thus follow him in belief and practice or else renounce their association with him, but not to fake understanding and continue under his leadership as with an illusion. 'There are a thousand fields in which we can serve the country. Why then remain in charkha work and sail under false colours. Please do not therefore remain under an illusion. Let me go my way alone. But if it were found that I was myself suffering from an illusion and that my belief in charkha was mere idol-worship, either you may burn me to ashes with the wood of the charkha, or I myself would set fire to the charkha with my bare hands.'[84] He likened the disbanding of the *Sangh*, in this case, to the dispelling of a mist by the sun. He hoped that the remaining few volunteers of the *charkha* would be sincere believers and would become effective agents of change. He offered his considered thinking on the *charkha* to those who were confident of their faith in *charkha*, and with finality invited those who had really understood his philosophy of *charkha* to formally pledge themselves to faith such as he deemed necessary. 'Those of you who want to remain with me give me in writing that you regard the charkha from today as the emblem of non-violence. You have to make your decision today. If you do not or cannot regard the charkha as the emblem of non-violence and yet remain with me, then you will thereby put yourself in an awkward plight and also drag me down with you.'[85]

However, once again, his followers were to disappoint him. With his characteristic honesty of perception and position, Gandhi recognised facts as they presented themselves to him and was beginning to conclusively determine the abiding difficulties of creating any principled and

204 ❄ In argument: considerance of the political

enduring public activity, and he acknowledged within a month's time that the charkha had not really been used in the way he had envisaged:

> I first introduced khadi and only later studied its implications and experimented with it. I find that I have been deceiving myself. What I gave to the people was money but not the real substance – self-reliance. I gave money in the form of wages and assured them that it contained *Swaraj*. People took me at my word and believed me, and continue to believe me. But I have now my own misgivings as to how far such *Khadi* can lead to *Swaraj*. I am afraid that *Khadi* has no future if we continue it as today.[86]

Unfortunately, in 1925, Mahatma had responded to Tagore's remonstrance with an appeal to relinquish his doubts and spin like others, as it was the call of the times. Tagore had persisted with his disagreement, although it was 'extremely distasteful to [him] to have to differ from Mahatma Gandhi in regard to any matter of principle or method'.[87] He had noticed the hypocritical attitude of many a supporter of *Charkha*, which Gandhi tragically perceived later, and terming it a great wrong to the country appealed to his supporters: 'Not to deceive me in the evening of my life.' The fact, however, remains that in their basic approach the two men were in broad agreement, but their experience of *Swadeshi* and boycott was dissimilar. Their reluctance to engage in a debate which threatened to become unpleasant, perhaps limited the scope of dialogue on *Charkha*. It may do appear to some that in this debate, they occasionally fail to address each other and some of the issues raised were not adequately examined in their immediate context. However, Gandhi returns to Tagore's interrogation of the *charkha* even years after the debate and many of his positions indicate a broad empathy with Tagore's concerns. In his statements to the *Charkha Sangh* in the years around 1944, wherein he notes the perils of being accompanied by an unintelligent political community, Gandhi resembles so much like Dhanajaya admonishing his followers in *Muktadhara*. But it can hardly be over-emphasised that the issues in their debate over non-cooperation and *charkha* are intrinsic to the central concerns of their political thought which was, equally for both, the exploring of the means to institute ethics and truth as the first principles of political philosophy and action.

Interestingly, Tagore refused to endorse any relaxation in literary canon under accusations of elitism and in the pretext of people's culture. Being criticised since a couple of decades for being insufficiently sensitive towards mass literary sensibility, he retorted in a series of writings around the 1920s that the pursuit of literature was autonomous and not amenable to any criteria other than that of aesthetic bliss. The finest literature was universally salutary across social classes, and hopefully the common literary audience of the future would be able to appreciate what it had been unable to understand in the present. The prince and the peasant alike needed to apply themselves to deserving aesthetic delight, although the former had leisure to do so, whereas the latter had none. But this argument pertained to social systems, albeit necessitating appropriate social remedy. He felt that the true artist, while creating *rasa* (aesthetic impressions), was aware of only the categories of truth and excellence and did not recognise anything else. Tagore never believed that the aristocracy and the proletariat should be offered different qualities of artistic nourishment. Shakespeare might, in prevalent hearsay, be regarded as a public poet, but *Hamlet* was hardly a play appealing to common tastes. Similarly, notwithstanding the habitual approbation of Kalidas as a poet by the general public, a recital of his *Meghdoot* would probably be somewhat of an oppressive experience to an uninitiated village audience, Tagore opined. *Mehgdoot* was, in fact, equally intended for the common village audience, but that they should be enabled to artistically deserve and savour it was the responsibility of who had been positioned above the common public. Artificiality was undesirable for all art, but the proposition that genuineness consisted only in its being effortlessly understandable to everybody, and that anything requiring a refinement of the mind for its understanding was artificial, was for Tagore not worthy of deference. He believed that only a broad disrespect towards the people was evinced from the exclusion of the general public from the metaphorical aesthetic banquet where, like the servitors in the traditional feasts given by the *zamindars*, the populace were relegated to the outer courtyard and offered simply curd and parched rice, while the choicest delicacies were saved for those who were considered to be respectable.[88]

Tagore's position on art is relatable to his views regarding mass participation in politics, insofar as he was opposed to expedient circumvention of difficult questions during large-scale political mobilisations. Familiar arguments of public unpreparedness or eagerness cut no ice with him. He was, therefore, markedly reserved in his attitude to mass campaigns, such as *Swadeshi* and the non-cooperation movement, preferring a prior preparation of public agency against ethical and cognitive lapses such as violence. Gandhi, with an evident and complete similarity of position on ethical preparation, travelled beyond Tagore's reading of the present

206 ❧ In argument: considerance of the political

mental state of the political community. He regarded public preparation as subject to both mobility and versatility, and not necessarily because of this also prone to ethical leniency. For Gandhi, preparation and mobilisation were joined in complementarity and were well served by political exigence.

However, even with the distinctions that may be evident in their respective viewpoints on art and culture, a study of the argument between Gandhi and Tagore perhaps makes it fairly clear that some of their expressed differences of opinion regarding concepts and individuals, including those which have been frequently highlighted by critics, are incidental and essentially peripheral to their concerns and their dialogue.

One such peripheral but public difference of opinion occurred between them regarding Raja Rammohun Roy, with a rather sharp correspondence on the issue. Gandhi, earlier to his controversial reference to Rammohun in Cuttack in March 1921, had while writing a character sketch on the great reformer educationist Ishwar Chandra Vidyasagar in the *Indian Opinion* in 1909 referred to Rammohun appreciatively as a one of the 'heroic' reformers of Bengal. This sketch was one of a series of morally instructive writings on the lives of 'good men and women', the emulation of whom he thought to be desirable among the young generation, and notwithstanding this reference to Rammohun, the absence in this series of a sketch devoted entirely to him has puzzled scholars: 'Why he did not include Rammohun among these "good men" it is difficult to say.'[89] Admittedly, the omission of a separate article on Roy, along with a mention of his contribution with Vidyasagar, makes apparent both the facts that Gandhi was undoubtedly more reverential to the latter even when he remained respectful towards the former. Kripalani's speculation on the omission reflects the difficult nature of even scholarly perception regarding the Gandhi–Tagore relationship. It should be mentioned that Gandhi's reference to Rammohun during a public meeting in Cuttack was in a response to a sceptical comment to him, which pointedly questioned the core belief of Gandhi that the possibilities of Western education in reforming and modernising India were rather limited. One of his auditors had commented: 'English education has gone to the bottom of our national life, brought about unity among various Indian peoples and it can abolish untouchability. So is it an extra evil? Are not Tilak, Ram Mohan Roy, yourself products of English education?'[90] Gandhi's response was sharp and perhaps all the more so because, as he said, this was a 'representative view' in a large section of the people and was an active psychological obstacle to the national movement. 'We must conquer the battle of swaraj

In argument: considerance of the political   ❖   207

by conquering this sort of wilful ignorance and prejudice of our country-men and of Englishmen.'[91] He called the prevailing system of education an 'unmitigated evil', for the destruction of which he had deployed his strongest effort and he did not see India as having derived any advantage from it. 'The present system enslaves us without allowing a discriminat-ing use of English literature. My friend has cited the case of Tilak, Ram Mohan and myself. Leave aside my case; I am a miserable pigmy. Tilak and Ram Mohan would have been far greater men if they had not had the contagion of English learning.'[92] He called Rammohun and Tilak as pygmies compared to saints such as Chaitanya, Shanker, Kabir and Nanak. He referred to instances of martyrdom in Indian history and said that Western education by itself had been unable to generate such dedication as witnessed in Indians, who have been without the disadvantages that hampered those who had received Western education. He lamented his lack of knowledge of Sanskrit and Hindustani, the enablement of which would have otherwise given him access to epistemic resources so essential to any Indian. English education had, in reality, loaded the Indian society with weakness and curbed the natural flow of sensitivity and intellect and had tremendous potentialities of lasting enslavement. He, however, declared 'I highly revere Tilak and Ram Mohan. It is my conviction that if Ram Mohan and Tilak had not received this education but had their natural training they would have done greater things like Chaitanya.'[93] Some weeks later, explaining his censure of English education and pre-sumably also that of Tilak and Rammohun, he wrote in appreciation of the contribution made by them in adverse circumstances and this time and even though he maintained that to them English education was a disadvantage and that he believed personalities such as Chaitanya, Kabir, Shivaji were greater men, he desisted from using the term pygmy in their connection. 'Ram Mohan Rai would have been a greater reformer and Lokmanya Tilak would have been a greater scholar, if they had not to start with the handicap of having to think in English and transmit their thoughts chiefly in English. Their effect on their people, marvellous as it was, would have been greater if they had been brought up under a less unnatural system.'[94] He attempted to disabuse his readers of the illusion that the ideas of liberty could have been introduced to the Indian mind only by English education, saying that he considered the education system to be the most serious reflection of the misgovernance of the country by England and which would have the more lasting ill effects if not begun to be remedied at the earliest possibility. The official educational policy

208 ❀ In argument: considerance of the political

evidenced that the tendency of the colonial government has been to 'dwarf the Indian body, mind, and soul'. Clarifying that the aim of his comparison of Roy and Tilak with some other great personalities had not been an indication of disrespect on his part, Gandhi extolled the value of their contribution to Indian life: 'I know that comparisons are odious. All are equally great in their own way. But judged by the results, the effect of Ram Mohan and Tilak on the masses is not so permanent or far-reaching as that of the others more fortunately born. Judged by the obstacles they had to surmount, they were giants, and both would have been greater in achieving results, if they had not been handicapped by the system under which they received their training. I refuse to believe that the Raja and the Lokmanya could not have thought the thoughts they did without a knowledge of the English language.'[95] Critics have normally been unsparing to Gandhi over his controversial reference, with an obviously unnecessary and unhappy choice of word, regarding Rammohun. Krishna Kripalani, who has been a secretary of Tagore and a biographer of both Tagore and Gandhi, has even accused Gandhi of economising with the truth: 'The Mahatma was no doubt a votary of truth. But his truth had many angles and many facets, and he saw at any time what he chose to see. Like Nelson he had no compunction in putting the telescope on the blind eye. The utterances relating to Rammohun have many contradictions and half truths, and a half truth can be as misleading as an untruth.'[96] The impression is thus heavily inclined against Gandhi for allegedly indulging in slanted argument for scoring a political point, and that any reasonable account of Rammohun's career will dispel any notion of an anti-pathetical viewing, on his part, of Sanskrit and the vernaculars regarding the future scheme of education in India. Critics have also identified, as has been hinted earlier, the significant similarity in the educational outlook of Gandhi and Tagore:

> In hindsight, the Mahatma's critique and the subsequent backtracking seem quite unnecessary, for, over the question of the alienating effects of Western education, there is really little to separate Gandhi from Tagore. Indeed, in his autobiographical fragment (*Jeebonsmriti*, 1912), Rabindranath had observed that Western education had acted like a heady intoxicant which excited the mind without also producing enduring convictions that could meaningfully change people's lives. Both Gandhi and Tagore bemoaned the fact that this education had led the new intelligentsia to look outside itself for strength and inspiration, rather than inward at its own intellectual and cultural resources.[97]

In argument: considerance of the political   ❧   209

It is apparently perplexing why Gandhi chose to ignore the well-known facts regarding Rammohun's early education and his proficiency and writings in classical languages and some of the Indian vernaculars. It is appropriate to mention at this point that in addition to his well-known writings in the classical languages, Rammohun was a versatile author in the vernacular and significantly for the discussion on cultural nativity is credited with the authorship of some of the earliest Hindi writings.[98] It is in this context that Sen has observed: 'Historically speaking too, Gandhi's critique appears to have suffered from certain apprehensions. First, the Mahatma erred in assuming that his advocacy of the English language and Western-style institutions precluded Rammohun Roy from using the vernacular. Quite to the contrary, for it is now established that Roy consciously used the vernacular to democratize knowledge that had hitherto been the captive of upper-caste society. In the process, he had hitherto contributed meaningfully to the development of modern Bengali prose.'[99] It was perhaps the outcome of the political climate of the times and the deliberate, and misplaced, pointedness of the question addressed to Gandhi that led him to take an absolute position in Cuttack, as it was the intensity of political discourse that caused his repeated affirmation of his respect for Rammohun's greatness and contribution to be obscured among the allegations of angular statement. That Rammohun was a great venerator of tradition and Indian philosophy and learning is recorded and incontestable. It might, therefore, be helpful towards understanding Gandhi's comment on Rammohun's predominant advocacy of Western education, to locate Rammohun's forceful petition to Governor General Amherst in 1821 in the context of the intense aspiration of the times for the modernisation and uplift of Indian society and its unshackling from the constraints of aged doctrines. Rammohun's appeal to Amherst, arguably this petition that must have provoked Gandhi to include him with such conviction in the genealogy of Western education in India, was singular in its advocacy against governmental standardisation of traditional education, particularly Sanskrit and philosophy:

> The Sanscrit language, so difficult that almost a life time is necessary for its acquisition, is well known to have been for ages a lamentable check to the diffusion of knowledge, and the learning concealed under this almost impervious veil, is far from sufficient to reward the labour of acquiring it. But if it were thought necessary to perpetuate this language for the sake of the portion of valuable information it contains, this might be more easily

210 ❖ In argument: considerance of the political

accomplished by other means than the establishment of a new Sanscrit college; for there have been always and are now numerous professors of Sanscrit in the different parts of the country engaged in teaching this language, as well as the other branches of literature which are to be the object of the seminary. Therefore their more diligent cultivation, if desirable, would be effectually promoted, by holding out premiums and granting certain allowances to their most eminent professors, who have already undertaken on their own account to teach them, and would by such rewards be stimulated to still greater exertion.[100]

Rammohun proceeded to reject any contemporary general virtue in the study of Indian philosophy, which he thought to be most unhelpful for instituting a modern society for which he wholly preferred English instruction and traced English improvement directly to the discarding of medieval scholastic philosophy for the progressive Baconian philosophy. 'In the same manner the Sanscrit system of education would be the best calculated to keep this country in darkness, if such had been the policy of British legislature.'[101] Rammohun made a noticeable exception to the specialised study of classical language and philosophy in his general criticism of traditional education. His criticism of classical philosophy, in general, followed surprisingly his mastery of the Sanskrit language and extensive conversancy with the classical texts that included his writing of the *Vedantasara*, a Sanskrit edition of the *Brahmasutras*, a Bengali version of the *Atmanatmaviveka* and, arguably, the *Vedanatagrantha*. These works were not, however, uncritically accepted by the contemporary cognoscenti. Robertson, in his erudite analysis of Rammohun's religious thought, has referred to his 'controversial career as an interpreter of the vedanta'.[102] It is noticeable – while being descriptive of the colonial context of the cultural interaction between East and West – that in the changing world Rammohun, the harbinger of the Indian Renaissance, did not consider classical learning to be a normally possible means for general 'improvement', even though it is generally acknowledged that 'Sanskrit was necessarily a part of the intellectual life of those who created the nineteenth century Indian Renaissance'.[103] It can be said that his view of the possibilities of socio-economic improvement did not entail a personal assessment of the value of classical learning. It might also be easily demonstrable that beginning his effort of national uplift in the early days of the colonial situation in India, and even while contributing to the creation of a modern indigenous political consciousness, Rammohun, as with many others of his generation, did not actively seek to effect

In argument: considerance of the political ❖ **211**

immediately a radical change, whereas Gandhi was committed not only to the political liberation of India, but equally to enact a comprehensive change in the climate of the Indian mind. Tagore's commitment was similar. The urgency of their situation occasionally imperated on the reformers a choice of terms that signalled a break within their views, whereas the undertone had all along been one of detectable convergence.

Truth and democracy

A discussion on the Gandhi–Tagore debate naturally confronts the possibility of any degree of bitterness between the two, because of the level of their disagreements regarding basic principles of policy, and the feeling that the warmth and veneration that otherwise characterised their relations may not have been entirely genuine and that there could have been effectively an element of hypocrisy in their professed regard for each other. The detailed discussion of their debate as above perhaps helps to dispel any possibility of insincerity in their respect and affection for each other. Zepp has designated the Gandhi–Tagore differences over non-cooperation as a 'lover's quarrel': '[b]oth words are to be emphasised, but "love" is the stronger and enduring term' (parenthesis as in the original).[104] Rolland's letter, written on 19 October 1925, to Kalidas Nag is an insightful portrayal of the sincerity of Gandhi and Tagore towards their own ideals, which compelled disagreements in their intimate friendship and which make the considerable differences testamental of the richness and the moral quality of their imagination of modern India. Rolland writes of the sadness and solitude of Tagore's mental seclusion from Gandhi concerning the political movement of the times. 'I understand him; they each have their own mission, and neither of them can or may give it up. That of Tagore is loftier and more remote; it is aimed at the soaring human spirit, beyond all barriers of classes, nations and centuries. That of Gandhi seeks to adapt itself to the passing necessities of one people and one age (yet without renouncing for himself and his Ashram disciple the strict observance of an intransigent faith). It is natural that this mixture of holiness and politics should often shock you. (In reality it is not a *mixture*, but a *juxtaposition* of these two different "orders".)'[105] Rolland argues that this juxtaposition is not uniquely incongruent in human history and some of the greatest saints in the West, such as St. Benedict, St. Theresa and St. Francis of Assisi, were inspired to combine the two missions.

212 ❖ In argument: considerance of the political

Individuals such as Tagore and Rolland himself were unable to do so, as their 'mission' was more in the realm of contemplation and knowledge than in that of thought and action, and Rolland referred emotively to Pascal's definition of the latter mission as the 'order of charity', mentioning at the same time that the order of knowledge was in the case of the evolved souls the 'supreme charity'.

> But we should be grateful to the saints who are capable of other missions, less pure and more stained with concessions to human weakness, for without them, to what depths would human weakness fall! It needs an ideal within its reach, an ideal whose practice is easy and workaday, an ideal which can be achieved by men's hands (for most men think only with their bodies, in action). It is in this sense that I believe Gandhi's charkha useful (in the religious sense) despite everything, like the more or less mechanical exercises of the monastic orders. The supreme ideal of man is Liberty. But there is a whole hierarchy of Liberty (as in living souls), from the infinitely small which is hardly distinct form automatism, to the limitless and formless liberty of the victorious Buddha. Life is of infinite richness and diversity; none of us can reduce it to a unity.[106]

That the relationship, founded as it was on the reverence for the truthfulness of the other, endured perfectly the divergence of views is avowedly communicated in this exchange during a time of mutual disagreement, as Tagore wrote to Gandhi on 27 December 1925: 'You have my assurance that even if you ever hit me hard in the cause of what you think as truth our personal relationship based upon mutual respect will bear that strain and will remain uninjured.'[107] Gandhi acknowledged this letter in kindred spirit: 'I am thankful for your sweet letter. It has given me much relief.'[108]

The debate also has explicit significance for the meaning of democratic imaginings of the nation. It might be useful for a history of ideas to refer to a representative comment on the genealogy of the idea of the nation as perceived with regard to the emerging nationalities of what has been rather inadequately termed as the 'Third World'. Edward Said, a theorist whose ideas regarding evaluations of identities in the colonial world have had enormous influence, and not only in the West but also in the erstwhile colonial world itself, offered a controversial definition of the nationalistic idea in India. According to Said: 'In India, for example, the Congress party was organized in 1880 and by the turn of the century had convinced the Indian elite that only by supporting the *Indian* languages,

In argument: considerance of the political ☀ 213

and commerce could political freedom come; these are ours and ours alone, runs the argument, and only by supporting our world against *theirs* – note the us-versus-them construction here – can we finally stand on our own.'[109] The Gandhi–Tagore debate contradistinguishes the plurality and inclusivity of Indian nationalism from the axiomatic and motivational animus that is embedded in the definition of Indian nationalism in the formulation of Edward Said.

As indicated earlier in this study, the issue of the imagining of an ethical state is intrinsically linked to the necessity of truthfulness in politics. Michel Foucault has so valuably demonstrated, in the context of ancient Athens, the crucial importance of the notion of *parrhēsia*, which he translates as truth telling, in the functioning of democracy. Foucault has underlined and described the relationship that is essential to make *parrhēsia* possible in a society, and this can be typified by such conversation between two individuals.

> Thus the true game of *parrhēsia* will be established on the basis of this kind of pact which means that if the parrhesiast demonstrates his courage by telling the truth despite and regardless of everything, the person to whom this *parrhēsia* is addressed will have to demonstrate his greatness of soul by accepting being told the truth. This kind of pact, between the person who takes the risk of telling the truth and the person who agrees to listen to it, is at the heart of what could be called the parrhesiastic game. So, in two words, *parrhēsia* is the courage of truth in the person who speaks and who, regardless of everything, takes the risk of telling the whole truth of what he thinks, but it is also the interlocutor's courage in agreeing to accept the hurtful truth that he hears.[110]

The correspondence between Tagore and Gandhi testifies to their willingness to speak the truth for what they thought were the first principles of politics – ethics and truth. Foucalt has distinguished between mere rhetoric, which he feels imposes a constraining bond between the partners in dialogue, and truth telling which requires very different conditions of correspondence. '*Parrhēsia*, on the other hand, involves a strong and constitutive bond between the person speaking and what he says, and, through the effect of the truth, of the injuries of truth, it opens up the possibility of the bond between the person speaking and the person to whom he has spoken being broken . . . The parrhesiast, on the contrary [to the rhetorician], is the courageous teller of a truth by which he puts himself and his relationship with the other at risk.'[111]

214 ❖ In argument: considerance of the political

Judging by what they had to say to each other, and how each received what was said between them, the debate between Gandhi and Tagore signifies their devotion to truth and democratical values and also the scope for future theoretical possibilities regarding ethical politics that is contained in the conversation.

❁

Notes

1. Alasdair MacIntyre, *A Short History of Ethics* (London: Routledge, 2002), 12.
2. 'Extract from Romain Rolland's Diary', in *Romain Rolland and Gandhi Correspondence* (Delhi: Publications Division, Government of India, 1976), 44–45.
3. Tapan Raychaudhuri, 'Gandhi and Tagore: Where the Twain Meet', in Tapan Raychaudhuri, *Perceptions, Emotions, Sensibilities: Essays on India's Colonial and Post-Colonial Experiences* (New Delhi: Oxford University Press, 1999), 148.
4. Raychaudhuri, 'Gandhi and Tagore', 143.
5. 'Romain Rolland to Rabindranath Tagore on 2 March, 1923', in eds. Alex Aronson and Krishna Kripalani, *Rolland and Tagore* (Calcutta: Visva-Bharati, 1945), 36–37.
6. Sabyasachi Bhattacharya, 'Introduction', in ed. Sabyasachi Bhattacharya, *The Mahatma And The Poet: Letters and Debates Between Gandhi and Tagore 1915–1941* (New Delhi: National Book Trust, 2005), 216.
7. Rabindranath Tagore, *Rabindra Rachanabali* (125th anniversary edition), 15 vols. (Kolkata: Visva-Bharati, 1986–1992 [1393–1398 Bengali Era]), [hereafter *Rachanabali*], 5: 678. All citations are in translation from Bangla and have been translated by myself, unless otherwise specified.
8. *Rachanabali*, 5: 678.
9. Ira G. Zepp, Jr., 'Tagore and Gandhi on Non-Violence: A Lover's Quarrel Represented by Dhananjaya', in Ira G. Zepp Jr., *Rabindranath Tagore: American Interpretations* (Calcutta: Writers Workshop, 1991), 173.
10. Bhattacharya, *The Mahatma and the Poet*, 7.
11. Sean Scalmer, *Gandhi in the West: The Mahatma and the Rise of Radical Protest* (New Delhi: Cambridge University Press, 2011), 82–83.
12. Bhattacharya, *The Mahatma and the Poet*, 55.
13. Bhattacharya, *The Mahatma and the Poet*, 55.
14. Bhattacharya, *The Mahatma and the Poet*, 57–58.
15. Bhattacharya, *The Mahatma and the Poet*, 59.
16. For a discussion on political method particularly, see *Rachanabali*, 12: 652–664.

In argument: considerance of the political ❖ **215**

17. Rabindranath Tagore, *Selected Letters of Rabindranath Tagore*, eds. Krishna Dutta and Andrew Robinson (Cambridge: Cambridge University Press, 1997), 261.
18. Bhattacharya, *The Mahatma and the Poet*, 62.
19. *The Collected Works of Mahatma Gandhi*, 100 vols. (Delhi: Publications Division, Government of India, 1958–1994), [hereafter *Collected Works*], 20: 158–159.
20. *Collected Works*, 20: 162.
21. *Collected Works*, 20: 162.
22. *Collected Works*, 20: 163.
23. *Collected Works*, 20: 164.
24. For details, see Krishna Kripalani, *Tagore: A Life* (Delhi: National Book Trust, 2001), 167–172.
25. *The English Writings of Rabindranath Tagore*, 4 vols. (Delhi: Sahitya Akademi, 1994–2007 [hereafter *Writings*]), 3: 413.
26. *Writings*, 3: 414.
27. *Writings*, 3: 416. Tagore mentioned some of the revolutionaries turning to yoga: 'From the writings of the young men, who have come out of the valley of the shadow of death, I feel sure some such thoughts must have occurred to them. And so they must be realizing the necessity of the practice of *yoga* as of primary importance; – that form which is union in a common endeavour of all the human faculties.' *Writings*, 3: 417. He was probably referring to Aurobindo Ghosh.
28. *Writings*, 3: 417.
29. *Writings*, 3: 418.
30. *Writings*, 3: 418.
31. *Writings*, 3: 419.
32. *Writings*, 3: 418.
33. *Writings*, 3: 421.
34. *Writings*, 3: 421.
35. *Writings*, 3: 422.
36. *Writings*, 3: 423.
37. *Collected Works*, 21: 288.
38. *Collected Works*, 21: 289.
39. *Collected Works*, 21: 289.
40. *Collected Works*, 20: 432.
41. *Collected Works*, 20: 433.
42. *Collected Works*, 21: 291.
43. His English translation, *The Waterfall*, appeared the same year in the *Modern Review*. The complete English version was produced by Marjorie Sykes as the *Free Current*.
44. Kripalani, *Tagore*, 175.

216 ❖ In argument: considerance of the political

45. *Writings*, 2: 197.
46. *Rachanabali*, 7: 743.
47. *Rachanabali*, 7: 743.
48. *Rachanabali*, 7: 743.
49. Zepp, *Rabindranath Tagore: American Interpretations*, 174.
50. Zepp, *Rabindranath Tagore: American Interpretations*, 184.
51. *Collected Works*, 23: 5.
52. The English translation of Ray's writing can be found in the *Young India* of 2 February 1922, carried with Gandhi's approbation as a 'closely reasoned preface of Sir P. C. Ray to a Bengali booklet on charkha'. *Collected Works*, 22: 316. The text of the preface, not reproduced in the *Collected Works*, does not refer to Tagore by name. It, however, has a similar analytical evaluation as Tagore's on *Swadeshi*. Gandhi, in his aforementioned comment, also concurred with the evaluation: 'I entirely endorse Dr. Ray's remarks that Bengal gained nothing during the first swadeshi agitation by bringing cloth from Bombay or Ahmedabad instead of Manchester or Japan. In order to enable us to feel the full and immediate effect of swadeshi, we must manufacture yarn and cloth in our millions of scattered homes. Swadeshi will bind them as nothing else can.' *Collected Works*, 22: 316.
53. *Writings*, 3: 538.
54. *Writings*, 3: 539.
55. *Writings*, 3: 541.
56. *Writings*, 3: 541.
57. *Writings*, 3: 541.
58. *Writings*, 3: 542.
59. *Writings*, 3: 544.
60. *Writings*, 3: 546.
61. *Writings*, 3: 547.
62. Bhattacharya, *The Mahatma and the Poet*, 122.
63. Bhattacharya, *The Mahatma and the Poet*, 123.
64. Bhattacharya, *The Mahatma and the Poet*, 124.
65. Bhattacharya, *The Mahatma and the Poet*, 125.
66. Bhattacharya, *The Mahatma and the Poet*, 126.
67. Bhattacharya, *The Mahatma and the Poet*, 126.
68. *Collected Works*, 25: 593.
69. *Collected Works*, 25: 577.
70. *Collected Works*, 25: 21.
71. *Collected Works*, 25: 23.
72. *Collected Works*, 25: 274.
73. *Collected Works*, 25: 274.
74. *Collected Works*, 36: 218.
75. *Collected Works*, 36: 223.
76. *Collected Works*, 70: 316.

In argument: considerance of the political ❖ **217**

77. *Collected Works*, 70: 316.
78. *Collected Works*, 70: 377.
79. *Collected Works*, 72: 192.
80. *Collected Works*, 78: 64.
81. *Collected Works*, 78: 66.
82. *Collected Works*, 78: 66.
83. *Collected Works*, 78: 77.
84. *Collected Works*, 78: 78.
85. *Collected Works*, 78: 78–79.
86. M. K. Gandhi, 'Discussion' at the conference of the Charkha Sangh, 7–14 October 1944, in *Khadi Why and How* (Ahmedabad: Navjivan Publishing House, 1955), 203.
87. *Writings*, 3: 547.
88. For the details of Tagore's argument, see Nepal Majumdar, *Bharate Jatiyota o Antarjatikata ebong Rabindranath*, 6 vols. (Kolkata: Dey's Publishing, 1996 [1403 Bengali Era]), 6: 250–264.
89. Krishna Kripalani, 'Rammohun Ray and Gandhi', in ed. B. P. Baruah, *Raja Rammohun Roy and the New Learning* (Calcutta: Orient Longman, 1988), 10.
90. *Collected Works*, 19: 476.
91. *Collected Works*, 19: 477.
92. *Collected Works*, 19: 477.
93. *Collected Works*, 19: 477.
94. *Collected Works*, 20: 42.
95. *Collected Works*, 20: 43.
96. Baruah, *Raja Rammohun Roy and the New Learning*, 16.
97. Amiya P. Sen, *Rammohun Roy: A Critical Biography* (Delhi: Penguin Books, 2012), 3.
98. For an authoritative discussion of the Raja's Hindi writings, see Hazari Prasad Dwivedi, 'Hindi Bhashaye Rammohun', in Satish Chandra Chakrabarty ed., *The Father of Modern India: Commemoration Volume of the Rammohun Roy Centenary Celebrations, 1933*, part II (Calcutta: Rammohun Roy Centenary Committee, 1935), 465–468.
99. Sen, *Rammohun Roy*, 3–4.
100. Rammohun Roy, *The English Works of Raja Rammohun Roy*, ed. Jogendra Chunder Ghosh, 4 vols. (Delhi: Cosmo, 1982), 2: 472–473.
101. *The English Works of Raja Rammohun Roy*, 2: 474.
102. Bruce Carlisle Robertson, *Raja Rammohun Ray: The Father of Modern India* (Delhi: Oxford University Press, 1999), 30.
103. R. K. DasGupta, 'Rammohun Roy and the New Learning', in ed. B. P. Baruah, *Raja Rammohun Roy and the New Learning* (Calcutta: Orient Longman, 1988), 37.
104. Zepp, *Rabindranath Tagore: American Interpretations*, 174.

218 ❧ In argument: considerance of the political

105. *Romain Rolland and Gandhi Correspondence*, 49.
106. *Romain Rolland and Gandhi Correspondence*, 49.
107. Sabyasachi Bhattacharya, *The Mahatma and the Poet*, 98.
108. Sabyasachi Bhattacharya, *The Mahatma and the Poet*, 98.
109. Edward Said, 'The Clash of Definitions', in Edward Said, *Reflections on Exile and other Literary and Cultural Essays* (New Delhi: Penguin Books India, 2001), 575–576.
110. Michel Foucault, *The Courage of Truth: The Government of Self and Others II*, ed. Frederic Gros; trans. Graham Burchell (New York: Picador, 2012), 12–13.
111. Foucault, *The Courage of Truth*, 14.

Bibliography

Ahmed, Aijaz. 'Azad's Careers: Roads Taken and Not Taken', in Aijaz Ahmed, *Lineages of the Present*, Delhi: Tulika, 1996, pp. 133–190.

Améry, Jean. *At the Mind's Limits: Contemplations by a Survivor on Auschwitz and Its Realities*, trans. Sidney Rosenfeld and Stella P. Rosenfeld, Bloomington: Indiana University Press, 1980.

Anderson, Benedict. *Imagined Communities: Reflections on the Origin and Spread of Nationalism*, London: Verso, 2001.

Arendt, Hannah. *Between Past and Future*, New York: Penguin Books, 2006.

Arendt, Hannah. *Eichmann in Jerusalem: A Report on the Banality of Evil*, New York: Penguin Books, 2006.

Arendt, Hannah. *Men in Dark Times*, San Diego: Harcourt Brace and Company, 1968.

Arendt, Hannah. *On Violence*, London: Allen Lane, 1970.

Arendt, Hannah. *The Life of the Mind*, San Diego: Harcourt Inc., 1978.

Aronson, Alex and Krishna Kripalani, ed. *Rolland and Tagore*, Calcutta: Visva-Bharati, 1945.

Aronson, Alex. *Rabindranath through Western Eyes*, Calcutta: Riddhi-India, 1978.

Atharvaveda. Pardi, Valsad: Svadhyaya Mandal, 4th edition, not dated.

Baumer, Rachel Van M. 'The Reinterpretation of Dharma in Nineteenth-Century Bengal: Righteous Conduct for Man in the Modern World', in ed. Rachel Van M. Baumer, *Aspects of Bengali History and Society*, New Delhi: Vikas Publishing House, 1976, pp. 82–98.

Bayly, C. A. *Origins of Nationality in South Asia: Patriotism and Ethical Government in the Making of Modern India*, in *The C. A. Bayly Omnibus*, Delhi: Oxford University Press, 2009.

Benhabib, Seyla. *Another Cosmopolitanism*, ed. Robert Post, New York: Oxford University Press, 2006.

Bergoglio, Jorge Mario and Abraham Skorka. *On Heaven and Earth: Pope Francis on Faith, Family, and the Church in the 21st Century*, trans. Alejandro Bermudez and Howard Goodman, London: Bloomsbury Publishing, 2013.

Berlin, Isaiah. *Personal Impressions*, ed. Henry Hardy, Princeton, NJ: Princeton University Press, 2001.

Berlin, Isaiah. *Russian Thinkers*, eds. Henry Hardy and Aileen Kelly, London: Penguin Books, 1994.

Berlin, Isaiah. *The Crooked Timber of Humanity: Chapters in the History of Ideas*, ed. Henry Hardy, Princeton, NJ: Princeton University Press, 1990.

220 ❖ Bibliography

Berlin, Isaiah. *The Power of Ideas*, ed. Henry Hardy, Princeton, NJ: Princeton University Press, 2002.

Berlin, Isaiah. *The Sense of Reality: Studies in Ideas and Their History*, ed. Henry Hardy, New York: Farrar, Strauss and Giroux, 1999.

Berlin, Isaiah. *Three Critics of the Enlightenment: Vico, Hamann, Herder*, ed. Henry Hardy, Princeton, NJ: Princeton University Press, 2000.

Bhattacharya, Sabyasachi. ed. *The Mahatma and the Poet: Letters and Debates between Gandhi and Tagore 1915–1941*, Delhi: National Book Trust, 2005.

Blaut, James M. *The National Question: Decolonizing the Theory of Nationalism*, London: Zed Books Ltd., 1987.

Boehm, Max Hildebert. 'Nationalism: Theoretical Aspects', in Edwin R. A. Seligman *et al.* eds. *Encyclopaedia of the Social Sciences*, vol. XI, New York: The Macmillan Company, 1963, pp. 231–240.

Bondurant, Joan. *Conquest of Violence: The Gandhian Philosophy of Conflict*, Princeton, NJ: Princeton University Press, 1988.

Bose, Nirmal Kumar. *My Days with Gandhi*, Delhi: Orient Longman, 1987.

Burckhardt, Jacob. *History of Greek Culture*, trans. Palmer Hilty, New York: Dover Publications, Inc., 2002.

Cesaire, Aime. *Discourse on Colonialism*, trans. Joan Pinkham, Delhi: Aakar Books, 2010 [1955].

Chandra, Sudhir. *Dependence and Disillusionment: Emergence of National Consciousness in Later Nineteenth Century India*, New Delhi: Oxford University Press, 2011.

Chatterjee, Bankim Chandra. *Essays and Letters*, eds. Brajendranath Nath Banerji and Sajani Kant Das, New Delhi: Rupa, 2010.

Chatterjee, Bankimchandra. *Prabandha o Onnanya Rachana*, Kolkata: Sahityam, 2007.

Chatterjee, Bankim Chandra. *Bankim Chandra Chatterjee – Sociological Essays: Utilitarianism and Positivism in Bengal*, trans. and ed. S. N. Mukherjee and Marian Maddern, Calcutta: Rddhi-India, 1986.

Chatterjee, Bankimchandra. *Bankim Rachanabali: Upannyas Samagra*, Kolkata: Shubham, 2009.

Clark, T. W. 'The Role of Bankimcandra in the Development of Nationalism', in ed. C. H. Phillips, *Historians of India, Pakistan and Ceylon*, London: Oxford University Press, 1961, pp. 429–445.

Congress Presidential Addresses, ed. A. M. Zaidi, 5 vols. New Delhi: Indian Institute of Applied Political Research, 1986–1989.

Constituent Assembly Debates: Official Report, 5 Books. New Delhi: Lok Sabha Secretariat, 1950; rpt. 1999.

Dalton, Dennis. *Nonviolence in Action: Gandhi's Power*, New Delhi: Oxford University Press, 2007.

Das, Sisir Kumar. *The Artist in Chains*, Delhi: New Statesman Publishing Company, 1984.

Dasgupta, R. K. 'Rammohun Roy and the New Learning', in ed. B. P. Baruah, *Raja Rammohun Roy and the New Learning*, Calcutta: Orient Longman, 1988, pp. 24–42.

Desai, Narayan. *My Life is My Message*, trans. Tridip Suhrud, 4 vols., New Delhi: Orient BlackSwan, 2009.

Draper, Alfred. *Amritsar: The Massacre that Ended the Raj*, London: Cassel Ltd., 1981.

Datta, Bhupendra Nath. *Bharater Dvitiya Swadhinata Sangram*, Calcutta: Burman Publishing House, 1949.

Datta, Bhupendranath. *Swami Vivekananda: Patriot – Prophet*, Calcutta: Nababharat Publishers, 1993.

Dwivedi, Hazari Prasad. 'Hindi Bhashaye Rammohun', in Satish Chandra Chakrabarty ed., *The Father of Modern India: Commemoration Volume of the Rammohun Roy Centenary Celebrations, 1933*, part II, Calcutta: Rammohun Roy Centenary Committee, 1935, pp. 465–468.

Einstein, Albert. *Ideas and Opinions*, ed. and trans. Sonja Bargmann, London and New York: Crown Publishers, 1954.

Fanon, Frantz. *A Dying Colonialism*, trans. Haakon Chevalier, New York: Grove Press, 1965.

Fine, Robert and Robin Cohen. 'Four Cosmopolitan Moments', in ed. Steven Vertovec and Robin Cohen, *Conceiving Cosmopolitanism: Theory, Context, and Practice*, New York: Oxford University Press, 2002, pp. 137–164.

Fisher, Louis. *The Life of Mahatma Gandhi*, Mumbai: Bharatiya Vidya Bhavan, 1990.

Foucault, Michel. *The Courage of Truth: The Government of Self and Others II*, ed. Frederic Gros, trans. Graham Burchell, New York: Picador, 2012.

Gandhi, M. K. *An Autobiography or The Story of my Experiments with Truth*, Ahmedabad: Navjivan Publishing House, 1988.

Gandhi, M. K. *Hind Swaraj and other Writings*, ed. Anthony J. Parel, Delhi: Cambridge University Press, 1997.

Gandhi, M. K. *Non-Violence in Peace and War*, 2 vols. Ahmedabad: Navjivan Publishing House, 1942.

Gandhi, M. K. *The Collected Works of Mahatma Gandhi*, 100 vols. Delhi: Publications Division, Government of India, 1958–1994.

Gandhi, Rajmohan. *Mohandas: A True Story of a Man, His People and an Empire*, Delhi: Penguin Books, 2006.

Ganguli, B. N. *Concept of Equality: The Nineteenth Century Indian Debate*, Simla: Indian Institute of Advanced Study, 1975.

Gellner, Ernest. *Nations and Nationalism*, Ithaca, NY: Cornell University Press, 2008.

222 ❖ Bibliography

Gokhale, Gopal Krishna. *Speeches and Writings of Gopal Krishna Gokhale*, 2 vols. Delhi: Anmol Publications, 1987.

Gonda, Jan. *Change and Continuity in Indian Religion*, 1965; rpt Delhi: Munshiram Manoharlal Publishers, 1997.

Griswold, Charles L. *Forgiveness: A Philosophical Exploration*, New York: Cambridge University Press, 2007.

Halbwachs, Maurice. *On Collective Memory*, trans. and ed. Lewis A. Coser, Chicago: The University of Chicago Press, 1992.

Hardimon, Michael O. *Hegel's Social Philosophy: The Project of Reconciliation*, Cambridge: Cambridge University Press, 1994.

Heehs, Peter. *Sri Aurobindo: A Brief Biography*, Delhi: Oxford University Press, 2003.

Heehs, Peter. *The Bomb in Bengal: The Rise of Revolutionary Terrorism in India 1900–1910*, Delhi: Oxford University Press, 2004.

Heimsath, Charles H. *Indian Nationalism and Hindu Social Reform*, Princeton: Princeton University Press, 1964.

Herman, Arthur. *Gandhi and Churchill: The Epic Rivalry that Destroyed an Empire and Forged our Age*, London: Hutchinson, 2008.

Hilberg, Raul. *The Destruction of the European Jews*, Teaneck, NJ: Holmes & Meier Publishers Inc., 1985.

Hilberg, Raul. *The Politics of Memory: The Journey of a Holocaust Historian*, Chicago: Ivar R. Dee Inc., 1996.

Hilberg, Raul, Stanislaw Staron and Joseph Kermisz. ed. *The Warsaw Diary of Adam Czerniakow: Prelude to Doom*, Chicago: Ivan R. Dee Publishers, 1999.

Himmelfarb, Gertrude. 'The Illusion of Cosmopolitanism', in Martha C. Nussbaum, *Love of Country*, ed. Joshua Cohen, Boston: Beacon Press, 1996, pp. 72–77.

Hoare, Quintin and Geoffrey Nowell Smith, trans. and ed. *Selections from the Prison Notebooks of Antonio Gramsci*, Chennai: Orient Longman, 1996.

Hobsbawm, E. J. *Primitive Rebels: Studies in Archaic forms of Social Movement in the 19th and 20th Centuries*, New York: W. W. Norton & Company, 1965.

Hochhuth, Rolf. *The Deputy*, trans. Richard and Clara Winston, New York: Grove Press, 1964.

India's Foreign Policy: Selected Speeches of Jawaharlal Nehru, September 1946–April 1961, New Delhi: The Publications Division, Government of India, 1983.

Isherwood, Christopher. *Ramakrishna and His Disciples*, Kolkata: Advaita Ashram, 2007.

Jacob, Margaret C. *Strangers Nowhere in the World: The Rise of Cosmopolitanism in Early Modern Europe*, Philadelphia: University of Pennsylvania Press, 2006.

Bibliography ❖ 223

Jordan, William Chester.' "Europe" in the Middle Ages', in ed. Anthony Pagden, *The Idea of Europe: From Antiquity to the European Union*, New York: Cambridge University Press, 2002, pp. 72–90.

Joshi, Lal Mani. *Discerning the Buddha: A Study of Buddhism and of the Brahmanical Hindu Attitude to It*, Delhi: Munshiram Manoharlal Publishers, 1983.

Kalghatgi, T. G. *Study of Jainism*, Jaipur: Prakrit Bharati Academy, 1988.

Kant, Immanuel. *Perpetual Peace* [1795], Minneapolis: Filiquarian Publishing, LLC, 2007.

Karim, Rezaul. 'In the Eyes of a Non-Hindu', trans. William Radice, in ed. Bhabatosh Chatterjee, *Bankimchandra Chatterjee: Essays in Perspective*, New Delhi: Sahitya Akademi, 1994, pp. 177–181.

Kaviraj, Sudipta. *The Unhappy Consciousness: Bankimchandra and the Formation of Nationalist Discourse in India*, Delhi: Oxford University Press, 1995.

Kaviraj, Sudipta and Sunil Khilnani. *Civil Society: History and Possibilities*, Delhi: Cambridge University Press, 2002.

Kazantzakis, Nikos. *Report to Greco*, trans. P. A. Bien, London: Faber and Faber, 1973.

Kedourie, Elie. *Nationalism*, Malden, MA: Blackwell Publishing, 1993.

Khadi Why and How, Ahmedabad: Navjivan Publishing House, 1955.

Khilnani, Sunil. *The Idea of India*, London: Penguin Books Ltd., 1997.

Kingston, Maxine Hong. *The Fifth Book of Peace*, New York: Alfred A. Knopf, 2003.

Kohn, Hans. *The Idea of Nationalism: A Study in its Origins and Background*, New Brunswick, NJ: Transaction Publishers, 2005.

Kopf, David. *British Orientalism and the Bengal Renaissance: The Dynamics of Indian Modernization 1773–1835*, Berkeley: University of California Press, 1969.

Kripalani, Krishna. 'Rammohun Ray and Gandhi', in ed. B. P. Baruah, *Raja Rammohun Roy and the New Learning*, Calcutta: Orient Longman, 1988, pp. 1–23.

Kripalani, Krishna. *Tagore: A Life*, Delhi: National Book Trust, 2001.

Levi, Primo. *Moments of Reprieve*, trans. Ruth Feldman, London: Penguin Books, 2002.

Levi, Primo. *The Drowned and the Saved*, trans. Raymond Rosenthal, New York: Vintage International, 1989.

Levinas, Emmanuel. *Totality and Infinity: An Essay on Exteriority*, trans. Alphonso Lingis, Pittsburgh, Pennsylvania: Duquesne University Press, 1969.

MacIntyre, Alasdair. *A Short History of Ethics*, London: Routledge, 2002.

Majumdar, Bimanbehari. *Heroines of Tagore: A Study in the Transformation of Indian Society 1875–1941*, Calcutta: Firma K. L. Mukhopadhyay, 1968.

224 ❀ Bibliography

Majumdar, Bimanbehari. *History of Political Thought from Rammohun Roy to Dayananda*, vol. I, Calcutta: University of Calcutta, 1934.

Majumdar, Nepal. *Bharate Jatiyota o Antarjatikata ebong Rabindranath*, 6 vols., Kolkata: Dey's Publishing, 1996 [1395 Bengali Era].

Margalit, Avishai. *The Decent Society*, trans. Naomi Goldblum, Cambridge, MA: Harvard University Press, 1996.

Marx, Karl. *The Eighteenth Brumaire of Louis Bonaparte*, Moscow: Progress Publishers, 1967.

Memmi, Albert. *The Colonizer and the Colonized*, trans. Howard Greenfeld, Boston: Beacon Press, [1957]1967.

Moore, Margaret. *The Ethics of Nationalism*, New York: Oxford University Press, 2001.

Mukhopadhyaya, Prabhat Kumar. *Rabindrajibani*, 4 vols., Kolkata: Visva-Bharati Granthanbibhag, 2008 [1415 Bengali Era].

Nandy, Ashis. *Regimes of Narcissism, Regimes of Despair*, Delhi: Oxford University Press, 2013.

Nandy, Ashis. *The Illegitimacy of Nationalism*, in *Return from Exile*, Delhi: Oxford University Press, 1998.

Nayar, Sushila. *Mahatma Gandhi: India Awakened*, Ahmedabad: Navjivan Publishing House, 1994.

Nehru, Jawaharlal. *Jawaharlal Nehru: an autobiography*, London: The Bodley Head, 1942.

Pande, G. C. *Jaina Political Thought*, Jaipur: Prakrit Bharati Sansthan, Centre for Jain Studies, University of Rajasthan, 1984.

Pande, G. C. *Life and Thought of Sankaracharya*, Delhi: Motilal Banarsidass, 2004.

Pande, G. C. *Studies in the Origins of Buddhism*, Delhi: Motilal Banarsidass, 1995.

Pasternak, Boris. *Dr. Zhivago*, trans. Max Hayward and Manya Harari, London: Vintage Books, 2002.

Pinch, William R. *Peasants and Monks in British India*, Delhi: Oxford University Press, 1996.

Payne, Robert. *The Life and Death of Mahatma Gandhi* [1969], New Delhi: Rupa, 1997.

Plato, *Crito*, reproduced in Jewett's translation, in Doris A. Hunter and Krishna Mallick eds. *Nonviolence: A Reader in the Ethics of Action*, Delhi: The Gandhi Peace Foundation, 1990.

Phule, Jotirao. 'Slavery', trans. Maya Pandit, in G. P. Deshpande ed., *Selected Writings of Jotirao Phule*, New Delhi: LeftWord Books, 2002, pp. 22–99.

Putnam, Hilary. 'Must We Choose?', in Martha C. Nussbaum, *Love of Country*, ed. Joshua Cohen, Boston: Beacon Press, 1996, pp. 91–97.

Radhakrishnan, S. trans and ed., *The Bhagavadgita*, Bombay: Blackie & Son, 1982.

Bibliography ❖ **225**

Valmiki, *Ramayana*, Gorakhpur: Gita Press, 1976 [2033 Vikram Era].

Raychaudhuri, Tapan. 'Gandhi and Tagore: Where the Twain Meet', in Tapan Raychaudhuri, *Perceptions, Emotions, Sensibilities: Essays on India's Colonial and Post-colonial Experiences*, New Delhi: Oxford University Press, 1999, pp. 141–151.

Raychaudhuri, Tapan. *Europe Reconsidered: Perceptions of the West in Nineteenth-Century Bengal*, Delhi: Oxford University Press, 2006.

Renan, Earnest. 'What Is A Nation', in Geof Ely and Ronald Grigor Suny eds. *Becoming National: A Reader*, New York: Oxford University Press, 1996.

Rigveda, Poona: Vaidik Sanshodhan Mandal, 1946.

Robertson, Bruce Carlisle. *Raja Rammohun Ray: The Father of Modern India*, Delhi: Oxford University Press, 1999.

Rocker, Rudolph. *Nationalism and Culture*, trans. Ray E. Chase, California: Rocker Publications Committee, 1937.

Romain Rolland and Gandhi Correspondence, Delhi: Publications Division, Government of India, 1976.

Roy, Rammohun. *The English Works of Raja Rammohun Roy*, ed. Jogendra Chunder Ghosh [1906], Delhi: Cosmo, 1982.

Said, Edward. *Reflections on Exile and other Literary and Cultural Essays*, New Delhi: Penguin Books India, 2001.

Sandburg, Carl. *Abraham Lincoln: The Prairie Years*, New York: Dell Publishing House Co. Inc., 1960.

Sean Scalmer, *Gandhi in the West: The Mahatma and the Rise of Radical Protest*, New Delhi: Cambridge University Press, 2011.

Sehanobis, Chinmohon. *Rabindranath o Biplabi Samaj*, Calcutta: Visva-Bharati Granthanbibhag, 1985 [1392 Bengali Era].

Sen, Amartya. 'Foreword', in Krishna Dutta and Andrew Robinson eds., *Selected Letters of Rabindranath Tagore*, Cambridge: Cambridge University Press, 1997, pp. xvii–xxv.

Sen, Amiya P. *Rammohun Roy: A Critical Biography*, Delhi: Penguin Books, 2012.

Sen, Amiya P. *Swami Vivekananda*, Delhi: Oxford University Press, 2013.

Sen, Kshitimohon. 'Rabindranath o Tilak', in ed. Pronoti Mukhopadhyaya, *Rabindranath o Santiniketan*, Kolkata: Punascha, 2009, pp. 217–225.

Sen, Sukumar. *History of Bengali Literature*, Delhi: Sahitya Akademi, 1992.

Seton-Watson, Hugh. *Nations and States: An Enquiry into the Origins of Nations and the Politics of Nationalism*, London: Methuen & Co., 1977.

Sharma, Arvind. *Modern Hindu Thought: The Essential Texts*, Delhi: Oxford University Press, 2002.

Shirer, William L. *The Rise and Fall of the Third Reich: A History of Nazi Germany* [1950], New York: Ballantine Books, 1983.

Shklar, Judith N. *The Faces of Injustice*, New Haven: Yale University Press, 1990.

226 ❖ Bibliography

Sil, Narasingha P. *Swami Vivekananda: A Reassessment*, Selinsgrove: Susquehanna University Press, 1997.

Stalin, Joseph. *Marxism and the National and Colonial Question*, London: Lawrence & Wishart, 1936.

Steiner, George. 'The Cleric of Treason', in George Steiner, *A Reader*, Harmondsworth: Penguin Books, 1984.

Swami Vivekananda, *The Complete Works of Swami Vivekananda*, 9 vols. Mayavati/Kolkata: Advaita Ashrama, 1947–1997.

Tagore, Rabindranath. *Four Chapters*, trans. Rimli Bhattacharya, Delhi: Shrishti, 2001.

Tagore, Rabindranath. *Rabindra Rachanabali* (125th anniversary edition), 15 vols., Kolkata: Visva-Bharati, 1986–1992 [1393–1398 Bengali Era].

Tagore, Rabindranath. *Letters from Russia*, trans. Sasadhar Sinha, Calcutta: Visva-Bharati, 1984.

Tagore, Rabindranath. *Nationalism*, ed. and intro. Ramachandra Guha, Delhi: Penguin Books, 2009.

Tagore, Rabindranath. *Selected Letters of Rabindranath Tagore*, eds. Krishna Dutta and Andrew Robinson, Cambridge: Cambridge University Press, 1997.

Tagore, Rabindranath. *The English Writings of Rabindranath Tagore*, 4 vols., Delhi: Sahitya Akademi, 1994–2007.

Tendulkar, D. G. *Mahatma: Life of Mohandas Karamchand Gandhi*, 8 vols., Delhi: The Publications Division, Government of India [1951–1954], rpt. 1962.

Terchek, Ronald J. *Gandhi: Struggling for Autonomy*, Lanham: Rowman & Littlefield Publishers, Inc., 1998.

Toynbee, Arnold. *A Study of History*, London: Thames and Hudson, 1995.

Trivedi, Harish. 'Tagore on England and the West', in eds. G. R. Taneja and Vinod Sena, *Literature East and West: Essays Presented to R K DasGupta*, New Delhi: Allied Publishers, 1995, pp. 163–176.

Van der Veer, Peter. 'Colonial Cosmopolitanism', in ed. Steven Vertovec and Robin Cohen, *Conceiving Cosmopolitanism: Theory, Context, and Practice*, New York: Oxford University Press, 2002, pp. 165–179.

Vertovec, Steven and Robin Cohen. 'Introduction: Conceiving Cosmopolitanism', in ed. Vertovec and Cohen, *Conceiving Cosmopolitanism: Theory, Context, and Practice*, New York: Oxford University Press, 2002, pp. 1–22.

Walzer, Michael. *Just and Unjust Wars: A Moral Argument with Historical Illustrations*, New York: Basic Books, 2006.

White, Hayden. *Metahistory: The Historical Imagination in Nineteenth Century Europe*, Baltimore: The Johns Hopkins University Press, 1975.

Wiesel, Elie. *A Beggar in Jerusalem*, trans. Lily Edelman and Elie Wiesel, New York: Shocken Books, 1985.

Wiesel, Elie. *Dawn*, trans. Frances Frenaye, in *The Night Trilogy*, New York: Hill and Wang, 2008.

Wiesel, Elie. *From The Kingdom of Memory*, New York: Shocken Books, 1995.

Wiesel, Elie. *Night*, trans. Marion Wiesel, in *The Night Trilogy*, New York: Hill And Wang, 2008.

Williams, Bernard. *Morality: An Introduction to Ethics*, Cambridge: Cambridge University Press, 1993.

Williams, Bernard. *The Sense of the Past: Essays in the History of Philosophy*, ed. Michael Burnyeat, Princeton: Princeton University Press, 2008.

Williams, Bernard. *Truth and Truthfulness*, Princeton: Princeton University Press, 2002.

Wolfenstein, Eugene Victor. *The Victims of Democracy: Malcolm X and the Black Revolution*, New York: The Guilford Press, 1993.

X, Malcolm. *By Any Means Necessary*, New York: Pathfinder, 2008.

Yajurveda, Delhi: Motilal Banarsidass, 1978.

Young, Iris Marion. *Responsibility for Justice*, New York: Oxford University Press, Inc., 2011.

Zepp, Ira G., Jr. 'Tagore and Gandhi on Non-Violence: A Lover's Quarrel Represented by Dhananjaya', in ed. Ira G. Zepp Jr., *Rabindranath Tagore: American Interpretations*, Calcutta: Writers Workshop, 1991, pp. 167–187.

Index

agitation 131, 136, 146
ahimsa 58, 82–3, 83, 85, 89, 191
Ambedkar 33, 166
Amery, Jean 6
Anandamath 16
Andrews, C. F. 42, 131, 133, 134,
140, 175, 177, 180, 183
Antipov, Pasha 66
Arendt, Hannah 42–4, 48, 64, 79,
89–91, 93–5, 100, 101
Aronson, Alex 52
assassination 83–4, 162
Atharvaveda 10
Atmaparicahaya (Self-Introduction)
124

Bangadarshan 11, 17
Bangadesher Krishak 14, 15
Bangalakshmir Bratakatha 154
Bengal 7, 14, 15, 17, 28, 31, 46,
52–4, 59, 61, 154, 155, 159, 183,
185, 190, 197, 206
Berlin, Isaiah 24, 29, 50, 52, 57, 93,
95, 152, 153, 155, 156, 160
Beware of Ourselves 158
*Bharatbarsher Swadhinata o
Paradhinota* 12
Bondurant, Joan 91
Bonnerjee, W. C. 4
boycott 72, 84, 131, 157, 158, 177,
178, 181, 182, 185, 186, 199, 204
Brahmin 11, 14–15, 25
Buber, Martin 72–4, 76
Buddhism 183

The Call of Truth 183
caste oppression 3–4, 13–14

censorship 134–5, 140–2
Cesaire, Aime 30
Champaran 96–8
Char Adhyaya (Four Chapters) 41, 52,
53, 59, 60, 62, 65, 67
charkha 83, 177, 186–8, 190,
193–204, 212
Charkha Sangh 201, 202, 204
Chatterjee, Bankim Chandra 1–33
Chatterjee, Sharat Chandra 60–1
Chatterjee, Suniti Kumar 63
Chauri Chaura 98, 99, 138, 158,
159, 192
'Chhoto o Boro' ('Small and Big') 61
civil disobedience 136, 140–3, 178
colonialism 13, 14, 30, 182, 194
communalism 130
Congress 3, 4, 46, 82, 98, 117, 122,
128, 131, 134, 136, 144–6, 158,
161, 174, 175, 189, 192, 193,
201, 202
conscience 1, 7–18, 40–69; freedom
of 69–85
cosmopolitanism 48, 50, 119–33
The Cult of Charkha 128, 193
cuspidal imaginings 1–33

Das, C. R. 128–9, 134, 145, 175
Das, Sisir Kumar 7
debate, contemporary 68–9
democracy 211–14
deprivation 25, 27, 189–90, 193–4
'Desher Katha' 66
The Destruction of the European Jews
90
dharma 8, 43, 53, 62, 67, 68, 97,
119, 137

230 ❖ Index

Dharwar Social Conference 4
dignity 25–6, 76–7, 187, 189, 194
disagreements 176–7, 196, 204, 211
Discourse on Colonialism 30
Durgeshnandini 17
Dutta, Bhupendra Nath 61
A Dying Colonialism 55

education 4, 15, 25, 48, 51, 114,
    120, 132, 155, 178, 179, 182,
    184, 186, 197, 202, 206–10
Eichmann, Adolf 89
*Eighteenth Brumaire of Louis
    Bonaparte* 32
ethical politics 5, 9, 23, 40–1, 180,
    214
ethics 16, 18–20, 23, 27, 31, 32,
    40–69, 72, 73, 93, 114–62;
    of community 69–85; and
    responsibility 114–62
ethnolatry 116
extremism 59, 61, 62, 72

Fanon, Frantz 55, 56, 62
forgiveness 59, 60, 133
Foucault, Michel 213
freedom 41–3, 52–4, 60, 63, 75,
    135, 140–1, 146, 149, 152, 156,
    184, 186–8, 191; of conscience
    69–85; political 50, 62, 119, 156,
    185, 202, 213

Gandhi, M. K. 41, 69–85, 195, 204;
    concept 69, 98, 161; movement
    5, 72, 173, 183; non-violence 69,
    72, 78; position 42, 74–8, 80, 98,
    175, 177, 184, 189; statement 70,
    83, 98
Gandhi, Rajmohan 79–80, 108
Gaurdas Babajir Bhikshar Jhuli 17
Gelder, Stuart 161
Germany 2, 69–75, 78–80, 82–91,
    93, 95, 100

Ghaire Baire 59, 62
Ghare Bhaire 61
Gokhale, Gopal Krishna 4, 5
Government of India 121
Greenburg, Hayem 87–9
Griswold, Charles 2
Grynszpan, Herschel 84
Grynszpan, Zindel 84
Gujarat 137, 161
Gulamgiri (Slavery) 3

Haldar, Gopal 63
Hardimon, Michael 2
Herzen, Alexander 57
Hilberg, Raul 86, 90, 92, 93, 95
himsa 58, 82, 83, 89, 179
Hind Swaraj 69, 80, 83, 89, 129,
    131
Hitler, Adolph 70–4, 76, 78, 79, 82,
    83, 85–7, 90, 91, 96
Holocaust 69, 77–8, 87, 89–90, 93,
    95, 100, 111–12, 125
Hunter Commission 42

Jewish Frontier 87
Jews 69–76, 78–85, 87, 89–96,
    100–1, 106–7, 109–10, 117, 132,
    169; extermination of 86–7, 91,
    95
Jinnah, M. A. 33, 133
Jordan, William Chester 122

*Kant as an Unfamiliar Source of
    Nationalism* 153
Kazantzakis, Nikos 6

Lakhnavi, Majaz 56
Levi, Primo 77

Magnes, Judah L. 72–4, 76
Mahatma 41, 73, 178, 186, 187,
    191, 193, 195, 204, 208, 209
Memmi, Albert 30

modernity 7, 8, 18, 22, 43, 124, 129, 184, 196
Moonje, B. S. 130–1
moral responsibility 93–4, 93–4, 143, 147
movement: non-violent 82, 143; political 82, 126–7, 179, 211; swadeshi 153–8
Muchiram Gurer Jibancharit 14
Muktadhara 190, 192, 204
Muslims 7, 12–13, 17–18, 33, 49, 79, 111, 121, 126, 130, 149, 160

nation 5, 6, 8–11, 13, 19, 27–33, 35, 47, 49–50, 90–1, 114–21, 128–33, 150–3, 157, 160–4, 166, 169–70, 211–12
nationalism 2–3, 35–6, 50, 65–6, 105, 114–72, 175, 181, 219–21, 223–6; and cosmopolitanism 119–33; defined 115; ethics of 162–3, 224; pathology of 158; qua reform 2–6; responsible 147–62; violence and state 133–47; violent 29, 131
national movement 177–211
Nazi 69, 77–8, 82–3
non-violence 40–102; political 69, 84; pragmatism of 69–85; resistance 69, 71, 76, 78–9, 81, 83, 87, 89, 96, 98; and truth 40–102

Pande, G. C. 20, 21, 57, 58
Paramhansa, Ramakrishna 23, 26
parrhēsia 213
Pather Dabi 61
patriotism 16, 27, 31, 35, 62, 120, 128, 157, 179, 181, 183, 189
Phule, Jotirao 3, 13
Plato 43, 58, 60, 116, 175
political community 1–33

politics 40–102; ideological 116; mass 186; philosophy 4, 35, 52; violence 53–5, 83, 177
poltical ethics xvi, xvii
pragmatism 69–85
Prasna 59
protest 1, 2, 21, 40, 50, 60, 61, 66, 68, 69, 72, 76, 80–3, 87, 91, 93, 95, 96, 98, 99, 101, 133–8, 140, 154, 158, 176
Punjab 133–5, 137, 139, 141–3, 145, 167–8

Rabindranath o Biplabi Samaj 61
Ranade, Mahadev Govind 4
rashtra 10
Raychaudhuri, Tapan 174
renunciation 20–2, 20–7, 74–5, 184, 190
Report to Greco 6
resistance 72, 82, 88–9, 168
responsibility: ethics and 18–20, 114–62; nation 27–33
retaliation 58, 80, 191
revolutionaries 28, 54–5, 57, 59, 61, 63–4, 201, 215; violence 52, 54–6, 59, 62–3, 68, 72
Rigveda 10, 11
Rolland, Romain 42, 162, 173, 175, 211, 212
Rowlatt Act 139, 141, 143
Roy, M. N. 72
Roy, Rammohun 7, 26, 31, 34–5, 206, 217, 221, 223, 225

sacrifice 48, 63, 95–6, 100, 138, 149, 174, 179–80, 184–5, 189, 196, 198, 202
Sanskrit 8, 10, 207–10
Santiniketan 51, 114, 115, 120, 134, 140, 157, 159
sanyas 20–2, 28, 29

232 ❧ Index

satyagraha 71–3, 75, 78, 87–8, 91, 97, 102, 136–44, 150, 159, 177, 178, 191
Schirach, Gauleiter 96
Sehanobis, Chinmohon 61
Sen, Surya 63, 68
shastras 17, 18
shudras 3
Sitaram 16
social conscience 7–18
social/reform 2–6, 13, 19, 23, 26
swadeshi 151–60, 172, 176, 183, 185, 204, 205
swaraj 144, 147, 148, 150, 178, 183, 184–7, 200, 201, 204, 206

tabula rasa 116
Tagore, Rabindranath 26, 37–8, 40–69, 102–5, 114, 124, 153, 157, 162–4; attitude 148, 157; criticism 173, 175, 177–8, 195; letter 134, 142; opposition 50, 61, 174–5; relationship 133, 153; response 52, 133, 135
Tilak, Bal Gangadhar 157, 206–8
Tocqueville, Alexis de 9
Trivedi, Ramendra Sunder 134, 154

truth 40–102, 211–14; and conscience 1, 67; courage of 213; and non-violence 40–102; and politics 43
truthfulness 44, 46, 49, 103, 212–13
Tyabji, Badruddin 4

Upanishad 48, 176, 183, 197

van Baumer, Rachel 8
Vidyasagar, Ishwar Chandra 7, 17, 206
violence 54–60, 62–3, 65, 67, 75, 77–9, 83, 85, 92–4, 96, 107–8, 112, 137–42, 158
Vivekananda, Swami 1–33, 38–9, 61, 124

Weltsch, Robert 84
Wiesel, Elie 77
Williams, Bernard 31, 68
women 11, 15, 17, 40, 52, 62–3, 96–7, 139, 182, 187, 198–9

Yajurveda 10–11, 35, 227
Young India 96, 98, 143, 177, 187, 196